What folk a

"…Very funny from the start and has you laughing out loud." *S Ashford, UK*

"Brilliantly funny. Laughed out loud!" *E Davies, UK*

"... pure entertainment ..." *B Brislin, UK*

"Pitchforks happily brought to mind the tone and style of a Tom Sharpe novel. Comedy this is and deliciously observed..." *A Fry, New Zealand*

"I was laughing out loud in places... I've been up all night with sick kids and reading your work has given me a great lift." *F Ferris, Australia*

"Well done - dry like a good wine - with a punch."
S Wnukowski, Poland

Other books by GK Kingsley

Illustrated paperback 'Pick-me-up Pearls' books of verse:

The Bust in Dust… – And other pick-me-up pearls for when wisdom is waning

Ticks For a Fix – And other pick-me-up pearls for when the will is wilting

Visit www.gkkingsley.com

GK loves connecting with people online, either via her website, Facebook, Twitter, LinkedIn or Pinterest, and if you'd like to receive her 'Latest Scribblings' weekly email update, you can subscribe to her mailing list via her website. She'll also keep you updated on new releases and announcements. Please do seek her out and connect with her. She doesn't bite!

About GK Kingsley

GK Kingsley is a Northamptonshire based writer of both fiction and what she calls Pick-me-up Pearls (aka weeny bits of verse). In her own unique way, she regularly shares illustrated bite-size bits of upbeat poetry that lift your day. Taking every day challenges, she turns the pesky mites upside down and leaves you with a new thought to make you smile. Not content with 'just' writing fiction for your pleasure, along with snippets of humorous poetry, she also regularly appears on BBC Radio Northampton with Rob Adcock, summarising the week's events and news in a fun and lively poem. If your spirits are in need of a lift, a quirky dose of GK Kingsley won't let you down.

GK Kingsley asserts the moral right to be identified as the author of this work

Front cover illustration by Nathan Ariss

Front cover design by Martin Streets, Brightspark Design

Published by GK Kingsley Limited

Copyright © 2015 GK Kingsley

ISBN 978-0-9930777-5-3

PITCHFORKS
&
PIÑA COLADAS

GK Kingsley

To my wonderful son. Just remember – never give up on your dreams.

And an important word of thanks…

Firstly, to Nicky Fitzmaurice of SatinPublishing, I would like to say what a brilliant editor you are and what a fabulous writer's pal too. Without you, the finished version of this beast just simply wouldn't be. Thank you.

And secondly, of course I also want to thank the dear friends and family who have encouraged and supported me over the years. Writing is my passion and, at times when I've lost sight of what I'm doing, you've - quite simply - not let me stop. Thank you one and all. You know who you are…

Chapter One

When Derek Fitztumbleton sat down for breakfast with his wife that November Monday morning, he had no reason to believe he'd be dining with a transvestite by the end of the week. He also had no reason to believe he'd be staring at a stripper's buttocks by elevenses; but then that was an understandable assumption for a headmaster to make. So what Derek focused on, whilst he buttered his toast, were the more pressing issues that could occupy an ambitious man.

"I think I'll have to back down on the scarecrows," he announced, as he jabbed at his scrambled eggs. "Sandra Lovelock has a point when she says *The Call* could come from Ofsted any day now. We need to be prepared."

Miranda stood up as he said it, her chair scraping across the mock-tiled floor, and walked surprisingly gracefully for a woman of her generous size over to the sink. As she left the table, a waft of perfume sauntered up Derek's nose and he found himself distracted by the novelty of the smell; but it was only for a split second. After that he discarded the thought. Things like perfume were mere fripperies to occupy the minds of the underwhelmed and he really did have more important things to deal with.

1

She began to wash up.

"That flasher struck again outside M&S this weekend you know, Derek," she muttered. "Pippa Nelson was there. She said it made her day."

Derek frowned. A wistful tone had crept into her voice which was beginning to seep through to a deeper level in his consciousness. But fifteen years of marriage were not to be sniffed at, so he concluded that a wistful tone could also be ignored and picked up the pupil progress figures by his side instead.

None of this was unusual, of course. Miranda and Derek had ignored each other's conversations for so long it had reached a point where it might have appeared rude if one of them had suddenly taken an interest. It would certainly have destroyed the status quo.

However, Miranda then began to hum.

As Derek surveyed the peaks and troughs of his graphs, his wife's tuneless melody writhed its way across the hills and dales of a song and ate into his psyche like a maggot. Squirm, squirm, squirm, it went, wriggling like a nagging doubt, gnawing and biting, until finally, the moment arrived.

Something, he realised at last, required his consideration. He gave his balding head a good scratch.

First off, Miranda never wore perfume unless it was an important occasion. He'd always been relieved that deodorant was included within her daily routine, but perfume had seemed an unnecessary expense; he had also appreciated her thrift.

Secondly, she never talked about flashers. However this was so beyond the blueprint of their normal conversations that Derek decided it should be put to the side for the time being.

Which still left the third yet most notable item; namely that she absolutely never, ever hummed.

He put his report down on the table and cleared his throat.

"You're looking all dressed up today, darling. Women's Institute? Or have I forgotten something important?"

Miranda turned to look at him and frowned. "I've put your clean underpants in the airing cupboard," she replied, and then dropped her marigolds into the bin and hummed her way out of the room.

* * *

By eight o'clock, Derek had left the civilised sanctuary of Cockerby Town, bracing himself for another working day in the rural backwater of Lower Bushey, blissfully unaware of what was yet to come.

By ten to nine, the playground was packed with screaming children.

From their lofty location five feet three inches above the ground, Derek's eyes surveyed his financially famished domain, and he prepared himself for another week.

Fuck 'em! Fuck 'em all! he thought in quick succession, and then waited for the calming wash of

3

indifference to soothe his soul. It was a daily ritual he had carried out ever since he'd been appointed and it had served him well for seven years. Some might think it to be a disturbing strategy for an educationalist, but in truth it had nothing to do with a troubled mind yet to be ensnared by the CRB checking system. No, in fact Derek had a lot of time for fastidious record keeping, and he therefore wholly approved of the spending of millions of pounds each year to verify that nobody was a problem. That sort of thing meant that a box could be ticked and he liked ticking boxes, very much. He also liked percentages, pie charts, and graphs that went up on the right hand side... But all that was by-the-by. For what Derek had really struggled with as soon as he'd started at the school – besides the mildew and peeling paint – was a frustration that knew no bounds. Despite all that he had scrutinised, measured and tracked, the young buggers within had pursued a passion for mediocrity that had fought his efforts at every turn.

And so, as with seven years' worth of previous Tuesdays, Wednesdays, Thursdays and Fridays, he felt that this Monday was no exception.

As the phrase formed in his head for a second time, a pair of enormous four year old eyes frowned back. With an awkward flush, Derek realised that he had unwittingly mouthed his thoughts. In an effort to cover his tracks, he said out loud, "Fun, fun, fun," making a big play of shaping the word carefully with his lips, and then waved to the Reception teacher who was on duty. She shot him an unforgiving glare and looked at her watch. Only ten minutes playtime left, the gesture said; 'why don't you focus on your paperwork, Mr Fitztumbleton, and leave the kids' stuff to us?' Derek nodded. Perhaps she was right. A coffee would put him back on track and he could show his face again in a few minutes for the sake of a bit of PR.

His decision took him back inside, past his secretary's office, and on towards the musty hub of the school. As the front door clunked shut somewhere far behind, Derek hoped without conviction to find the staff room empty, and was amply rewarded for his realism to find it wasn't. Sandra Lovelock's sloping hanger-like shoulders came into view and he stopped in his tracks with a shudder.

Her beady eye froze him to the spot.

"Ah, Mr Fitztumbleton, I was hoping you were in. There is something I need to discuss with you."

Derek cringed under the withering stare and braced himself. What Miss Lovelock's bony middle-aged exterior hid was not to be underestimated. It was said that she could sniff a lie from forty metres; could spot an articulated dodge several seconds before it occurred; and had inclinations that only the most unlikely looking people could have, which she also pursued.

For two whole seconds he withstood the severity of her glower, dying a little inside as each one ticked by, but finally its power became too strong. His eyes darted south and landed squarely on her chest. Despite his years of training, Derek did a double take.

"Well, quite," slipped from his lips. There was little of note to the frilly shirt, but the same could not have been said of the leather clad 'A' cup covertly poking through an unbuttoned gap underneath. If its nose had been any pointier, he'd have sworn it was giving him a sniff.

Horrified, he diverted his gaze to a set of instructions on how to unblock the photocopier and cleared his throat.

"I'll get us a drink, shall I?" he mumbled, and watched from the corner of his eye as she looked down at her chest and flushed. It took a while for Sandra to nod and Derek gave his chin a thoughtful rub; this was not an opportunity to miss. "Not sure if I've got time for a chat though, Miss Lovelock," he added slyly, striking whilst her confusion was hot, and then felt himself relax a little further as she continued to try to reacquaint one side of her shirt with the other. He let one more second tick by for the sake of good manners, and turned, relieved, to do battle with the drinks machine instead.

The options presented were predictable, but this was as far as the contraption ever allowed one to take things for granted. He cast his eye down the list, giving it some careful thought. Two days of unbroken peace across the space of a weekend tended to make this purveyor of refreshment a flamboyant but unreliable affair. Derek made his selection and crossed his fingers for good luck.

A disconcerting gurgle erupted from the appliance, and he gingerly reached in and pulled out a steaming brown plastic cup. He looked at the contents with consternation.

It had to be said that the liquid inside was not what he was expecting. True, it was hot and wet, but at that point depiction and reality then diverged. Concern for customer satisfaction clearly stopped at mouth watering descriptions and depended, thereafter, on some sort of warped equivalent of the placebo effect. Derek risked a sniff from a distance and grimaced. Well, he knew nothing about consumer rights, but the Geneva Convention would surely have condemned the stuff as a breach of human rights.

It was a sobering notion, and one that also then made him wonder just how many people it took for a conflict to be termed a war; for Miss Lovelock's furious stare had begun to burn a sizeable hole in his back. What had felt like a minor conquest the week before, when he'd boldly refused to let her remove the infants' scarecrow exhibits, was now mutating into a foolish attempt at bravado.

Derek heaved a deep and heartfelt sigh, and resigned himself to his lot. There was only one way to move forward; to assume that accepted rules of engagement were in play, the Geneva Convention being, after all, a well respected modus operandi. It was time to wave the white flag.

"Do you have milk in your coffee?" he asked, turning round to face Sandra properly, aware that she would have recovered from her embarrassment by now. "I'm sorry. I didn't think to ask if you preferred black or white." He glanced briefly again at the strange fluid purporting to be Costa Rica's finest and scowled.

"I don't drink coffee, I drink tea," she replied, her clothing all ship shape and Bristol fashion once more. "But you never thought to ask that either, did you?"

Her eyes challenged him and then broke away, flicking with derisory disdain towards the ceiling. Derek looked for a third time at the contents of his cup and finally realised with abstract relief that he must have chosen chicken soup by mistake. Well, at least the floating green bits now made sense.

About to offer her a tea instead, he bent over to read the instructions more carefully just as the sound of sensible shoes squelched on the hall linoleum. Mrs McFreece, the school secretary a.k.a. The Fridge, to those in the know, which didn't include Mrs McFreece, appeared at the doorway and even Sandra seemed to sink into the background.

"Ashley Milner's mother has just called. They are running late," she announced, the Scottish tone of disapproval unmistakeably evident.

Mrs Milner had not endeared herself to the daunting secretary when Ashley had arrived three weeks before, and with Mrs McFreece now looking with such disdain upon the poor child, Derek had not yet plucked up the courage to ask to see the previous school's pupil notes. He sighed and allowed divine inspiration to descend.

"Well, we'll have to mark Ashley down as late, Mrs M. I don't like the effect it will have on our statistics any more than you do, but honesty is the best policy. The data must be accurate, otherwise what point is there in collecting it in the first place?"

He knew it was the right thing to say. There weren't many similarities between him and Mrs McFreece, but a love of all things measurable was at least one. The Fridge issued a curt nod of approval and then turned and swayed her ample hips back to her office.

"Well, quite," Derek sighed for the second time, taking advantage of the lull in Miss Lovelock's headlong attack, and sidestepped his way to the door. "Perhaps a swing around the playground in the name of public relations before the day starts will help things along, eh?"

Sandra's eyes narrowed. She had clearly recovered her momentum now that the secretary had disappeared and it was a look that shouted, 'You lily-livered coward, I've asked for a couple of minutes of your time and you're dodging me.'

It was a fair appraisal of the situation, and Derek felt it should be granted recognition, but only once he'd escaped out of the room.

* * *

Taking a deep breath, Derek stepped outside for the second time that day and felt the chill sting his cheeks.

He looked around. It was a scene he'd surveyed more times than he cared to acknowledge, and his eyes bounced over the patchy tarmac and decaying basketball net and spotted instead that only a few children were wearing outside clothes. He made a mental note to send a letter home. It never hurt to remind the parents that coats, hats and gloves were recommended. Such actions like that provided excellent evidence to the powers-that-be, a.k.a. Ofsted that he regularly communicated with his flock. They also reinforced the notion that the school sat at the heart of the community. It would be another tick in a box.

"Mr Fitztumbleton!" the caustic cry of The Fridge broke his train of thought.

As one, the groups of chattering mothers instantly huddled together, sympathetic looks darting in his direction. Mrs McFreece never graced the playground with her presence unless it was absolutely necessary; something was afoot.

"There's a phone call for you!" she added, and Derek, having now spotted the fierce anticipation glowing in her eyes, realised that the playground empathy was misplaced.

Oh.. My.. God... he thought to himself. This is it. This is the call. *The Call!* The glint of suppressed excitement shining across at him, a glint so clearly out of place on such an unenthusiastic face, was surely proof enough. He raised an eyebrow and Mrs McFreece nodded back. Derek's heart skipped a beat. At last! His chance to show the rest of the world how much he had achieved was finally at hand.

Barely aware of the skip in his step, he trotted across, thanking The Fridge as he went for holding the door open for him, and darted into his office.

"He's on line three," she puffed, following closely behind, and then bent down to put the call through before adding in a rare moment of solidarity, "I'll go and get us a coffee, shall I?"

Under normal circumstances such an offer would have thrown Derek off the mark, but nothing was going to distract him now. He managed an almost casual nod, straightened his jacket out unnecessarily, and then leant across to grab the handset.

It was a short call, abrupt and perhaps intended to intimidate, but to Derek it meant the answer to all his prayers. They, a Mr Barnaby de Ravel and a Ms Diana Bonniface, would be arriving on Thursday. It would be a full two day inspection. No stone would be left unturned.

* * *

To all but the most foolhardy it was a call that would have spelled impending doom, but to Derek Fitztumbleton it meant redemption. On paper, well, more on screen and particularly in multicoloured graphs, the school looked in reasonable shape. The bar charts and scatter diagrams for the recently completed academic year were all sloping upwards, past national norms and up into the cloud topped peaks of pretty good.

Derek had watched with patient but mounting excitement as this astonishing performance had shone through despite the pupils' best efforts. He had spotted the statistical aberration early on. And, not daring to question openly what had happened in Lower Bushey eleven years before, had wondered if a nomadic group of geniuses had somehow affected the gene pool. However, he was also aware that a travelling circus boasting a bearded woman and some reject clowns must have followed closely behind. The figures he'd been looking at only that morning had made it clear that all would be counterbalanced when the following July arrived. Next summer's school leavers were going to be the worst there'd ever been. With the official statistics looking fantastic for only another eight months, the time for an inspection was now or not at all.

He replaced the handset and breathed in, almost smelling promotion and the overpopulated corridors of a thriving urban school.

"Mrs M.!" he called, the lift of his voice unnecessary as she was already hovering by the door. "Rally the troops. Our time has finally come."

Like Rumpelstiltskin, The Fridge did a little jig and scrunched her fists up with glee.

"Shall I call your wife to let her know you will be late tonight?" she asked.

Derek nodded. Monday nights were WI nights, she wouldn't mind a bit. Although, he then pondered, feeling the glow of success beginning to warm his belly, it might be nice to give her the news himself.

"Actually, Mrs M.," he mused, pausing only briefly before making up his mind, "ask Miranda to call me back. I'd like to tell her the news myself after I've spoken to the staff."

If nothing else, he thought with satisfaction, it would give her a decent reason to hum.

* * *

Having briefed the teachers, fielded their horror-struck questions, and once again congratulated himself on being so well prepared, Derek decided to give his head some air.

All was going to plan so far.

John Bentwick, the school's Chair of Governors, had been bumbling but supportive.

"Don't worry," he'd said. "Yer yields 'ave been good; yer tracking yer productivity; and yer don't get involved in the teaching." Derek had wondered what he'd meant by the last comment, but consoled himself by acknowledging that the man had never been one for words. Teachers teach, he thought, leaders lead, and governors around here tend to farm.

And now, with a petrified hubbub buzzing within the school, a bit of calm was what was needed to prepare his thoughts for the next leg of his career.

He stepped back into the chilly morning, his breath puffing great billows of warm air into the ether, and cast a disparaging eye across his current realm. This may be my domain for now, he contemplated, but it won't be for much longer.

"Fuck 'em, fuck 'em all," he muttered to himself, smiling; and for once the words were coated with a smug sheen.

A wood pigeon sounded from the other side of the playground, but Derek ignored it and continued to revel in his projected success. Now was not the time to worry about a lurking dive-bomber. The little sod may have bombarded him all summer but that sort of rural stuff would soon be at an end. For a couple of minutes, he could allow himself to dwell on the exciting things ahead; things that had nothing to do with country life; things that meant he could once again be proud of his career. Things like concrete and lots of classrooms. That was what he was looking forward to. Pupils by the hundred; parents by the score; respect and admiration by the...

Ching! The sound of the school gate clinked in his ears.

Derek dragged himself from his reverie and took in the attractive, heavily made up blonde now strutting his way. His eyes widened in surprise. The loincloth length skirt was one thing; the flouncy, fly away material acting suspiciously like a blouse certainly another. But the tuning knobs pointing outwards were what really proved this woman was in touch with nature on a chilly autumn day. Inexperienced in such sophisticated ways, Derek did the only thing a man could do; he stared.

"And who is this handsome devil, Ashley?" she cooed to the child scuttling by her side. The overly emphasised 'aitches' landed in his ears and, to his chagrin, Derek felt his face turn pink. The pair of long tanned legs came to a halt in front of him.

"I'm Derek," Derek managed, but only just. For as he said it, he found he had to look up and quickly realised just how tall this corker was.

Her lipstick-laden lips spread wide into a smile.

"Well, hello… Derek. I'm delighted to make your acquaintance. My name is Mabel Milner."

"Mum," Ashley whispered, frowning with embarrassment, "this is Mr Fitztumbleton. He's our head teacher."

Dazzled by the wanton sexuality now pointing directly at him, Derek barely registered the introduction.

Mabel Milner now lifted an eyebrow "Ooooh," she groaned. "I like a good 'ead, meself. Makes all the difference, don't you think?"

It took a second for the complimentary nature of the words to sink in but Derek had already found his blush deepening to a crimson glow. Desperate to regain his composure, he dragged his eyes away from the bewitching sight and looked instead at the clean black trousers, sensible shoes and androgynously laid out features of the youngster he'd been ignoring. An unexpected panic ballooned.

Oh my god! he thought. Was this a boy or a girl? So unisex were clothes these days he realised he had no idea. Cursing his cowardice for not reading the pupil notes earlier, Derek armed himself with what he hoped would elicit a gender specific response.

"So, Ashley," he muttered, praying, "are you involved in the training tonight?"

Football training always took place on a Monday and for a second Derek was sure that, despite the politically incorrect assumption, the youngster's reply would tell him all he needed to know. Unfortunately, the dismissive shrug that came back didn't even give him a clue.

"Not into footie, then," he struggled on, but Mrs Milner's hand had already begun to reach across to grasp the child's fingers and guide them both towards the front door. Two innocent eyes stared back and to his despair Derek realised that he had little choice but to give up. "Well, do take yourselves inside. Mrs McFreece will register you in," he muttered, regretfully aware that it would mark the end of this extraordinary exchange.

As the words slipped out, a vision of Miranda appeared in his mind, her bountiful proportions and regal hairstyle the antithesis of what was before him now. There was no doubt, he conceded, that both women had their strengths. But the devoted nature of his wife was not to be overlooked. She needed him, and although it felt an onerous duty at times for one who had so many other responsibilities, he liked being needed. Yes, he rallied internally, whilst one eye continued to linger on the toned brown thighs walking off, he should be grateful for the angel fluttering in his conscience. It was an appropriate reminder to have. And despite his wife's inexplicable humming earlier, he was struck by a tiny tinge of guilt.

"On second thoughts," he mumbled, pulling himself together and suddenly becoming aware of the weightier implications of what he'd just said; The Fridge was going to need to be kept under control for the next few days. "Let me see you in."

But as this magnanimous offer reached its audience, a series of not entirely unpredictable but still unfortunate events then occurred.

Mrs McFreece opened the front door. A gust of wind eddied across the playground. A piece of loose material fluttered upwards and Derek's last thought, before The Fridge condemned a rare pleasure to the annals of never-to-be-mentioned-joys, was: Good Lord! Buttocks before break...

Chapter Two

Mabel Milner threw her handbag onto the kitchen table in disgust and throated a growl that would have made a Doberman proud.

Who did that poxy little man think he was? She hadn't run away from a lousy East End home, pregnant, destitute and clinging onto the coattails of a wayward older sister, just to be treated like that now. This pathetic little village, with its dung ridden streets and pint-sized school, was neither London nor Cockerby Town. No! It was blinkin' Lower Bushey, a rural backwater that was still clearing up after celebrating women gaining the vote. Nothing within it, including its only headmaster, warranted delusions of grandeur!

Mabel recalled the look of disgust chiselled into McFreece's face and growled again. The fat hog had blatantly given her the once over. "I've seen nudists with more clothes on," the sow had muttered, and all the Headmaster had done was shift from one stumpy leg to the other, opening and closing his mouth like a clam. Mabel could remember, even now, how she had watched him in astonishment. Waiting for some sort of rebuke to issue from his lips, she'd flattened down her skirt until she'd eventually given up and marched out of the school, chin, chest and nipples held high.

So what if it's a windy day! She now fumed, and let her breasts wobble indignantly as she plumped her hands onto her hips. And so bloody what if I'm not wearing any knickers either! If Fitztumbleton couldn't appreciate a touch of natural beauty when it was presented to him, then he was more of a prawn than she'd originally thought.

She felt her left boob slip out of its flimsy holder and absentmindedly tucked it back in.

Well ok, she conceded, feeling the tickle of lace as it brushed against her skin. Perhaps her work attire wasn't the most appropriate clothing for school. A stripper's garb definitely looked better through drunken eyes under conditions of subdued lighting... But Ashley had been late enough as it was. The choice had been stark; be there or be square. Old Titzfumble couldn't have it both ways, and if his self-righteous secretary could just keep her thoughts to herself for one more month, Mabel would no longer be a *Removals Executive (Clothing Division),* the current job title she had accorded herself on her latest application form, for she'd have a proper job, proper clothes and a proper h-h-h-accent. Tomorrow's interview was but a minor detail.

As she weighed up the likelihood of this future, an elephantine thump sounded upstairs. Mabel lifted her gaze and raised a despondent eyebrow. Whatever the miracle was that she was planning to pull off the next day, however, it was unlikely that other things in her life would improve quite so swiftly. Not only was she stuck renting an ex-council house that hadn't been redecorated since the Sixties, but Dwayne, her transgender lodger, was obviously up and getting ready for the day. The sound of the toilet flushing after the third attempt gurgled through the pipes in the wall, and was then followed by the hiss of air freshener. Mabel humphed. There was only one thing for it. She grabbed the broom, rammed the handle up at the ceiling, and gave it a bang three times.

"Oi! You'd better bloody well not 'ave used all the 'ot water!" she yelled, hoping the unnecessary volume would make her feel better, but then huffing in frustration when she realised her ploy hadn't worked. After a night of smiling, poling and pleasing, all she wanted was a nice hot bath and the opportunity to sleep the sleep of the just had it; fat chance.

Dwayne's fluffy-slipper clad footstep sounded on the stairs and he appeared at the kitchen door. Mabel noted the silky thigh length dressing gown and frowned. It wasn't the first time he'd pinched it, and it was unlikely to be the last, but the smudged makeup and bleeding lipstick were a very different matter.

"Is that my eye shadow you're wearing?"

Dwayne flushed, or at least it seemed that way; it was hard to tell through the thick 'cover-my-six o'clock-shadow foundation'. Mabel waited patiently whilst he stalled, and watched him pull a blond curl behind his ear, investigate a nail, give his bollocks a scratch, and then run an 'ok-you've-caught-me' tongue across his lips. *Sea-grass green!* the gesture implied. Who wouldn't have borrowed it? Eventually, things culminated in an awkward cough.

"How about I let you use my Prada clutch, Mabe?" Slipped out pathetically, whilst regret flitted across his features.

Mabel snorted. "If that bag is Prada, I'll eat Marmite for a month, but I'll borrow it tomorrow for my interview, if you don't mind. It'll go nicely with the dress I bought on Saturday."

Dwayne squinted, imagining the outfit she was proposing, and then nodded his considered agreement.

"Wear your Jimmy Choo fakes..."

Despite her annoyance, Mabel winced. He'd got her there. Those shoes had been an eBay faux pas. Her dad's market-trader motto of *caveat emptor* sprang to mind every time she thought of them, and she was quite prepared to *'buyer beware'* the bloody bastard who'd sold them to her. But she had at least hoped that no one else had spotted it. Dwayne obviously read her mind. He smirked and raised an eyebrow.

"Oh, darling, you didn't expect me to think they were real, did you? I can spot a Choo shoe from a hundred paces. Still, you'll be alright *here*..." The word came out coated with disdain and Mabel winced again. "Let's face it," Dwayne finished off, "nobody in Cockerby would know the difference, and the inhabitants of Lower Bushey think that steel toe caps are the latest thing. So wear them and be proud, Mabe. I won't tell a soul."

Dwayne had made no secret of despising the rustic surroundings in which he'd now found himself but equally so, in this instance, he wasn't talking cobblers. He was absolutely right; they were fakes and there was nothing Mabel could do about it. It wasn't a palatable reminder of her financial position, but then life didn't often fit together palatably for her anyway. So, keen to find a distraction, she focused on the ghoulishness of his makeup again and scowled.

"Did you 'ave a bad night or something?"

Dwayne let his hands fall limply at the wrist and smirked.

"Well, not as bad as yours by the looks of things," he replied, and sauntered across to the sink to fill the kettle. "By the way, did you hear the news? That Father Christmas flasher's struck again. I'll bet a tenner the police will be knocking on our door tomorrow, sniffing around... The bastards can't tell the difference between a nutter and a cutter, can they? Well they can confiscate my knob any time; save me the job. Fancy a cuppa before you hit the sack?"

As he bent across to turn the tap, a pair of nice tight buttocks peeked out from under the pink dressing gown and, despite herself, Mabel envied him. Why is it that men get all the perks? she thought. Gravity was already making a beeline for her buns so how the hell did a trannie five years her senior manage to keep in such good shape? I'm only twenty-six, she then cursed silently. *Give me a sodding break!* And as though he'd read her mind, Dwayne turned around, adjusted his G-string and raised another dopey eyebrow.

"So what's got you all grouchy then?"

Mabel plumped herself down on the nearest chair.

"Oh nothing," she puffed disconsolately, and then contradicted herself. "I'm 'aving a crisis, as usual, and in the meantime my poor daughter 'as to put up with a mum like me. Oh Dwayne," she added, and let out a long, sad sigh, "I'm just worried that I'm not doing enough for Ashley." She paused, feeling excessively sorry for herself, and then scrunched up her forehead as the moment passed and another more pressing thought sprang back to mind. "'Ang on a minute..."

As she said it, Dwayne's unkempt appearance suddenly fell into place.

"'Ow come you look like Morticia Adams this morning?" she continued, the furrows now deepening further. "You were meant to be babysitting Ashley last night. When I left for work there wasn't a drop of foundation on your skin. And," she then added, fully aware of the androgynous nature of her daughter, "don't try to tell me that you and Ash 'ad a girlie night in 'cos that ain't gonna wash and you know it."

Dwayne swallowed heavily and bit his lip. Lying had never been his forté. Even when he'd been pretending to himself that he was *all* man he'd done an appallingly bad job. Mabel could tell that something was up. And it now struck her that he'd been dodging a certain subject ever since he'd come downstairs.

Suddenly her eyes widened.

"You did that gig with Sasha last night, didn't you?" she accused, pointing an angry finger in his direction. Dwayne bit his lip again but shook his head.

Mabel lifted a dubious eyebrow and probed further. "But the word is that *Dominantics* are short staffed at the moment, Dwayne. And," she then added, "bearing in mind that you and Sasha aren't fussy about S&M, are you sure you're not lying to me?"

This time Dwayne winced.

"Well," he started and then sniffed, "yes I'm sure, err... I didn't do that gig *with* your sister."

Mabel gasped in fury. "Then you did it *for* 'er, didn't you?" His lack of reaction told her all that she needed to know. She clenched her fists in frustration. "Oh, Dwayne," she wailed, "you promised me you'd stay in with Ashley last night. 'Ow long was she alone?"

Grasping the nub of it at last, Dwayne flapped his hand to counter the manically escalating note in her voice. "No, no, no!" he pleaded. "It's not like that, Mabe, really. Ashley was never alone."

Clearly expecting his words to put Mabel's mind at rest, his eyes then widened in surprise as her face turned a menacing plum purple instead.

"No!" she screamed, and launched herself at him, her chair flying sideways onto the floor.

Dwayne stepped back.

"I'm sorry..." he managed, and ran a hand awkwardly through his ruffled curls. "Sash babysat for me," he explained quickly, and sidestepped a mistimed swipe. "But please, Mabe, don't be angry. I did it as a favour for her 'cos that awful perv has been following her around again, and besides," he then conceded, as she clearly remained unconvinced, "I need the extra money, and that, and that..." Mabel let her hand fall back to her side as she waited for him to justify the unjustifiable. "… And that is all your fault," he finished off, and crossed his arms victoriously.

It was often said that attack was the best form of defence but Mabel wasn't having any of it.

"My fault?" she gasped, foolishly allowing herself to be distracted. "And 'ow do you make that out?"

Dwayne let out a gratified snort and shuffled around to pick up her chair.

"Well, Ashley made me book another appointment with my gender reassignment consultant, and you know how much he costs, so I need all the cash I can get. Sash fancied a night off and it seemed that the circumstances suited everyone. She did promise she would behave," he added finally, clearly not convinced himself.

Mabel screeched.

"But you know I don't want that woman anywhere near my daughter! She's… she's… she's a bad influence," she rasped, and then realised the absurdity of her words. Mabel collapsed back into her chair.

Who was she trying to kid? She and Sasha were both Removals Executives. She had no right to be righteous, even if there were differences between them. Mabel may well have been the one changing her outlook, accent and dreams, but at the end of the day, regardless of their differing desires and prospects, they both still currently did the same job. The only silver lining was that nobody other than Dwayne knew it.

Well, nobody other than the punters at the club.

And the management.

Then there was Frank the barman.

Oh, and of course the bouncers on the door and the little old lady who made their outfits.

But apart from them, absolutely nobody else knew that Mabel and Sasha took their clothes off for a living, and only Dwayne and Ashley knew that Sasha was her sister. The very same sister she'd followed away from home when she was pregnant, hungry and scared. And the very same sister who, despite their differences, was still her closest friend, very closest friend, so close that they could read each other's minds.

"She did promise to keep out of your wardrobe," Dwayne added, just before realising that this was the fatal error.

As soon as the words had left his mouth, both he and Mabel made a dash for the stairs.

It wasn't a pretty sight.

Two fluffy slippers, four breasts - two real, two fake - and a lone unwanted penis, flew in directions physicists had never thought previously possible. It was a desperate scramble to see who could get to the top first.

"If she's pinched my new dress," Mabel gasped, "I'm going to kill you!"

The threat reached Dwayne's ears and his eyes widened in panic. With the strength that only sheer terror can bring, he launched himself off the final step and slammed her bedroom door in her face.

Mabel glared at the wood three inches from her nose and then pressed her ear against a panel. She listened hard. The scrape of a drawer sounded. Swiftly followed by the ting of an empty hanger. Silence then reigned for three seconds, until the rattle of a gummed up first floor window was finally finished off by a suppressed whimper of fear.

"Dwayne," she growled, "if that cow 'as taken it…"

A thump the other side of the door told her Dwayne had collapsed to the floor.

"No, she hasn't taken it," he moaned, just as Mabel wrenched the handle open and launched herself into her own bedroom.

She found him crumpled in a heap, struggling to retain his dignity and hide the new silky saffron coloured dress at the same time. A growl snarled in her throat.

"Oh give it up," she bristled. "My dressing gown is too short to cover an arse that size."

As Dwayne pulled at the hem, Mabel lunged to grab the dress, but failed.

"It's not so bad, Mabe," he yowled, tucking it further under his arm. "It could be worse. She's just added a twist of her own, that's all."

Narrowing her eyes, she pounced again, this time adding a strategic kick, and the dress came away in her hands. For a second, Mabel felt the weight of the material between her fingers, the garment's chic beauty hanging in her mind's eye, and then braced herself and held it up cautiously to assess the extent of the damage.

At first, things didn't look too bad, just the odd yanked button and crushed pleat. But as her eyes adjusted, it soon became clear that the work undertaken by an expert such as her sister was actually subtle yet devastating.

Mabel's mouth went dry.

Not so noticeable in the dullness of a bedroom, Sasha knew only too well what baby oil could do to silky material. She had cleverly judged how it would appear in the cold stark strip lighting of an office. "You crafty little bitch," Mabel muttered, now realising that the mangled folds were but artful distractions set to guide her eye away from the real *pièce de* résistance. And as she stared harder, two greasy painted Halloween faces grimaced back; their rampart-like grins stretching hideously across the contour of each bodice cup.

"All I did was rip 'er tassels off." Mabel gasped, suddenly remembering the incident from two weeks before that had triggered this disturbing turn of events.

"Yes, but she had nipple rash for a week afterwards..." Dwayne reminded her, and pulled himself into a more respectable kneeling position. "If you remember, it was harvest festival, Mabe," he continued. "You'd said to bring melons and stuff to the church service. Sash just hadn't heard you properly."

"Oh, don't you go defending her, Dwayne," she bit back, unable to control her temper any further. "You know what I thought of the courgette and two onions you took to the service."

Dwayne shrank into her dressing gown as she said it.

"That was below the belt."

"It was meant to be," she murmured, and disconsolately threw the ruined dress in the bin. "This is all your fault, D. None of it would 'ave 'appened if you 'adn't gone out last night. You do know that, don't you?"

Suitably sheepish, Dwayne smoothed an eyebrow with the tip of his little finger and nodded.

"Which means I owe you one, I suppose," he murmured.

"Too bloody right, and you can start by babysitting for me tonight," she replied, glad to have something positive at least to announce for the day so far. "Because believe it or not, you little sod, I've got a date."

* * *

Mabel listened to Dwayne's crashing and banging as he got ready to go to his gender-reassignment appointment, glad that she was holed up in her room. Her relief naturally extended in two directions.

First, of course, it meant that she could be curled up in bed, alone and free to drop off to sleep, and boy did she need that. Being up all night, shaking her booty into the early hours and then persuading already pissed punters to spend more money on drinks, was not where she wanted to be. But she had plans for dealing with that which included interviews and self-improvement.

What was currently more important, with respect to retreating to the comfort of her bedroom, was that Dwayne couldn't raid her makeup or wardrobe.

For a short while her life was looking ok. Her belongings were safe; she had an interview the following day, lack of outfit notwithstanding, and most significantly of all; tonight she had a date.

A date!

My god, how long had it been since she'd had a proper one of those? True enough, this one was likely to have its eccentric moments, that was patently clear now from the few times she had met John Bentwick but, well, how could she put this politely? ..He was loaded!

Dropping her head back into her pillow, she smiled at the memory of her and John's first meeting in the local shop just three weeks before.

"When I were a lad, I 'ad a rockin' 'orse with a bigger dick than that," he had announced to her as they had both been perusing the cucumbers. It had been fair to say that the Co-Op often offered a less-than-Brussels-approved selection of vegetables, but even Mabel had had to agree that these were a particularly pitiful collection of gourds. She had looked at his thirty-something weather beaten face, noted the gentrified tweeds, and wondered quite how to respond.

A swift appraisal of the situation had been required.

Her trench coat covered her 'work' clothes, so it was unlikely that any knob-based references had been elicited by the hope of a little how's-your-father. The thick farmer's fingers that had tested the spongy cucumber had made her wonder briefly what hidden delights had yet to be revealed, but she hadn't felt compelled to voice those thoughts. It had been a long night of being felt up and down and the bull sized appendage that no doubt accompanied such well-developed digits, had been low on her list of priorities.

And that had been about as far as her thinking had got before he had beaten her to the next stage.

"Do yer like riding?" he had then asked, and for a split second Mabel had been prepared to tell him what to do with the cucumber still in his hand, until she'd realised that he'd genuinely meant it. "I've just bought a new mare, yer see," he'd continued, oblivious of her confusion. "Pretty little thing she is, and I'm looking for a lady to try 'er out. Most of the farmers' wives around 'ere," he'd then added conspiratorially, "would be far too big for 'er, but you m'dear; you'd be perfect."

That had been the first time she'd met John Bentwick, just after she and Ashley had moved into Lower Bushey. Their second meeting had consisted of a brief but animated exchange on the intricacies of artificial insemination, as they'd queued to pay at the till. And as a result of their third, which had taken place only that morning, she had learned that his ram's scrotal circumference was well over forty centimetres, an exceptional development, apparently. Mabel had managed to express such interest in this new and extraordinary fact that John had suddenly taken her by surprise.

"Do yer fancy a visit to The Tupping Paddock?" he'd asked.

Even now, as she was lying at home in her bed, she could remember the sense of worldly empathy that had flooded her soul as he'd stood there, all flushed and harassed. Some men seemed to find it so hard to ask a sophisticated city girl out on a date. Well-crafted invitations, with meaningful sentences in tow, were simply beyond their grasp. But then who was she to criticise? *The Tupping Paddock* wasn't a pub she'd heard of, but these rural inns were renowned for their funny names. So she'd accepted the invitation gracefully, and John had beamed from ear to ear and informed her that he'd pick her up at six.

"It'll be getting dark, I'm afraid, but I can't make it any earlier," he'd added finally, which had struck her as slightly odd, but it had been so long since she'd been asked out on a proper date that she was prepared to overlook a quirky approach.

Thinking it through now though, she'd have to play it coy. He had no idea what she currently did for a living and she had no intention of telling him. *They* always experienced a shift in attitude once *they* found out the truth. So a rich, admittedly odd, farmer had to be played just right. The right outfit was critical. These men weren't necessarily conservative, just easily embarrassed. They were fully au fait with cows' wombs and bulls' balls, but the female of their own species was an entirely different matter. Cheek blushing pink would inevitably clash with any foxy red number she had, so it would need to be a demure but pleasantly provocative little black shift instead. Four inch heels could perhaps be one concession to ultimate femininity and, she decided suddenly, Dwayne's Prada clutch could be another. With a name like The Tupping Paddock; the dress code could swing either way.

Chapter Three

Sandra Lovelock turned to write the heading '*Henry VIII*' carefully on the blackboard, and then underlined it twice. He had, after all, been one of the most dominating characters in history, second only to her absolute favourite, Genghis Khan, so the emphasis was deserved. Having reviewed her handiwork, she then allowed herself a second of reverence for the great man, before turning back to face her class.

"Right!" she barked, ensuring that every head was looking to the front before she continued. "Who can tell me the name of King Henry's first wife?"

Ashley Milner's hand shot up and waggled in the air. Sandra relished this child's keenness. It stood out like a beacon in the desert of ignorance and the pall of indifference surrounding her. But sadly her years of experience as a teacher demanded that someone else be given a chance to answer. So she waited for the others to respond.

"Come on," she snapped, "this isn't a trick question. Who, other than Ashley, can tell me the name of King Henry's first wife?" she repeated, and ran her eyes across the group.

As her stare moved round, it snagged on a terrified face. The owner's hand was hovering at shoulder height, twitching to lift further and battling against the rest of its body -which was adamantly holding it at bay. She stared at Peter Drayton's fraught expression, and raised an eyebrow.

"Peter," she tried, knowing that even this nominal attempt was a rare event. "You look as though you know the answer. Why don't you give it a go?"

Peter swallowed hard, clearly also aware of the significance of the occasion, and plucked up the courage to speak.

"Beryl," he managed finally, his shoulders sagging with relief as the name tumbled out of his mouth. "Beryl, Beryl, Beryl," he then added for good measure, unstoppable now that he'd started.

Sandra lifted her hand to shut him up and he obeyed.

She cleared her throat. Really? she thought. Beryl?

It was a question she had asked many times, but this reply was a new one on her. It was also difficult to fathom from whence it had been spawned. But then Peter's arch enemy, Billy Barber, kindly clarified the matter.

"No it were never Beryl, yer tosser," Billy exclaimed, and shot Peter a condemning stare. "Beryl were 'is second wife. It were Maggie Thomas that were 'enry King's first wife. But she caught 'im copping off with Beryl in the cow shed and ditched 'im after that. My mum says 'enry King's a right randy little bugger."

Sandra winced. There was much about that, much on many levels, that didn't hit the spot. Billy and Peter were well known rivals in the playground, but here, in the classroom, they were more like squabbling kindred spirits. Such a response needed to be treated with the contempt it deserved.

"Well, that's all very interesting, Billy," she sighed, at least relieved that his Tourette's was in a low key mood. "But what I'd really like to know is: Who was King Henry the Eighth's first wife?" Both Billy and Peter now looked nonplussed, but she ploughed on anyway. "So can anyone tell me that?"

She threw the question back to the class for a third go.

This time, only Ashley's hand shot up and, despite herself, Sandra felt a flush of admiration in her relief.

Already she held this girl in high regard. Ashley had the makings of a strong woman and Sandra Lovelock liked strong women. Of course, she tolerated strong men too, but only as long as they behaved, and Ashley had more than just strength, she had potential. Ashley was bright. Ashley was mature. Ashley wasn't afraid of trying new things. And most significantly of all, Ashley was confident in her inner self.

In Sandra Lovelock's more introspective moments, Ashley Milner was, in fact, everything she wanted to be.

Yes, she was a troubled lady was Sandra Lovelock, her brain wanted one thing, but her heart wanted something completely different. And her undernourished exterior and inflexible, stern features did little to defuse the situation.

As she listened to Ashley give the correct answer, she thought back to the brief but futile exchange in the staff room only that morning; it was a perfect illustration of what she had suffered all her life. As soon as she'd seen the fall of Derek's handsome features, she'd realised that she should have started the conversation with a more direct approach. It would have been far better to have taken control and not allowed him room to manoeuvre. Only then would she have removed the responsibility of decision making from the poor man's shoulders, and given him the chance to just blindly agree.

For a split second, she wondered why she couldn't put into practise what she excelled at every Monday night, when she had full control of a populace that did exactly as it was told. On Monday evenings she wasn't Sandra Lovelock, but Lady Lovelick; Mistress and Minister to the Minions at hand. Wise overseer. Worthy warmonger and commander of a clan that followed a different set of rules to those commonly accepted by civil society. A set of rules clearly spelt out at the entrance to *Dominantics – The Club!* for those interested enough to get their reading glasses out.

Sadly, the answer was all too clear. What happened on a Monday night stayed within the confines of a Monday night; thems was the rules. And the remaining seven days and six nights had to be filled with their own dreams and longings; dreams and longings that had over time, mutated into grief and heartache. For what motivated and propelled this tortured woman through every second of this undesignated time… What gave her hope when the rest of her aspirations were falling by the wayside… What made her heart pound with red blooded palpitations was a deep rooted adoration for the man at the top of her pile.

Yes, Derek Fitztumbleton *B.Sc.(Hons), PGCE. M.Ed. NPQH. Promotion Please ASAP*, a man with more letters after his name than a Welsh railway station, was the man around which her world revolved. He was the yang to her yin; the tonic to her gin; the needle to her pin; the shake to her tin; the kith to her kin; the whisker to her chin; if only he could but also be her love...

Completely lost in her thoughts, Sandra sighed and clenched her fists.

Oh why, oh why, was he still with that woman? she bemoaned. What did he see in someone who barely acknowledged his existence? Miranda Fitztumbleton was a wife as dour as the teaching day was long. She despised all that was dear to his heart. She spoke to him as though he were a dog, which in itself was not the problem, as Sandra fully approved of that sort of behaviour; it was the fact that Miranda then gave him no little treats in return that broke all the rules, and despite it all, he still thought the sun shone out of her Playtex covered arse.

Really, he was the most perfect material for a faltering dominatrix like Sandra. If only he would just choose to obey the right woman.

"Miss?" The voice of Peter Drayton cut in, and interrupted Sandra's thoughts; "Miss, I've cut my finger again."

Sandra closed her eyes, just for a second to gather her patience, and then turned to inspect the offending digit now being thrust in front of her face.

An initial glance suggested a visit to the first aid box was needed, and she was about to usher him out when she spotted a dribble of bloodied snot making a slow descent from his nose.

Any other pupil would have received instant short shrift; but not Peter. Peter was special. Peter needed careful handling regarding matters of health. Peter was the child who had come to her crying one break time, petrified that he'd caught some horrible disease.

"What ever makes you think that?" she had asked on that miserable chilly day, just a couple of weeks before. And Peter had gone on to explain.

"Where ever I seem to poke meself it 'urts," he'd wailed. "'Ere on my 'ead," he'd demonstrated. "'Ere on my arm. And 'ere on my leg an' all. I've tested every part of my body, Miss Lovelock, and every time I poke it, it 'urts."

As he'd spoken, the tear stained face had reached out and resonated with a single heart string; which, in turn, had then twanged with more fervour once she had realised Derek was watching, and although the obvious answer had been to tell Peter to stop prodding himself, Sandra had swiftly concluded that that would not have solved the problem anyway. Peter wasn't the brightest of bulbs, but once he had got a hold on a concept, he found it hard to let go.

Taking his hand and holding his right index finger up for him to see, she had tried to help him to understand the error of his ways.

"Peter," she had said, as patiently and kindly as she could, bearing in mind her audience, "tell me; what can you see?"

"My finger," he had replied, and his eyes had stared innocently back.

"Take a closer look," she had advised, and had let him peer a little harder to allow his brain to catch up with the proceedings. "You've cut the end of your finger, haven't you?" she had tried next, but his face had creased into a frown, and at that point Sandra had then resigned herself to providing a more detailed explanation. "You've cut the end of the finger you're poking yourself with, Peter. That's why it hurts every time you prod. It's your finger that's hurting," she'd added finally, "not the rest of your body."

The dubious look on his face had stubbornly held for a short while as he'd worked out the implications of what she'd said, and it was only as she had been about to give up, that he had finally nodded and then taken steps to resolve the problem by thrusting the gory tip into his mouth.

It may have taken Peter a while to put two and two together that time, but since that day it had become a concept that was available for use in his mind at any opportunity.

He now poked his recently bloodied fingertip a little higher for her to see and wiped the beginnings of a tear away with his other hand.

"I don't even know 'ow I done it this time," he whimpered and a sniff made a heartfelt escape.

"How I *did* it," she corrected automatically, and was about to impart an additional piece of advice but he interrupted her.

"'Ow *you* did it?" he asked in wonder. "*You* didn't do it, did you?"

And for one awful moment, Sandra actually contemplated engaging in this particular thread. But Peter's little brain could only conceive of so many things at one time, so it wasn't worth the lengthy diversion.

"Now listen to me, Peter," she stated very deliberately instead. "Have you tried giving yourself a poke this time? If not, why don't you give it a go?"

Perplexed, but obedient to the core, which was a small but very necessary bit of nourishment for Sandra's flagging patience at this moment, he followed her instructions, and then looked back.

"Did that hurt?" she asked.

He thought about it and then shook his head.

"Well then you haven't cut your finger, have you?" Finally the logic sank in and he shook his head once more. Sandra sighed. "No, what you've been doing is picking your nose, Peter, and now you have a nose bleed," she explained, before ushering him out of the class room, grabbing a box of tissues as she went.

* * *

Sandra led Peter along the hall and into the tiny staff room, carefully avoiding the office as Mrs McFreece never tolerated anybody less than four feet tall in her room. Encouraging him to hold a bunch of tissues up to his nose, she then decided it would be prudent to note it in the accident log immediately, rather than wait until the end of the day, just in case she forgot.

It was a thought that made her bite her lip.

The official procedure stated that the log had to be kept with the office administrator, and her decision to add an entry, therefore, brought with it a particular set of misgivings.

Mrs McFreece was a problem; she was a conundrum that neither Miss Lovelock, nor Lady Lovelick, had yet been able to solve. Whilst Sandra liked to believe that she, her good self, was the most dominating and commanding personality in the building, The Fridge seemed to hold that sought after position in the minds of all those around her instead. It had been a disconcerting confession to have to make, to admit that she, too, was scared of a lowly secretary, and not one that her core dominatrix personality cared to accept too openly. Yet whenever the woman was around, Sandra couldn't help but meld into the background, and she hated herself for it. It was a weakness; an aberrant bit of behaviour, and when she was being totally honest with herself, Sandra acknowledged that it was horribly akin to being submissive.

But that was no excuse for dereliction of duty. So, feeling vaguely empowered, she stepped out into the corridor and braced herself for the acerbic glower that would no doubt be sculpting itself soon.

The scrape of an imperious, unwelcome voice grated in her ears as she walked along the hall.

"Is Derek around?" its owner asked, out of sight and already ensconced within the office. A Fridge-like sniff followed swiftly in response.

Sandra stopped in her tracks. She knew that voice. It was a voice that haunted her dreams by night, and plagued her lovesick broken heart by day. It wasn't just *a* voice, but *the* voice; *The* Voice that belonged to *She* who should not be named.

A question immediately sprang to mind. What was *She* doing here?

Sandra's tormented brain began to weave its ugly thoughts. Please, please, please, it begged. In the name of all universal unlikelihoods, please don't say that Miranda Fitztumbleton has come to offer her support. The idea made her stomach knot. Now that *The Call* had come in, it wasn't what Sandra had planned. This week was supposed to be *her* moment of glory, when she would became Derek's pillar of strength. Seven years of hard labour couldn't just be thrust to the wayside simply because the Viyella worshiper had suddenly decided to add her weight to things, significant though it was.

To Sandra's relief, Mrs McFreece was one step ahead.

"I'm afraid he's carrying out a lesson observation in Year One, Mrs Fitztumbleton. I couldn't possibly interrupt him. You'd be best to telephone him later."

The Scottish lilt did its damndest to dismiss the woman, and for once Sandra caught herself offering a slither of gratitude to the secretary. She took a couple of steps closer to the doorway.

"No of course," Miranda replied, unperturbed, and then carried on. "I know the way things are around here, and I certainly wouldn't want you to disrupt his work on my account. But, could you give him this for me?"

The rustle of paper sounded, and then the tap, tap, tap of The Fridge's fingers on her keyboard resumed, as the Head's wife was summarily dismissed.

Before she realised what she was doing, Sandra took another pace forward and bumped headlong into the woman as she retreated out of the office. The padded collision sent them both staggering backwards, and a look of horrified surprise flitted briefly across Miranda's face.

"Oh, I'm dreadfully sorry," Sandra muttered, before she had a chance to curb the unintended words of apology, and then flushed.

One would normally have expected a similar message of contrition in reply, but it wasn't the first time Miranda had implied that she thought polite society stopped at the exit sign out of Cockerby Town. Manners in a place like Lower Bushey were not required. Obviously keen to escape, she pulled herself together instead, and began to bustle past without so much as a word. A sturdy, overfilled suitcase trundled along on its wheels closely behind.

Sandra let her eyes follow the struggling luggage and frowned. That was odd; it didn't fit the scenario she'd just painted in her mind. Miranda spotted the look of confusion and stopped walking. An awkward glow spread across her face.

"Old clothes for the second hand shop," she burbled unnecessarily. "Been having a clear out," she added, equally without reason, before then giving up on any further pretence at politeness and heading out of the school.

The front door clunked shut.

Sandra peered through the window, perplexed, and watched the case trundle along obediently behind its mistress, its tiny wheels struggling under the weight of the oversized clothes within.

If she is off to the second hand shop, Sandra now posed, why bother bringing the case into the school? Why not just leave it in her car? Perhaps she doesn't have a car, her mind answered. Women like that often don't drive, for they expect their slaves to do all that stuff for them. But then why come all the way out to Lower Bushey on the bus, dragging that bloody thing with her? she then reasoned. Just to give Derek an envelope? It still doesn't make any sense.

Sandra pondered further.

There was no way that Miranda was dressed for a quick dash to the second hand shop.

The smart little hat simply didn't fit the bill.

The gloves and shoes were items the Queen Mother would have died for. And...

And!

And; she was overpoweringly sprayed with *Anaîs Anaîs*!

Even if one put aside the clumsily applied makeup, it didn't add up to a trip to the second hand shop. In fact, it didn't add up to a trip to any shop at all.

Her heart rate rose. There was nothing for it; she'd have to follow.

Casting a quick glance back at the staff room to check that Peter was still there, she tip-toed through the front door, and closed it quietly behind her.

Miranda had already reached the other side of the playground, "I have to see this through," Sandra mumbled, her pulse beginning to race. "If it's what I've been waiting for, I need to know for sure," and with that hopeful thought, she scuttled off after the woman.

By the time she had reached the playground gate, Miranda was already tottering along the pavement, a distinctive hum emanating back. Sandra crouched down behind a parked Land Rover, wrinkling her nose at the toneless tune, and craned her neck. Where on earth was the woman going? The bus stop was in the opposite direction; this simply didn't make any sense.

But then suddenly, as if in answer to the puzzle, the noisy rumble of the suitcase came to a halt, and Miranda bent over to peer through the passenger window of a shiny new Jag. She gave the glass a tap, and then followed the gesture with a saucy little wave. The dapper leg of a pinstripe suit swiftly appeared, and a lissom, middle aged man climbed out of the vehicle and ambled his way to the rear. With one click of a button, he flicked the boot open and leant inside. Sandra's eyes widened with surprise.

"Thank you for picking me up from here, Marcus," Miranda said, as she glanced nervously around. "It wouldn't have done to have you collect me from the house. The neighbours would have had a field day."

Marcus appeared to make an appropriate noise in response, and then planted the sloppiest kiss on the woman's mouth that Sandra had ever seen. Finally, once the king-sized smackeroonie had ended, he then hoisted Miranda's luggage into the car and slammed the boot shut.

As the Jag drove off, its throaty roar slowly dissipated away, and Sandra felt her pulse inexplicably drop to calm. This is it, she said to herself. This really is my chance.

* * *

Sandra casually veered into the office knowing that she could face Mrs McFreece now if she had to. The end justifies the means, she thought to herself as her confidence rallied. No amount of refrigeration was going to get in her way.

"Is Derek around?" she asked, wavering only briefly inside. The Fridge glared back.

"Mr *Fitztumbleton*," the woman stressed, stating the formal address as though Sandra were one of his pupils, "is otherwise engaged. He's in a lesson observation."

"Yes, yes, yes," Sandra interrupted, and then waved her hand dismissively for good measure. Mrs McFreece's jaw dropped in astonishment. Encouraged, Sandra ploughed on.

"Yes, yes, I know," she continued, spurred on by the lack of response. "Ofsted are here in three days..."

"Two days, seventeen hours and forty three minutes, actually." the secretary snapped at last, and pointed to a digital clock ticking backwards on her computer. "So you should only interrupt him if it really is very urgent."

The woman's eyes shone bright with re-established gusto, and Sandra realised that soon her nerve would fail; if there was ever a time to play her trump card, it was now.

"Well, I'd like to get a pupil fast tracked onto our Gifted and Talented programme." she announced. "For the sake of the Year Six statistics," she then added, convinced that it was an ace. The woman's jaw now plummeted for the second time.

"Really?" The Fridge gasped. And it was only then that Sandra realised quite how absurd the statement must have sounded. Her mouth stretched into a smug grin.

"I suppose you're wondering who I'm talking about, aren't you?" It was true to say that, until three weeks ago, it would have been hard to find a pupil gracing the heady echelons of just below average in Year Six. But that had been three weeks ago and now was different. Sandra met the derisory scowl head on.

"It's Ashley Milner," she announced, and waited for this second bomb to drop.

Three – two – one; Mrs McFreece's face twitched.

To hear that pupil's name in the same sentence as the words '*Gifted and Talented*' was clearly a difficult thing to assimilate. Sandra knew, however, that the woman would be battling with the contradictory pleasure of ticking a box as well. Stretching exceptional pupils until they snapped was good for the school's figures. The more the '*more-able*' were pushed, pulled, yanked and ranked, the better, so long as it was statistically and bureaucratically visible, of course. It was a tough call, but as Sandra had anticipated, the box ticking won.

Without saying another word, Mrs McFreece reached to her left, pulled out a form, and ceremoniously handed it across to Sandra. With a conspiratorial flick of her head, she then indicated for Sandra to go through to Derek's office without any further ado.

"He's actually in there," she whispered. "I just didn't want any old person interrupting him." And finished her announcement off with a wink.

Inside, Sandra's heart sang. Outside, her face sat as sourly in position as it ever did.

"Shall I take that through for him too?" she asked, trying to point at Miranda's recently deposited envelope without raising suspicion.

Mrs McFreece nodded her assent, and as though Sandra were being permitted to wander into VIP territory, she walked on, picking up the packet as she went by.

She found Derek sitting at his desk, perusing the latest statistics, papers lying everywhere. He looked so at home, almost at peace she thought; and suddenly Sandra faltered. Was now really the time to destroy his tranquillity? Should she wait until a little later?

As she pondered these life changing questions, she took in the balding scalp and hairy ears, and also wondered briefly why nature chose to distribute male hair in such an extraordinary way. The vagaries of female depilation were well known to all, but the hirsute nature of a middle aged man's nose and lug holes was still a mystery. What he needed was someone to notice these things. He needed someone to care. He also needed someone to ease the burden of accountability that all leaders felt, and make his decisions for him. And this was exactly what Sandra Lovelock wanted. She'd practised. She knew what had to be done.

Yes! She now realised, with a sudden clarity of mind; sometimes one had to be cruel to be kind.

She cleared her throat and Derek looked up, surprised.

"Ah, Miss Lovelock. Good to see you. I imagine you're bearing up well to the news we've had today. You have nothing to worry about, of course." He beamed a massive smile at her as he spoke, and her heart swelled. "By the way," he then added, his brow suddenly creasing, "Mrs McFreece left a message for Miranda to phone me some time ago, but I haven't heard back from her yet. You haven't taken a call from her today have you?"

As he asked the question, Sandra glanced through the window and spotted the scruffy collection of scarecrows they'd so vehemently battled over only the week before. They were nodding their ugly heads in the wind; tell him the truth, the motion said. Tell him what you know. She bit her lip and looked away. The envelope felt alien in her hand. She cleared her throat once more, only this time for a different reason.

"Err… no," she said, sniffing and shaking her head. "I've not taken a call from Miranda. Sorry." Well, it wasn't a lie. "I would like to talk to you, though, about putting Ashley Milner on the gifted and talented programme." She held up the G&T form for him to see as she said it. "But we can talk about it later if you'd prefer. I was going to ask you if you'd like me to stay behind to help prepare stuff for Thursday anyway."

Derek sighed and shrugged, clearly disappointed.

"Well I'm sure she'll call when she can," he muttered, and then pulled himself together. "However it's very good of you to offer your assistance later, thank you. I thought you went out on Monday evenings?"

Inadvertently adjusting the leather bra strap under her blouse, she managed as casual a shrug as she could, and shook her head.

"Oh no, it's okay. I'll happily change my plans for this evening if there's still a lot to be done."

Derek nodded his thanks, his attention already beginning to wander back to the reports on his desk.

"What is it you usually do?" he asked vaguely, as he eyes began to scan the graphs. "It's not WI is it? That's what Miranda does on a Monday." Suddenly he looked up from the papers and frowned. "No, you don't do WI, do you?" he exclaimed, and gave his ear a scratch. "I recall you mentioning it once. No don't tell me," he put his hand up to stop her from interrupting, and tapped his forehead for inspiration. "Some sort of cookery club. That's it, isn't it?" he announced, clearly pleased with himself. "I remember you grumbling that someone had poached your piece of cod!"

Inside, Sandra cringed. She remembered a rather different conversation, and she hadn't been talking to Derek at the time, she'd been complaining on the phone to *Dominantics - The Club* that someone had pinched Yuri's cod piece. But now was perhaps not the time to correct him.

"Yes, well" she tried instead. "Anyway. The children will be going home soon, so when they've gone, I'll do some sorting in my classroom. Let me know when you'd like to chat about Ashley."

Seemingly unaware that she'd dodged his question, Derek thanked her, and then reached over to take the envelope in her hand. For a split second, her fingers refused to let go. His pain would be deep and sharp. It would leave him exposed and vulnerable at a time when he needed his strength most. It would create the perfect scenario for her to step in. The question was though... would he let her?

Suddenly, Sandra realised that she'd never know unless she tried.

"I'm just going to log Peter's nosebleed in the accident book, Mr Fitztumbleton. But I'll be around if you need me," she said, and then finally allowed the envelope to pass across.

Chapter Four

John Bentwick watched from the safety of his Land Rover as Sandra headed back inside, and pondered the spring-like skip that had suddenly entered her step. She's an odd bird that one, he thought, as he took another bite of his Snickers. Walks as though she's got a rod up her arse, and what is it with the pointy teats? Yes, he decided finally, as he picked out a lump from his tooth, she's as nutty as a partridge. This is November not March; wrong season altogether to be hopping about like a lamb.

Reassured by the logic, and feeling magnanimously tolerant of these outsiders' peculiar ways, John then adjusted his backside against the thinly padded car seat and checked his watch. It was nearly ten past three. Probably best to wait for the bell to go first before heading in, as it didn't do to wander around a playground when teachers were at work. He'd been caught too many times as a lad, roaming aimlessly like a lost bullock, not to have learnt that lesson. And besides, he was in no rush. Roger, his overly-testiculated ram, had decided he didn't want an audience today, so it was best to leave him to it for a while. It didn't do to wander around a field when Roger was at work either.

The tenuous argument may have convinced a casual farm labourer of his motives for staying put, but John

Bentwick, reluctant Chair of Governors, was honest with himself, if nothing else. Deep down he knew he was procrastinating. He was a straightforward soul, with uncomplicated needs and ambitions. What he didn't know about sheep, cows and pigs wasn't worth knowing. But exactly the same could also have been said for what he did know about education; which wasn't worth knowing either. The kinds of challenges he relished, from one day to the next, involved worming tablets and prolapsed wombs. So this little matter of Ofsted, well that was unnerving. It had sat at the back of his mind all morning, whilst he'd tried to tantalize Roger with the prettiest ewe in the flock, and he'd come to the conclusion that there was only one thing for it; to consider this inspection in terms that he could understand.

It took time to breed a prize bull, so his rationale went; it wasn't something that happened over night, and it required constant attention and vigilance to make sure all the characteristics were primed to perfection. To raise a winner, one had to track growth, monitor development, and make adjustments as the need arose. The rules for success were extremely prescriptive, but take your eyes off the bull for one moment and all could be doomed to failure.

From the conversations he'd had with Bob the school caretaker, and therefore font of all accessible knowledge of education, at least as far as John was concerned, the concept of developing a successful school was no different. No different whatsoever.

"That's absolutely right, John," Bob had wisely confirmed to him only that morning. "The boxes are there to be ticked; you just need the right coloured pen."

Well, it was a logic that he could work with at least, so he now leant back, stuck a piece of straw in his mouth, and waited for time to tick by.

Before too long, children began to flood into the playground, frolicking hither and thither like lambs jumping free from a dipping pen, and John watched their happy escape with a heavy heart. Now that the plausible excuses were running thin, he had no choice but to force his legs to do what his brain was struggling to contemplate and as he headed towards the school gate, he allowed his mind to resort to a swift but significant mental debate regarding wellies.

It was important to get these things right. The distant recollection of his mother yelling, "Take 'em off, yer little bugger, or I'll tan yer backside till it's blue" was a poignant one, and had often provided the impetus he was looking for when all else had failed. As he reached the front door, he slid his feet out of his boots, carried out a last minute inspection for unwanted holes, and confirmed that his socks were holding fast. Just.

The Fridge eyed him suspiciously as he walked in, and stared with disgust at the sweaty footwear. Her piggy eyes narrowed.

"Oh it's you," she grunted.

John shifted his weight from one foot to the other and felt the chill of the lino seeping through to his soles. He'd had a sow like McFreece once; she'd also been bad tempered and a bully to the little ones. One day she'd rolled over and crushed a piglet, hadn't even heard the poor thing squeal its last squeal, and he had decided, then and there, that it would be her last litter. At this moment, he rather wished he could send The Fridge to the same abattoir. The paperwork wouldn't be a problem, for with a temperament like hers she was certain to have a livestock number.

"We weren't expecting you today, Mr Bentwick," she grumbled further, in her welcoming way, and John mentally moved the telephone number for the knackers' yard to the top of his to-do list. "Mr Fitztumbleton was under the impression that you were unavailable until tomorrow. So I'm afraid," she then huffed, as though he had committed the gravest of sins and, like any sin, there was a price to pay, "he won't have prepared yet the information that you'll no doubt be wanting to see."

It was at this point, that John's stomach clenched. It hadn't occurred to him that he'd *be wanting* to see *any* information. Farmers were renowned for wanting many things, but information wasn't one of them; for they tended to know it all already. Something had to be done.

"Err…" he replied, and then let the full import of the statement hang heavy between them. The Fridge waited briefly before replying.

"But I expect you're here to give a little moral support," she then suggested, and a swinish eyebrow lifted disparagingly above one eye.

Despite himself, John grabbed at the crumb of help.

"Um," he added with significance, and the swinish eyebrows leapt upwards in search of her hairline before swapping sides.

Silence reigned, momentarily, and then Mrs McFreece broke it with a crisp tut.

"Well," she sighed, evidently gratified that, once again, the school's Chair of Governors had fulfilled her every expectation, "as Mr Fitztumbleton would say, *carpe diem*. Although it's a little late in the day really to be doing any seizing, don't you think? Perhaps you can give him this note, though, when you go through," she then finished implying that, if nothing else, he could at least be of use as a messenger boy and folded the piece of paper in half and passed it to him. John's frown deepened.

"Carping what?"

Mrs McFreece smirked. "*Carpe diem*," she repeated, clearly happy that the phrase had done its worst. "It's Latin, Mr Bentwick. Mr Fitztumbleton uses it all the time." And then left the rest unexplained.

Feeling none the wiser, John skulked through to Derek's office like a dismissed collie and timidly knocked on the door. As a hoarse voice bade him enter, he walked into the tiny room, expecting at least a polite word of welcome, and was met instead by something that made him falter in his stride. Derek's face was as white as a sheep, and a particularly clean sheep at that, and it was shaped by a look of such vacuity that John was thrown. Derek had sounded so positive on the phone earlier; this didn't make any sense.

He decided the situation called for further consideration before he put his clammy socked foot in it.

Perhaps this was what headmasters did during school hours, he reasoned, as he sat down awkwardly. Perhaps they were paid to think and nothing else. Perhaps some thoughts made them smile, some thoughts made them frown, and others, like those that Derek was thinking at this moment in time, made them think of absolutely nothing at all. In its simplicity, the rationale had its attractions, but even John Bentwick could see it was lacking. People didn't just stare into space, looking like they'd seen a ghost, for no reason. There had to be a trigger.

It was only at this point in his internal meanderings, that he then spotted the letter clutched between Derek's fingers. Things potentially slotted into place.

He'd seen that look in himself in the mirror once, just after he'd received news that he was going to have to put his favourite mare down, and if that was what had happened, then it was no wonder that the man looked so miserable. John had not been aware that Derek was into horses, but as a result of having this new knowledge to hand, he decided that the fellow needed his sympathy.

"Are you alright, Mr Fitztumbleton?" he tried, believing he was now standing on sure ground. "It's just you look as though your prize 'unter's been given their marching orders. Which was something that 'appened to me once, but I shan't burden you with that story now, eh? You probably feel you *ought* to 'ave other things on yer mind, like this 'ere inspection really. You're meant to be *Carping the M*, apparently," he added, hoping that it at least made sense to someone in the know, if not to his own ears.

Carping or no carping, however, it mattered not. Derek didn't seem to hear a thing.

"Sorry, what was that, Mr Bentwick?" the despondent man muttered, sighing heavily. "I wasn't expecting you until tomorrow."

"Well, I know," John replied quickly, keen to move on from the Latin stuff now that he'd heard himself saying it; it seemed he'd got away with it this time, but it wasn't something to risk twice. "I know I said I couldn't join yer until tomorrer, but me tup's gone all shy. So I thought I'd pop in 'ere for a bit. Give 'im a bit of privacy, so to speak, and you a bit of moral support," he then added, thanking The Fridge mentally before he could stop himself.

Derek managed a frown. "Your... tup?"

"That's right, my tup, my ram; 'es down the paddock as we speak. 'Opefully doing 'is business, 'cos 'e prefers for me not to be looking on." John paused to check that all was understood before continuing and, when Derek nodded vaguely in verification, sighed and carried on. "Well, Roger is no showman," he explained, before scrunching his fist up in a ball and thrusting it up proudly. "But 'is scrotum's the size of a pumpkin, and 'is knob gets as 'ard as an 'ammer. So I can't get rid of 'im, can I?" And as he concluded his explanation with this stunning piece of logic, a corner of paper sticking out from his palm caught his eye.

"Oh, by the way," he added, oblivious to Derek's shocked expression. "Your," out of habit he wanted to use the phrase 'good woman', but it stuck in his craw, so he dropped the idea, "your, err… secretary asked me to give you this." He opened out the note and let his eyes glance across the words.

'*Sandra has G&T stuff waiting for you. She'll be in her classroom when you're ready.*'

Gordon Bennett, he thought to himself, as he passed the message across. Drinking at this time of day? Things were worse than he'd thought.

* * *

John checked the name of the street, and then let the Land Rover crawl along in first gear as he eyed the house numbers. He didn't know this part of Lower Bushey very well. Not that it was a large village, on the contrary, it boasted at most, a population the size of a small pig farm. It was just that this was the bit that had been built post war, generations after his family had moved into the area. The government had wanted a ghetto in every conurbation, and so Lower Bushey had got its quota of council housing just like the rest of them. Within a decade, having sucked in the urban stragglers who couldn't quite cut it in Cockerby Town, the cross cultural divide had been born. The '*thems*' lived on Bunting Hill, which was where John was now ambling along at five miles per hour, whilst the '*usses*' continued with life merrily where they'd always been.

He spotted number sixty-nine, and brought the car to a halt just to the right of an abandoned cooker. Looking at it, he ran his hand thoughtfully across his chin. Odd taste in garden decorations aside, this Mabel seemed a good 'un. She had an enchanting set of qualities that could compliment his crude ways well, given half a chance. Whereas he was a farmer used to fighting hardship with the simplicity of an incumbent landowner, she, on the other hand, had a style and panache that had never even singed his horizon before. Mind you, she also had a smile that could melt his heart and a nice set of ankles. But thoughts like that were a little bit advanced at this stage. She'd only said yes, so far, to seeing his ram...

The passenger door clicked open and shut, and a waft of flowery perfume slid pleasantly up his nose.

"Hi ya," Mabel muttered, settling into her seat, looking nervously back at her front door. "I saw you pull up, and thought I'd save you the walk. Shall we head off then?" she urged. "To The Tupping Paddock. Now. Before it gets too dark," she then added, before flicking another uncertain glance at her house, just as John caught sight of the swish of a curtain as it was pulled out of place. Despite the masculine looking, towel-clad, head staring out, Mabel's pleading expression tugged at his heart strings and he nodded and thrust the car into gear.

"Got a friend babysitting, 'ave yer?" he asked, and then got the shock of his life as the face in the window blew him a kiss. Disconcerted, he pulled away from the kerb as quickly as he could. "Nice to 'ave a girl friend you can turn to, isn't it? I should imagine it's difficult at the moment, you bein' new round 'ere, an' all."

Mabel smoothed her hair down.

"That's Dwayne, I mean Dawn," she corrected swiftly. "And *she's* a bit of a joker. But don't worry, she's harmless," she then explained, and shrugged as if in apology.

John risked a quick look across to his side and their stares locked. "Really," Mabel reassured. "Dawn's a bit unusual, but she's a good mate." The sincere yet imploring glint in her eyes begged him to leave it there, so he turned his attention to the road again.

With the ice now broken, they trundled along for a short while, both seemingly content to sit in silence, until John eventually allowed himself another quick peek to his left.

She had a nice profile, and he liked the way her hair was pulled back in a clip behind her neck. It gave her a look of subtle sophistication. His glance dropped down a bit lower and took in the tightly closed trench coat. The shadow cast by the dashboard made it impossible to see her legs, but he'd wager she had on a pair of those brightly coloured wellingtons that women seemed to go for these days. It was all a bit of fun, and he welcomed the thought of someone more light-hearted than the sour faced lasses he'd courted in the past. Yes, Mabel was different in so many ways; almost an enigma.

"So, what do yer do then?" he asked. And then quickly added, "Hold on, don't tell me. Let me guess."

She gestured for him to have a try. John pondered briefly before speaking.

"Well, I don't reckon yer from farming stock; sorry, don't mean to be rude," he then clarified; suddenly worried that she'd be offended at him making such a swift and condemning judgement. "It's just that yer've got the prettiest pair of fetlocks I've seen in a good while, and none of the fillies around 'ere 'ave 'alf as good a set of hocks as you." A quick rain-check indicated that she seemed mildly disturbed by the compliments, and he decided it might be better to tone things down a bit. It didn't do to be too forward early on. "Anyway, I reckon yer work in an office, or something like that. Yer've got the look of a clever mare."

Mabel cleared her throat, appearing to struggle with the flattering remark, but then managed a smirk.

"I'm going for an interview at the insurance brokers in Cockerby tomorrow, actually."

"What, Trotter, Ribley and Snouterton?" he asked, feeling a warm glow spread inside as he realised that they had something in common. Mabel's pretty smile broadened as he said it, and he noticed the fine set of teeth and grinned back.

"Yes, that's them," she replied, clearly pleased too. "They do agricultural insurance, don't they?"

He nodded. "I use 'em actually. I've been one of their main clients for years and they're a good company. I do 'ope it goes well for yer, 'cos you could do a lot worse than work for them. But what are yer doing currently whilst yer wait to see if yer get the job?"

He'd asked the question more to keep the chatter going, than for any other nosy reason, but, to his dismay, as the words slipped out of his mouth, the shine disappeared from her smile and she turned back to face the front once again.

"I'm a Removals Executive," she replied dryly, and the temperature fell rapidly ten degrees.

John bit his lip. He didn't know anything about moving house, he'd never done it, but he did sense he'd dropped a clanger without realising. His brain grabbed at a straw.

"Well, would yer like me to 'ave a chat with Mr Ribley tomorrer?" he tried, praying it would swing things back in the right direction. It had all been so pleasant before he'd opened his gob. "I could put a good word in fer yer, if it'd 'elp," he offered. "'E owes me one, does Mr Ribley 'E drove me spare the other day when 'e quoted my renewal. I 'ad to put my foot down and get Mr Trotter the senior partner involved."

"Don't tell me," Mable muttered glumly. "Mr Snouterton stuck his nose in an' all." And as she said it, John slammed his foot on the brake.

"Blimey!" he exclaimed, looking at her with something now akin to awe. "'Ow on earth did yer know that?"

* * *

It was only as John parked up on the grassy verge next to his tupping paddock, the village of Nether Bunting but a

65

stone's throw away, that the truth began to dawn on him. Ever since they'd hit the road, there'd been a terrier-sized voice yapping at the back of his mind. But, knowing what stubborn buggers terriers could be, he'd stolidly ignored it so far. Now though, as the frozen expression of horror on Mabel's face slowly sank in, the full length coat, the stylishly made up face, and the apparent lack of appropriate footwear, all urged him to acknowledge that things weren't adding up.

"So did yer bring yer wellies then?" he asked, still mentally blocking out the truth as though his life depended on it. "I'd wondered if yer'd forgotten them when yer got in, but I 'adn't wanted to say anything, what with yer seeming so keen to get going."

Mabel's forehead creased.

"My wellingtons?" she repeated back to him.

"Aye, yer gum boots," he tried, stumbling on like a blind bull, although the boundaries of the china shop were now making themselves felt. Inside, he cringed. As soon as he'd said it, an awkward look of realisation had begun to creep across her features, and the knot in John's stomach now tightened. He waited nervously for her response. Mabel bit her lip.

"Um," was the best she had to offer. But although it was clear that she was struggling to work out what to say next, as soon as the sound had left her mouth John melted with relief. With language like that they were sure to be kindred spirits.

Overjoyed, he offered her an, "Err…" in encouragement.

Finally, she found her voice.

"Silly me," she croaked, shrugging. "I forgot my dear old wellies in the rush to get out of the house. They'll be standing in the hallway, as we speak, wondering where I've gone."

John's jaw dropped. In all his years of farming, he had never known a woman refer to her boots as though they were old friends. It was more than he could ever have dreamed of.

"Are they nice pink ones, with 'earts on?" he risked, knowing it was cheeky but unable to stop himself now that he'd been given some hope. Mabel flushed. "Sorry, I just thought they would be; sophisticated lady like you," he furthered, hoping to reassure her. But then her forehead creased for a second time.

"But I thought you'd said we were going to The Tupping Paddock?" she stated, the deep furrows in her forehead beginning to bother him again. Despite his optimism, something wasn't right. "That is a pub, isn't it? Here in Nether Bunting," she added, and then pursed her mouth nervously.

John looked at her in dismay. Putting aside the backward step everything had unexpectedly taken, how did one answer such an inappropriate question?

"No," he resorted to eventually. "It's The Three Sided Thicket that's 'ere at Nether Bunting, and I 'ad 'oped you might join me." But then suddenly, as her face creased up even more, his words began to dry up. What on earth was he thinking? Why would a best in show winner like her want to spend time in Nether Bunting?

What could any of The Buntings have to offer such a woman? They may have been the whole world to him but, in reality, they were just a forgotten collection of villages that skirted the larger parish of Lower Bushey. Perhaps in their heyday The Buntings could have pulled a crowd. But since their decline in the early nineties, when Sky TV had declared that coverage would not reach them for a good while, The Three Sided Thicket had slipped downhill too. Such were the effects of Brazilian success at the 1994 and 2002 World Cups on the trimming of the population.

"Join you for what?" Mabel cut in, and broke his thoughts. John realised that his rambling gob had dug a hole he couldn't get out of. There was nothing for it but to ask her.

"Well I 'ad been 'oping you might join me at The Thicket – after; for a scampi and chips. But I can see that you've got other plans."

Her nostrils flared. "After? After what?"

"Oh no!" he cried, suddenly grasping why she looked so put out. "I've not brought yer 'ere to roll around in the 'ay, so to speak."

"Oh good," she mumbled, although her face didn't reflect the sense of relief that the words were supposed to imply. He backtracked one step further.

"No, it's not like that at all. I'd just wanted yer to meet Roger, and for Roger to meet you." He swallowed heavily, and realised that a full confession was necessary. "Look, I'll come clean. I did 'ave an ulterior motive." She raised an eyebrow, but he ploughed on. "I did think that it might 'elp 'im, Roger that is, to get into the mood if 'e saw me with a pretty lass by my side. But that weren't the only reason I asked yer, 'onest. Yer can borrow me niece's old boots, if it 'elps. She 'ad them when she was ten but she's a big lass now."

Mabel shot him a puzzled look.

"I mean she's tall for 'er age," he explained swiftly, and then leant across into the back of the car to grab them out. As he hoisted the size nine clod hoppers up for her to see, Mabel's eyes widened in surprise, and he realised further clarification was required. "What I meant," he added finally, "is I believe she's grown into 'er feet."

* * *

John was relieved to see that the flock had congregated near the gate for the night. It was a cloudless evening, and the moon was waxing well so the darkness was held at bay. But having to help a woman negotiate a field she didn't know, in boots five sizes too big, wouldn't have been ideal.

"So why's 'e," Mabel coughed, and then corrected herself. "Why's *he* got an apron on?"

John followed the direction of her finger with his eyes, and then clambered awkwardly over the gate after her. It was a good sign that she'd picked out his pride and joy so quickly, but was it really necessary to cast such aspersions?

"That's not an apron, that's an 'arness for the raddle," he replied, trying to keep his indignation to a minimum. "It's for marking the ewes when 'es, um," He paused, suddenly unsure how to put it a better way. "Well, it's for marking the ewes with dye when 'es 'ad 'em," was what he plumped for in the end.

Mabel shrugged.

"Well, I think he's been slacking whilst you've been away. There's not a painted arse amongst 'em," she announced, and as soon as the words had left her lips, her hand swept up to her mouth.

"Ooh," she exclaimed, mortified with herself, "I didn't mean to say arse. Oh no," she then added, her eyes widening with horror, "there I go again. Bugger. I'm sorry. What must you think of me?"

Bearing in mind that she was right about the dearth of decorated backsides, John would have liked to have had the opportunity to put her mind at ease. But it was exactly at this moment, unfortunately, that Roger decided it was time to prove his masculinity. Man on man, alpha male versus alpha male, he wasn't going to tolerate a rival amour on his patch. This was his flock and he had the tackle to prove it.

John knew the signs well and instantly went on guard. The quivering of the brute's upper lip meant Roger was spawning a plan, and a ram's brain that was devoted to one sole purpose didn't need much time to think. All raddled up and ready to go, the beast soon began to scrape at the grass, and then, with one final gut churning grunt, he set off.

For a big animal, he was surprisingly fleet of foot.

John snatched a hurried glance back. Mabel hadn't yet grasped the seriousness of the situation; still horrified, as she was, that she'd said the word 'arse'. Well that would soon to be the least of her worries, he realised. If he didn't do something fast, she'd be flattened.

As his mind raced, Roger's feet pounded across the grass and Mabel remained blissfully unaware. Closer and closer the fiend came, hooves hammering, nostrils flared with loathing, and John took in the wild eyed look of fury and realised that there was only one thing left he could do.

He ROARED.

With every pound to square inch of thrust he could muster, he roared with all his might, and sent the blood curdling noise out into the darkness. As the lion's growl thundered through the air, it tapped into the innate fear hardcoded into all beasts at the bottom of the food chain, and forced the ram to falter.

Roger skidded to a halt and snorted with disgust. That wasn't meant to happen. Everyone knew that when a ram had set his sights on a pretty little thing she never got away. His reputation was at stake. Humans were threatening the reason for his existence; If he wanted to retain his dignity, he'd have to take the ugly bastard out first.

Suddenly his emphasis shifted.

There could be no more of this namby-pamby honourable match amongst equals crap. This was now man versus beast. Two legs versus four; farmer versus farmed.

The complex calculation of momentum versus inertia rattled through his brain. Mass on mass, it looked to be a doddle. But this farmer was unpredictable, and that made it a tough call. Roger reworked the equation, to include centre of gravity and the reflexivity of a human brain, and then finished the cogitation off with a burp. Sorted; he was ready.

As the noise belched into the night, he dipped his head for the second time and set off.

Briefly, just before John found himself lying flat on his back in the mud, the farmer wondered whether wheat cultivation was more his thing. And within a few seconds, when he was lying stretched on the ground staring up at the sky, with The Plough twinkling back at him for comfort, he decided it probably was.

Ignoring the ache in his ribs, he drew in a slow deep breath. The troublesome thing, though, was this; much as he would have preferred to just curl up and die at this moment, there was still a small matter of a pair of oversized wellies hopping around needing to be saved. Action was still required, and regardless of the fact that his mind and body were currently unable to agree on what that action should be, the problem wasn't going away. It was a conundrum to be sure.

A concerned feminine voice sounded in his ears and temporarily stalled the internal debate. "Don't worry, John," it said. "I'll draw him away. Give you time to get up."

He searched for the sarcasm and then realised, to his horror, that there was none. She really meant it. She actually thought she could do something.

Panic now set in.

Overruling the mind/body stalemate, John battled to haul himself onto his feet. But before he had even had a chance to locate his knees, Mabel appeared out of nowhere parading the most bizarre display he'd ever seen.

Silhouetted against the horizon, her arms were whirling madly in circles whilst her body twisted and twirled around an invisible pole. Finding himself unable to move, John watched the flailing limbs in bewilderment, and tracked the madcap movements with his gaze as she wind-milled her way, backwards and forth. Eventually, she swirled right across his vision and out the other side.

As soon as she had vanished, a moment of calm befell.

The stars in his favourite constellation winked; a barn owl hooted for the hell of it; and amidst this sudden tranquillity, John glanced to his left and caught sight of Roger eyeing him with a malevolent leer. He was only a few feet away.

Their stares locked.

My field; *my* flock; *my* fun park; the ram's glare said. And don't you bloody forget it!

In a sophisticated meeting of minds, John stuck two fingers up, and whispered at him to *fuck off*.

Roger blinked.

It's still *my* field; *my* flock; *my* fun park; the blink said, and, and...

A shuffle of cloven feet tittered in the background.

And.

The brazen balled bugger's gaze shifted to see what was going on.

And.

John frowned for, although the ovine brain was short on attention span, the speed of this distraction was a surprise even to him.

And.

As the clomp of size nine wellies reached a thumping crescendo, the explanation for the change of focus suddenly made itself apparent.

Baaing with irritation, two ewes ambled across, pursued by a rear side wind that was eddying around their hormonal backsides and blowing their erotic pheromones towards the ram's nostrils.

Despite himself, Roger sniffed and then sniffed again. There was no doubt that this was a more enticing smell than that of a two legged trollop with no fleece. And, bearing in mind that his honour was still at stake, it was, he decided, a worthy justification for a change of plan. He gave John one final malicious gawp, scraped his hoof in a new direction, and then shot off towards the four footed fragrant beauties instead.

A look of awe crept across John's face. He and Mabel made it back to the gate at the same time.

"Blimey yer fleet of foot, missy," he puffed, before managing to then follow it up with the most supreme of compliments he could muster. "And boy, do yer 'ave initiative. What I'd give for a dog as good as that." Mabel frowned. "So 'ow about that scampi and chips, eh?" he added, slightly less sure of himself now that he could better see her face. "I'll chuck in a glass of sherry to say thanks, if it will 'elp to sway yer mind."

Now her face creased into a sneer.

"You can fuck off with your sherry," she snorted, and passed him the size nine wellies as she said it.

Crushed, John took them and opened the passenger door.

"Oh, right," he mumbled, unable to meet her gaze, and put his hand out to help her to climb in.

The warmth of her touch seeped through his calloused palms and he felt her fingers give his a squeeze.

"But I will have a Southern Comfort and lemonade if it's on offer," she said quietly, and swept his doubts away.

* * *

John and Mabel had a very pleasant evening. The Buntings did not let them down, and The Three Sided Thicket, empty as it was, welcomed them warmly into the fold. As he drove her back to her house, John tried to think of the last time he'd felt so relaxed at tupping time, and couldn't think of one; so easy to be with was his new companion.

"I would invite you in for a coffee," she explained sheepishly, and he fell in love with her even more. "But it's late and I have to get my daughter to school in the morning."

"It's no worry." he replied disappointed, but then felt his heart soar as she leant across from her seat.

"How about next time?" she whispered, her breath tickling his ear. "I've only got instant in the cupboard today, but I'll make sure I've got proper coffee beans in for when I see you again."

As far as John was concerned, a good grinding would be all that was needed to make that a success. But just as he was about to impart that sincere one liner, her babysitter rushed out of the house, and the moment was fortuitously lost forever.

"Well, hello handsome," Dawn cooed, and ran her tongue across her lips. "Mabe never let on you were this big."

Speechless, John tried to make sense of the extraordinary sight in front of him. Makeup, short skirt, heels and jewellery, none of those would not normally be a problem, per se. It was just that the particular combination visible through his passenger window was not what life had prepared him for. He mumbled something indecipherable, and then found that he was all percolated out.

Chapter Five

Sandra woke up three seconds before her alarm went off and felt the thrill of a new day flood through her veins. For once, this one had potential. It was the morning after the day before, and not only had she had an unusually invigorating evening for a Monday, but miserable Miranda's cowardly exit also meant that she could smile the biggest smile she'd managed in a very long time.

"Yes!" she shouted jubilantly, and thrust her arms into the air. "I've now got you in my sights, Derek Fitztumbleton. You will soon be mine!"

To her delight, the ecstasy continued to linger. So she turned to the mound bulging under the duvet next to her, and lifted her fist and walloped the unsuspecting lump as hard as she could. The material sagged where her arm had bashed down and hugged the impression like a lopsided smile. Oh, it wouldn't be long now. The need to play make-believe with a couple of old pillows would soon be over and Derek would be lying there next to her, the two of them living in leather bonded connubial bliss.

What a wonderful thought to wake up to.

As she slid out of bed, her buckskin corset creaked. She pulled the G-string out from between her cheeks and let it twang against a buttock. That was the one problem with these outfits; they needed to be kept under control.

A few hours of unconscious slumber and they could develop minds of their own. Absentmindedly, she caught herself wondering if Derek might prefer lace, and then mentally slapped herself. It wasn't his decision. Nothing in her life could have a mind of its own, unless she said it could; Derek would be no different.

Shivering as the November chill stroked her skin, Sandra slid on her jack boots and marched off to the kitchen. Down the stairs, along the hall and through the frosted glass doorway, she goose stepped her way straight across to the kettle and switched it on with a flick. Other than the obvious, there was nothing quite like a nice mug of tea to wake one up.

She grabbed the tea leaves, spooned out the necessary amount, and then tap danced over to the radio. A little local news would fill the time nicely, whilst she waited for the toaster to pop.

"...*Further complaints have been received by the police, of a flasher taking advantage of the season of good cheer...*" a disembodied voice informed the inhabitants of Cockerby Town. Sandra stopped to listen. "*... Dressed in Santa kit,*" it continued dryly, "*but sadly a mince pie short of a full load, the skinny imposter is baring his North Pole to unsuspecting pensioners in the ho-ho-hosiery department of M&S... Police have confirmed that they have narrowed down their search, as the suspect is unusually slight in build...*" She laughed, and waited for more. "*... However, they also 'sleigh' the public do not have 'Claus' for concern, for they expect* *to have the case wrapped up in the Saint Nick of time for Christmas."*

Poor buggers, she thought, chuckling further, and then piled her breakfast onto a tray; I bet they'll get more than they bargained for when they delve into his stocking. The suggestion made her giggle again and then she put the matter out of her mind and headed back upstairs, whistling. The law may have had its hands full, but she had more important things to think about than stories of policemen chasing a man with a big sack.

As she walked into her bedroom, a judgemental meow sounded.

"What are you looking at?" she snapped. But Mr Perkins ignored her and turned to lick his paw. "I'm allowed to whistle if I want to," she added for no reason, irritated by her companion's imperious nature. "You purr without permission."

The cat lifted his head nonchalantly to stare back at her from his vantage point on the window sill, and then blinked. It had always been an effort for Sandra to convince herself that she and Mr Perkins had settled on a mutual understanding for cohabitation, and she would also have liked to have been able to say that Mr Perkins had seen a few things during their time together. But she knew she'd be over-blowing her trumpet if she did. There was no doubt that Mr Perkins was a worldly beast, and he was certainly king pin in this area of Cockerby, she wouldn't have had it any other way, but the sordid sights upon which his eyes had lain had nothing to do with her life. Outside of *Dominantics*, Sandra Lovelock had made very little impact on the world, so far. Those who lived on the same street hardly noticed her. Her neighbours were barely aware she existed, and her bed had never, ever seen any action.

Mr Perkins' stare was clearly intended to remind her of that last poignant fact.

"Don't look at me like that, you mangy mog. You're just jealous," she growled. "I'll do more than have you castrated next time if you're not careful. Now bugger off. I'd like to get dressed in peace."

Despite the irritation in her voice, the cat carried on regally staring back for a couple of seconds longer than necessary, and then finally jumped down and paced silently out of the room. She waited for the tip of his tail to disappear, and only then did she allow herself to take a deep, calming breath. Right, back to the problem at hand; clothing.

It was a tough one. Although the usual just-about-acceptable-at-school things had never caught Derek's attention in the past, whatever she chose to wear today still couldn't have too much zing; Lower Bushey was a village with about as much imagination as a cow pat. What was needed, therefore, was something with understated style. Something that lacked the flowers, frills and froth that Derek had been living with for so long. Something that had humour, but with flair.

* * *

Sandra left for work an hour later.

The Wonder Woman outfit had been folded back up, the American overtones just too inappropriate for the English countryside. The Xena Warrior Princess number had been tried in combination with navy leggings, but had then been rejected because the rigid bustier top wouldn't fit neatly under a jacket. And Cat Woman's leather pants had been a touch too tight even by her standards. That had left a plethora of other more inappropriate outfits that she wanted to save for when she and Derek were alone. And there was one remaining acceptable piece; her 'pink panther', as she liked to call it, which was just what she was in the mood for today.

Plopping the Inspector Clouseau hat on her head, she pulled on the gloves and gave herself a final once over in the mirror. Wow! she thought. The tie, the coat, the briefcase, they were all just perfect, with the additional bonus that she could get away with her jack boots under the trousers as well. Oh, such a wonderfully neat little joke at herself it was; the hapless nature of Inspector Clouseau juxtaposed with her other more rigid personas. Derek's reference to the scene in the nudist camp would polish things off nicely and she'd left a guitar in the corner of the sitting room for that very reason. This was definitely an outfit that would provide a nice bridge between reality and her world. The start of the acclimatising process.

Donned in her favourite daytime costume, she reached the school a good hour earlier than normal, buoyant and ready to face her true love in style. As she walked in the front door, however, she was met with two undesirable problems that needed tackling before her morning could move on.

The first, and most pungent of the two, was an acrid aroma of sewage which was crawling up her nose ready to die.

The second, and more irritating, was the rural bouquet of John Bentwick, who was simply lacking the decency to not exist.

To her disgruntlement, it was the latter that had to be dealt with first.

Like any farmer, he had been up with the lark and done a full day's work by breakfast. Unlike any other farmer, though, he'd then come in to the school to have a word with Sandra about her *habits* – his word, not hers.

"So if you 'ave a moment to chat before Mr Fitztumbleton arrives, Miss Lovelock, I'd appreciate it. As I think 'e 'as enough on 'is plate at the moment, don't you?"

Sandra looked at him uncertainly. It would be natural to assume that the man was referring to the impending Ofsted inspection, when he said that Derek had enough on his plate. But with regard to his earlier use of the word '*habits*'; well that was bothersome for all sorts of reasons. She needed to know more before a course of action could be chosen.

"I don't want to take up yer time," he continued, and she mentally assured him that he need not worry on that score. John Bentwick obviously took her silence as permission to continue, and cleared his throat. "But there is something that I'd like to clarify with yer, particularly about *last night*."

Suddenly, Sandra's heart missed a beat. The implications of the timing now put a new slant on things; she definitely required more information.

"Well, I do have a lot to do, Mr Bentwick," she managed coolly. "However, I can spare you a couple of minutes. So tell me," she tried next, taking a leaf out of Mr Perkins' book and raising the imperious tone in her voice. "To which *habits* in particular do you refer?"

The look of surprise that flitted across his face was gratifying. It was clear that it had now struck him that she might have more than one type of '*habits*' about which he should be concerned. Sandra raised a taunting eyebrow just for good measure. The ruse did the trick and he looked away.

"Well, to put it blunt like, Miss Lovelock, seeing as yer appear to get my drift." he stuttered, and then risked a quick glimpse at her again, seeming to want a nod of confirmation. Sandra gave him a dismissive shrug. "Well, I don't approve of drinking in school, Miss Lovelock, and I don't believe I'm alone in thinking like that. So I'd therefore ask, if yer don't mind, that yer abstain from doing it on the premises from now on."

Sandra's forehead puckered. She had all sorts of little offbeat pleasures and secrets that she liked to keep to herself, but drinking wasn't one of them. This was good news. Inside, she let herself relax, just slightly.

"But I completely agree with you, Mr Bentwick," she replied, and the look of surprise on his face when she made this concession was so satisfying that she decided to carry on. "Although I'm not immune to the occasional *cock*tail," she added coyly, and watched him wince as the word 'cock' ushered from her lips. "But I'd never have one at school. And I'm surprised you feel it necessary to mention it to me."

Looking awkwardly at his socks, John cleared his throat.

"Well, I do include gin and tonic under the umbrella of alcohol, Miss Lovelock. Even if you sophisticated teacher-types try to cover it up by calling it a G & T." And at that, he ran out of steam.

This was quite an act of bravado on his part. Even Sandra could see that. But she knew she had to play the role of indignant employee, or he might start to wonder what was going on. If he didn't know by now that G&T stood for 'Gifted and Talented' in the world of education, then he was never going to know. So she decided to take a different approach.

"Look," she replied, and dropped her voice as though she was talking to Peter Drayton. "If I were to drink gin and tonic at school, I'd want ice and a slice to go with it, wouldn't I?"

John Bentwick's brow crumpled and he mouthed the words *ice and a slice* back. Sandra breathed a quiet sigh of resignation and waited for him to nod.

"Well," she continued, opting for a tone that now told him in no uncertain terms that he was about to hear a convincing explanation, "the freezer section in the fridge packed up two years ago, so there isn't a cube of ice on

the premises. And, with all our sophisticaaaaaaation..."
She stretched the word out as long as it would go, just
for extra emphasis, "we wouldn't entertain drinking gin
and tonic at school without ice, Mr Bentwick... Even if
we brought a lemon in from home."

His frown deepened, and drawing upon her decades
of experience as a teacher, she then went in for the kill;
utilising the deflective power of an alternative style of
expression.

"Look, one simply can't drink G&T without ice, can
one? It's Q.E.D, Mr Bentwick. Unquestionably Q.E.D."

"Kwed?" he muttered, not entirely to her surprise.
"But I thought yer always put a 'U' after the letter 'Q'."

Sandra smiled and then put him out of his misery.
"*Quod erat demonstrandum*, Mr Bentwick. It's Latin for
done-and-dusted. Your worries are unfounded."

A count to three ticked by as the language found its
place in his brain. Silently, Sandra applauded herself for
picking the right strategy. Chuck in a phrase several
diameters outside the circle of his world and a man like
John Bentwick would be flummoxed; but not so as he'd
want to admit it.

"Oh, that is good news," he said and then he paused,
as though allowing his belief to catch up with the
intended sentiment behind the words. "This Latin lark
certainly gives it a different complexion. I 'eard more of
it 'ere only yesterday, actually, but then this is a place of
learning, isn't it? I must 'ave got the wrong end of the
stick, Miss Lovelock. So I do apologise, and there was
me questioning your 'abits 'an all. You and Mr

Fitztumbleton make a good team," he added finally. "'E said as much to me only the other day, and I'm truly sorry to 'ave doubted yer."

Sandra felt her face flush. So Derek did think they made a 'good team', and not only did he think they made a good team, but he thought it enough to mention it to someone. The situation was shaping up nicely. Derek was shaping up nicely. On reflection, this strangely shaped Chair of Governors had now outstayed his welcome.

"Well, thank you very much, Mr Bentwick, but please don't worry about it any further. Now if you'll excuse me, I'd like to go and find out what that other awful smell is."

To her annoyance his face lit up.

"Ah, well, there I can 'elp yer, Miss Lovelock," he exclaimed eagerly, and delayed her escape. "The boys bogs 'ave flooded," he told her. "Turds are floating everywhere. Which reminds me of a time when they tried to install a portaloo in the shepherd's 'ut..."

But Sandra didn't wait around to hear the rest. She'd already got the gist of the story and the lack of aitches was beginning to hurt her ears.

The last words she heard as she marched away were, "Nice boots by the way. I like a good pair of boots, me. And I can tell yer, yer'll be needin' 'em."

* * *

What with John Bentwick's odd concerns, coupled with the faulty plumbing in the boys' loos, Sandra realised that it was a blessing that Derek hadn't made it in yet. She was acutely aware of the responsibility a 'dominant' adopts when accepting the role, and felt compelled to take control of the situation before her poor minion arrived.

It didn't take long to track down the epicentre of the flood. She found the caretaker's wiry form hunched over the offending toilet bowl, scowling.

"This is certainly an odd one," Bob sighed, wrinkling his nose in disgust, more at himself for running out of skill rather than the mess sloshing around his feet. "I expect someone's tried to flush their pants down the loo again. It wouldn't be the first time."

Sandra winced. Why parents couldn't train their brats to wipe their backsides properly she didn't know. People didn't tolerate skid marks on their drives, so why they tolerated them in their offspring's underwear was a mystery. But it was a conundrum she chose not to voice. Bob, with his simple approach to life, would struggle with the subject, thinking it was tantamount to paedophilia if he expressed an opinion on children and bottoms in the same sentence. What happened outside in the big wide world was one thing, but here, during the day, a strict protocol was always to be observed.

Despite her senses screaming to leave him to solve the problem on his own, however, her need to get things straight in time for Derek's arrival was more compelling.

"Let me give you a hand, Bob," she muttered, puckering her nose instead of risking a deep sigh. "Pass across that broom."

Bob's face lit up and he handed her the handle in relief.

"Many hands make light work, eh?" he said appreciatively, and then bent down with the shovel to scoop another brown floater into his bucket. "Mr Fitztumbleton will be impressed with you, Miss Lovelock. There aren't many teachers who would help out doing this."

"Well, Christmas is coming. I only work on logs at Yule time," Sandra mumbled, tapping into the essence of Clouseau as she said it – it was the one remaining lifeline she had left.

Bob straightened up and scratched his head. A joke from Miss Lovelock at any time was a rarity, but to hear one in the midst of such a challenging task was something else. Sandra felt the squirm of his puzzled stare and steadfastly carried on with what she was doing. Bugger! she thought. He's caught me out. The mention of Derek's appreciation of my efforts has done its worst whilst my guard is down, and I've let it catch me unawares. I need to be far more vigilant from now on.

Fortunately, Bob spotted her discomfort, misinterpreted it, and decided not to push his luck any further. One funny gag was all he was going to get to see them through this crisis. So instead, he pushed another soggy lump of loo paper onto his shovel, and then straightened up to change the subject.

"I love Christmas, I do. I know it's not everyone's cup of tea," he muttered, "and it is best when there are kids around... You don't have kids do you, Miss Lovelock?" She shook her head, and he shrugged knowingly. "But I'm chuffed to bits this year, 'cos you'll never guess what..." Sandra gave the brush an extra swift swipe to confirm that he was right, she hadn't guessed and wasn't about to try, and waited for him to divulge his good news. Bob carried on, oblivious. "The Working Men's Club have asked me to be Father Christmas!" he announced proudly. "And I said I'd be happy to do it as I already have the full costume – red hat, coat, beard and everything. So what do you think of that?"

Well. Sandra's penchant for dressing up was probably obvious to those with a keen eye, but Bob wasn't one of them. So if he wasn't trying to tap into her love of all things dramatic, then he had to be getting at something else. She swiftly decided that he was enjoying the pinnacle of his charitable career instead, and tried to picture him in full FC regalia.

The vision came up wanting.

Not only was Bob's stature an issue, but he was also going to need to work on his *'o, 'o, 'os.* The people attending such an event were likely to have mislaid a particular letter of the alphabet, and that, she realised caustically, was before they'd even encountered the concept of Noel.

"I think you'll need to pad yourself out with some pillows, Bob, otherwise they'll think that Santa has been on a diet."

As she said it, he scratched his chin sagely. "You're right, you know. I hadn't thought of that. I'd wondered why it had looked so saggy last night."

She shrugged regretfully and then sloshed a final broom load onto his spade.

"Well, I'm afraid I'm going to have to leave you to deal with the rest, Bob. I need to prepare some things before school starts."

The caretaker nodded and thanked her for her help. Sandra cast her eye over what she hoped would soon be a thing of the past, and beat a swift retreat. Realistically, her work here was done. She could now revert back to her original plan.

Before too long, she had written up her report and ticked the final box that ensured Ashley Milner was administratively gifted and talented. The smell of bleach that had begun to waft up her nostrils indicated that Bob was winning the battle against the brown bombs of Lower Bushey, and time was ticking by. She cautiously looked at her watch. Parents would be arriving soon to deposit their little darlings and Derek had still not yet arrived. It wouldn't do for the playground to be un-hosted, she thought. Really, it was her duty to greet the mums on behalf of her heart-broken hunk until he made it in. If, indeed, he did make it in; for she was beginning to wonder.

Still mulling things over, she stepped outside, Clouseau coat tightly belted around her waist, and breathed in the fresh morning air. As the clean unbleached oxygen filled her lungs, Derek's Ford

Mondeo nosed its way around the corner, and Sandra felt her heart leap. He hadn't let her down after all.

She watched as he pulled up to parallel park, and eyed with adoration as the ageing bumper deftly swung through one expertly judged arc and then straightened up. He is so adept at everything, she thought to herself; so magnificent. And, as if in solidarity, Percy suddenly swooped into view and planted his latest creation right in the middle of the windscreen of a car parked further up the road. That confirmed it. Derek was no longer a target.

Sandra's feet twitched on the leather layered soles of her boots. She was desperate to head across the road to greet him, offer her support and let him know that he need not fight the good fight alone. But parents were already beginning to filter in. She was torn. Should she stand her ground and remain where she was needed? Or could she give in to her whims and desert her post?

It was a tough call. All her instincts were telling her one thing, but all her passions were telling her another. And in an Olympic-sized tug of war, they began to pull and yank. Hustle and harry. Until, just as she realised with delight that her ardour had the edge, she suddenly spotted a passenger sitting next to her love. Her whole being froze.

It was a parent; female. A rival.

As she stared in disbelief, and her heart cracked into a million wretched pieces, Mabel Milner clambered out of Derek's car; fawn coloured trench coat and all.

Chapter Six

To say that Derek found Tuesday's journey into work a little more challenging than usual would have been an understatement.

To kick things off, he could still smell Miranda's perfume hugging the car seats. Its name always escaped him but he knew that it repeated itself. *Neigh, Neigh*, he tried, muttering the words sullenly as he changed up into third gear, no, maybe that wasn't it. When Miranda said it, it always sounded more exotic than that; far less equine.

But that was just for starters; there was more…

She'd also left a scarf on the backseat by mistake. Well, he'd initially assumed it was by mistake. But it hadn't taken long for him to then realise that it was the one he'd given her only the previous Christmas. She'd wryly whinnied her appreciation of it at the time, saying it could be her good luck scarf, which had seemed fitting as its principle motif was a horseshoe. Now however, it would appear that it had fulfilled its role and was no longer required. The shod, Derek surmised morosely, had been shed.

Yet on top of both of these poignant things, and as if to add salt to the suppurating wound that was his heart, he was still making this wretched journey out of

Cockerby and across to the festering wilds of Lower Bushey, and after seven years this was something that stabbed at his ego like a pitchfork in a haystack. Today, more than any other, Derek realised he was driving in the opposite direction to where he wanted to go; metaphorically, as well as literally. He was an urban boy deep down, not a country bumpkin. He had always preferred the clip of heels to the clop of hooves; the poop-poop of a horn to the doodle-doo of a cock; the cursing at dog poo to a heated debate about what made the finest manure. Those were the things that made him feel alive. And to have to admit that he resided in an unremarkable municipality; worked in the tiniest of primary schools, and was plagued by failed dreams of making it in a great throbbing metropolis was a difficult admission to make.

In reality, he reflected as the 'Welcome to Lower Bushey' sign came in to view, it was no surprise that Miranda had left him. The bud of the sweet girl he'd met in her early twenties had blossomed and outgrown her pot. She wanted the chance to spread her roots wider. Branch out and mature flamboyantly before she went to seed. Really, he sighed as he dropped his speed down to thirty miles per hour, the only chance he had of winning her back was to up his offering in the flowerbed department.

The floral analogy had had its attractions as he'd thought it through over breakfast, it had been so much more appealing than the countrified references to fillies and mares that he got from his chair of governors. And although it was true that it hadn't stretched successfully to incorporate a looming Ofsted visit, Derek could live with that. It made no difference whether he could describe an inspection in gardening terms or not. What needed to be done wouldn't change. He knew the first step towards promotion was to ensure his stats were all in order, and as he drove the last mile of his journey, he spotted one errant statistic ambling slowly next to its mother, sure to be registering as yet another 'late' if he didn't do something about it.

Derek freewheeled his Mondeo a few metres past Mabel and Ashley, and then pulled over. Out of the rear view mirror, he watched Mabel eye the vehicle suspiciously, yank at her collar, and then put a spurt of urgency into her stride. The tap of her heels quickened, and he waited patiently for her to open the passenger door as he ran a hand over his balding head.

On balance, he was relieved that she was fully clothed today. It wouldn't do for the neighbourhood to see a pair of fishnet stockings climbing into his car. And besides, he caught himself thinking, Miranda wouldn't like it, would she? She'd hate to think of a woman like that getting a lift. She'd, oh, bugger, he then brooded, and his heart sank to the soles of his shoes. Who was he kidding? At this moment, Miranda wouldn't care.

As the troublesome thought gnawed, he pulled the handbrake up and distracted himself with the vagaries of social etiquette instead. Would a joke or a polite 'hello' work best? Anything too flippant could give this woman the wrong idea; yet anything too stern could put her off getting in at all. It was critical to get it right, otherwise a man in his position could so easily be misconstrued - mistaken - or simply misunderstood.

Whilst the debate oscillated in his head, Derek floundered, and Mabel and Ashley walked past. He watched them vacantly for several paces, as they bobbed up and down, and only then realised what had gone wrong.

It appears he concluded grumpily, that a man in his position could *most* easily just be missed. But pride had to be the least of his worries at this juncture. So he leant across to open the door, stretching to reach the knob and fighting against the pull of the seatbelt until, realising that it was no good, he finally undid the restraint and fumbled with the window winder instead.

"Mrs Milner!" he cried, but she simply picked up pace and scurried forward even faster. "Mrs Milner!" he repeated, louder this time, and then gave up and stuck his head fully out of the window.

"Ashley!" he yelled.

And only then did it hit him, the same suffocating and overwhelming horror that had swooped in the day before. Was this a girl or a boy? A Janet or a John? It was impossible to tell. So in a pathetic attempt to backtrack, Derek swivelled back across into his seat and tried to hide behind the sun visor. But it was too late. The child had already turned around and grabbed its mother by the sleeve.

Mabel leant forward and followed the pointing finger with her gaze. Derek watched her nod as Ashley asked a question, and then the two of them headed back towards the car. To his dismay, her pale face soon appeared at the passenger window.

"Can I give you a lift?" he burbled, plumping for the obvious in the absence of anything sophisticated springing to mind, but then checked himself. Was this the right person after all? The woman peering back looked nothing like the one from the day before. This one was demure, with subtle lipstick, breath-taking eyes and neatly pinned back hair. This one was wearing a smart calf length raincoat and stylish shoes. There was none of the hideous gaudiness that he'd been introduced to yesterday; none at all. In fact there was only beauty, and it took his breath away.

"Oh, Mr Titzfumbleton..." Mabel cooed, but the child growled and she quickly corrected herself. "Sorry, Mr Fitztumbleton, I didn't realise it was you. Do you always 'ang around picking up unsuspecting women?" A jokey glint sparkled in her eyes as she spoke but Derek still blushed.

"Err... well, quite," he attempted, but failed even to achieve that with grace, and Mabel laughed.

"Ash and I would love a lift. Wouldn't we, Ash?" She turned to look at Ashley, who nodded whilst Derek's stomach tied itself in knots.

Girl or boy? Girl or boy? his mind raced, as they climbed into the car. But no answer was forthcoming.

"You'd better 'urry," Mabel urged, and pointed across to the other side of the road as she straightened out her coat. "There's a police car over there. He's watching you."

Distracted, Derek turned to see where she was pointing, froze momentarily, and then managed a deep panic stricken sigh. Right, he thought to himself, as the click of Ashley's seatbelt sounded in the back, perfect pulling away manoeuvre required; nothing but the best will do. He checked his rear view mirror, flicked the indicator on, and then gently drew away from the curb. Faultless, he thought with satisfaction, but then noticed Mabel's raised eyebrow.

"You 'aven't done your seatbelt up, Mr Fitztumble," she whispered, leaning coyly towards him, "and I think the copper's clocked yer."

Derek glanced across to his right and caught sight of the shiny metal clasp smiling provocatively back. His mouth went dry. *Why me? Why today? Why...* But it seemed that god was concentrating on more pressing issues elsewhere. So in a desperate bid not to highlight his faux pas by rectifying it, Derek quickly shoved the car into second gear and steamed down Bunting Hill instead. Maxing out at thirty miles an hour, they reached the roundabout at the bottom within seconds.

Any moment now, he thought panicking. Any moment now there'll be flashing lights and sirens everywhere; should I brake or escape? Should I stay or should I go? The clash of choices was stark, if scant in number. But as the 'Give Way' sign loomed, the decision was taken out of his hands, by his foot, which floored it, and the Mondeo lurched forward. With an

97

obstreperous buck, the exhaust crunched noisily as the vehicle tumbled across the central mound, and then suddenly all was calm once more. They'd made it across unscathed.

Dazed, Derek manoeuvred them back into the left hand lane and risked a look to his side.

"Has he followed us?" he asked nervously, and licked his lips.

Mabel glimpsed behind and then stretched round to get a better look. "Well if 'e 'adn't planned to at the start," she muttered, "'e sure as 'ell must be thinking about it now." She paused, waiting a little longer, and then shrugged. "But, I think you might be alright. 'E 'asn't budged," she replied and gave him a little smile. "Lady Luck must be on your side today, Mr Fitztumbleton," she added and pointed to Miranda's discarded scarf. "Cos I can tell you now, she's never bloody well been on mine."

* * *

It was the extraordinary lack of bitterness in the statement that caught Derek's attention. Blew him away, actually, and humbled him to the core. For if what had just happened was what this woman considered to be good luck, then he dreaded to think what she'd been through elsewhere. Sitting next to him in his car was a single mother and her fatherless child, that much he did know, even if he hadn't read the file, and the former spoke with the syntax of the worldly weary, whilst the latter spoke with the diplomacy of the worldly wise. He could only guess what Mabel Milner had run away from for her to have ended up in a place like Lower Bushey, and although some said that when you made a bed you had to lie in it – and Mabel Milner had clearly lain in several – he decided, taking inspiration from her gutsy inner strength; she at least now appeared to be making her own.

* * *

They pulled up at the school just in time to catch the bell. Kids streamed in from all corners of the playground, the girls skipping, whilst the boys dragged their feet with their hands in their pockets. Realising that he'd seen Ashley do neither, did nothing to improve Derek's mood.

As he yanked at the handbrake, a familiar figure parked a few cars up the road caught his eye. What on earth was John Bentwick doing here? he wondered; bearing in mind the man was normally poking about with sheep at this time of day. They'd only spoken the previous afternoon as well. And to be fair, although it hadn't been the most meaningful of exchanges, someone like John Bentwick tended to need time to recharge. Derek tried a wave to catch his attention, but the farmer didn't see him and instead seemed to be focussing on the stragglers walking down from further up the street. Derek followed the direction of his stare but could see nothing of particular note and so gave his chin a scratch.

The workings of that man's mind were a mystery at the best of times but something didn't feel quite right today.

"Thanks for giving us a lift," Mabel said, interrupting his thoughts as she opened the passenger door.

Still disturbed by the disconcerting look on Bentwick's face, Derek pulled himself together. "Oh. It's not a problem. I'd not realised we take the same route," he added, thinking that it was no bloody wonder he'd never realised; he was always at school a good hour before she was. He was obviously much better at getting out of the bed he had made for himself, he concluded; it was all a matter of practice, perhaps.

Mabel smiled her thanks and turned to her child, "Come on, Ash," she muttered and began to clamber out, "We're early, for once."

Derek only just stopped himself from loudly snorting, and then realised by John's expression that the farmer's focus had now honed in on their position and his face had taken on a new look. *What-are-you-doing-there?* it was asking, a perplexing question, seeing as this was where a headmaster would be every day. But, more significantly, it was asking it with disconcerting menace. A shiver passed down Derek's spine. Clearly something was bothering the farmer, and he dreaded to think what the man's ram had, or hadn't, been up to this time.

"Well you should be heading in for registration, Ashley," he sighed, putting his concerns aside, before noticing Sandra's poker straight face also glaring across. "Miss Lovelock will be waiting for you," he added, and shivered again. For her stare too was now sizzling between him and his passenger.

Mabel noticed it as well and gave the teacher a wave, winking back at him as she did so.

"Stale old loaf, isn't she?" she mumbled, and wiggled her fingers for a second time. "Ash says she's a good teacher, but I just think she's weird. I mean, look at 'er."

Derek did as suggested, and suddenly noticed the odd apparel that Sandra had chosen to wear. Inspector Gadget meets Bugsy Malone; it was a new one on him. Admittedly less vexing than the contraption she had donned the day before, but peculiar all the same and just another reason why he needed to get out of this place.

"Thank you so much for helping us, Mr Fitztumbleton," Ashley's voice murmured from behind, and Derek took stock of himself and glanced back at the child in the rear view mirror. "My mum is always late for everything," *it* continued. "And I hate it, mind you, she hates me nagging her too, you know," *it* then concluded with childish logic, just before *it* smiled unrepentantly and climbed out of the car, "I think we really just hate each other."

The words landed like tiny incendiary bombs, exploding cruelly and incinerating the struggling mother's efforts in a dismissive puff of smoke. Derek hauled himself out of the car and eyed Mabel. The woman was struggling to retain her composure and he knew only too well what it felt like to have to deal with that sort of pain; but knowing a pain and being able to offer consolation were two different things. He was pitifully ill-equipped.

To Derek's embarrassed relief, and before he could make any attempt at a pathetic mumble, Mabel muttered something about being late for an interview and hurried off. He watched her trot along the road, demurely but awkwardly, as though she wasn't used to her clothes, and shrugged aside reminiscent feelings from his wedding day. Now was not the time to reflect on that, was it? No. Now was the time to don the mantle of headmaster once more and step across the road.

Which was exactly what he did.

By the time he'd reached the school steps, he'd shed the remaining vestments of misery in his life and had determinedly climbed back into character.

The last sound that Derek noted as he opened the front door was the roar of John Bentwick's Land Rover and the screech of tyres on the tarmac.

The last thought that Derek thought before he went inside, was *Fuck 'em. Fuck 'em all!*

* * *

Mrs McFreece eyed him dubiously and pointed to the backward counting clock on her PC.

"I was about to send out a search party," she drawled, but her dry Glaswegian brogue, although uncompromising as ever, was oddly lacking in disapproval for once.

Derek stopped. A lump formed in his throat. Did she know? It had perhaps been unreasonable to hope that he could patch things up with Miranda before word had got out that she'd left, but he hadn't wanted it to be quite this soon. He tried an exploratory excuse to test the water.

"To be honest, Mrs M.," he began, thinking of the unopened lever arch file on his kitchen table, and assuring his conscience that it wasn't a total lie, "I got caught up with checking through our policies and simply lost track of time."

Mrs McFreece raised an eyebrow, and then did something that after seven years of working with the woman frighteningly suggested might be a smile; Derek held his breath.

"I'd wondered as much," she replied shrugging, and he let out a sigh of relief. "Seeing the hole on the shelf up there this morning, and time ticking by as it is, I'd hoped you were at it elsewhere. Although not with that crusty old bun," she added conspiratorially, and flicked a look behind him at what he guessed was Sandra Lovelock's classroom. "She's been a right royal pest since The Call came in, Mr Fitztumbleton. Won't leave me alone. Wants to get things just right for you, she says. Well I *told* her," The Fridge added, as though he would know exactly what it was that she had proclaimed to his most able teacher.

It took Derek a second to weigh things up. If caution was the better part of valour, then it was worth trying a zero reaction as a starter for ten. However, he was also aware that the look of anticipation peering back at him actually suggested that a noncommittal shrug would better suit the job. To his astonishment it worked. The Fridge divulged.

"I explained that you have everything under control," she confided smugly. "I *told* her, I did. I said that you are organised. I said that you are prepared. I told her that she should keep her nose out of it. And that's right, isn't it, Mr Fitztumbleton? You haven't let me down, have you?" This time he shook his head automatically; the rhetorical nature of the question being enough of a clue. She nodded with satisfaction and continued. "You're a good man and a credit to this school, and don't let anyone make you think different.

'*Differently*' hovered on his lips in correction, but remained unsaid. A Scottish compliment was a rarity. The merest hint of a thing called flattery from The Fridge had never been heard of before.

"Well, we have forty seven hours and thirty two minutes until our fate is decided," he tried instead, and the contorted grimace on the McFreece face broadened further.

"Oh, Mr Fitztumbleton there is just one thing though," and her expression lifted apologetically as she said it. "You might want to take a look at the hedge that runs along the bottom of the playing field. I overheard Billy Barber boasting about pushing Peter Drayton through it yesterday. We might have a hole."

He nodded, thinking that it wouldn't make it high on his agenda just yet, and then wrinkled his nose in disgust. Mrs McFreece smirked. Now that the stench of sewage and bleach had finally registered in his consciousness, she went on to explain what had happened.

Within a couple of minutes, Derek knew that Bob had done his best so far, but was waiting for Sid the plumber to come in. Only god knew when Sid would get there, however, as Mrs Bucklebraith's pussy had been tinkering with her neighbour's hosepipe. Their irrigation system had been wrecked and Sid was going to have to service the whole set up before he could get to the school.

"Although quite how her cat could have done that much damage," she finished off, "I really don't understand."

Even to Derek's distracted mind there was a clear message in this little story; Sid wasn't going to be rushing to the school too soon. Any anecdote that included a pussy, a hosepipe and the need for a full service, had to be a euphemism for 'sod off, I've better things to do with my time'. In a happier world, where Ofsted had already delivered the grading he deserved, and Sandra Lovelock's face actually smiled, he'd have sympathised with Sid; but it wasn't a happier world. Ofsted were still forty seven hours and twenty nine minutes away, and Sandra Lovelock's face was as chiselled as a raisin muffin. If Sid wasn't able to overcome his trouser-based concerns, somebody else would.

Thanking The Fridge for her supportive words, he decided his first task for the day would be to check with

Bob who they could contact instead. She nodded her approval, and he headed off along the corridor to seek his janitor out in the library.

He found Bob hunched over a low slung shelf, effing and blinding, as he tried to fix a socket. Derek caught sight of the skinny backside and briefly wondered how Sandra Lovelock could be in two places at the same time. But then he realised who it was. An inappropriate thought about a lunar eclipse rallied unwelcome in his mind, rebelliously challenging him to blurt it out. But, to his subconscious relief, it remained unsaid. At best, Bob would think that Derek thought the sun shone out of his arse. At worst, well, that didn't bear considering.

"Ah, Bob, I thought you were Miss Lovelock just then." It was a peculiar replacement statement to choose, but oddly accepted by the caretaker without question.

Bob straightened up, hitched his trousers back to his belt line, and nodded.

Derek bumbled on.

"I mean, I didn't recognise you," he corrected and then flushed; knowing that that sounded even worse. Bob remained unfazed.

"Oh, don't you worry, Mr Fitztumbleton. That Miss Lovelock of yours is a cracking bird. She did you proud this morning, and it's an honour for my arse to be confused with hers."

Derek had never associated Bob with coarse thinking, or any thinking at all, come to mention it, so for him to be proud that his buttocks were akin to those of Sandra's was an odd assertion to make.

"Well, quite," he managed, and then realised that any request for clarification would be futile. Sometimes one just had to know when to let a matter drop. He decided to move the subject on. "But what happened in the boy's toilets today, Bob?"

The caretaker's face turned white.

"Nothing," he gasped. "She swept and I shovelled. There was no hanky panky, Mr Fitztumbleton. Nothing happened at all in the boy's bogs, honest. Actually," he then managed as an aside, "I said she was a cracking bird just now, but she's not my type really. Too skinny for me. I like 'em a bit bigger." And as he said it, he cupped his hands melonically at chest height and winked.

"Well, quite," Derek managed again, and scratched his head in exasperation. "It would never have crossed my mind that there would have been any..."

"Hanky panky?"

"Err... untoward behaviour, Bob," Derek corrected for him. "I had just wondered..."

"No!" Bob interrupted, and put his hand up to stop Derek from saying another word. "She and I may have our similarities, Mr Fitztumbleton, but you know what they say; opposites attract, and I like 'em..."

"Well, quite," Derek resorted to for a third time, and finally caught himself wishing that he had more imagination. Miranda had mentioned it once. She'd said he had a passion for mediocrity, and he'd not really wanted to point out what that must have suggested about her. He decided to change tack. "But can you please tell me what that awful smell is, Bob?"

Prevented mid-flow from continuing his voluptuous description, it took Bob's brain a couple of seconds to catch up with the change of direction in the conversation. But once it had, the penny dropped.

"Someone tried to flush their pants again, Mr Fitztumbleton. It was a right mess down here this morning."

Bob then launched into a detailed account of the jetsam and flotsam floating around, utilising an impressive collection of adjectives even by Derek's standards, until Mrs McFreece appeared at the door wearing an expression that told the caretaker to put a toilet lid on it. Immediately.

"There's someone here to see you," she mumbled, and cleared her throat awkwardly. "It's the police," she mouthed, and then glanced behind her to check that no one was listening. As she said it, a pair of dark helmets came into view.

Derek froze. Mabel Milner's definition of good luck had obviously been a little premature. These officers must have followed him down the hill. Sat chuckling as they'd called in details of their next planned arrest, and then headed into the school, all high-hatted and full of themselves. Bastards.

"Mr Fitztumbleton?" the older of the two plods asked, as he stepped into the room marginally ahead of his acne. Derek nodded, his heart pounding, his face as red as a stop sign. "I'm afraid we need to have a quick word, sir."

Derek swallowed. "Well, quite," he managed and began to suggest that they speak in his office, but the officer shook his head.

"Thank you, sir, but that won't be necessary. Is this Bob Cartright?" The policeman pointed towards the caretaker as he said it and Derek nodded. "Bob Cartright," he then warbled, the voice undulating with uncontrollable pubescent disregard for its owner. "I'd like you to accompany us to the station, sir, to answer a few questions regarding an incident of indecent exposure at Marks & Spencer's last night."

The youthful voice droned on as Derek stared in horror back at his janitor.

"But," he managed as the policeman finished his spiel. "Bob?" he then tried.

Bob turned to him, aghast. "But I wasn't in M&S last night; honest," he croaked. "I was trying on my Father Christmas costume to see if it fitted right."

"Precisely, sir," was all that the officer then said, and the handcuffs clicked around his wrists.

Chapter Seven

Mabel could feel the tears pricking her eyes as she walked away; hot salty droplets that stung like acid as they broke their banks and burned their blackened trail. She lifted a finger to wipe them away carefully so as not to smudge her mascara any further.

Now was not the time for dwelling on Ashley's misjudged jibes. Her daughter was only eleven; she didn't know better. Mind you, Mabel rallied as she strode on, her East End pride never too far from the surface, that didn't mean a touch more appreciation wouldn't go amiss. Ashley was old enough to start thinking of others' feelings, at least. Charity began at home isn't that that what people said? Was eleven too tender an age to expect a touch of understanding? A touch of compassion? *I think we really just hate each other*, the girl had muttered. Words that had been flung so casually, and now clung and stung in Mabel's heart. They were words that had been flinging, clinging and stinging generations of mother/daughter relationships; that lesson never to be learned. If Mabel had ever heard of Charles Darwin, she'd have wondered what the bloody hell he'd have made of it all; for surely evolution would have been better off focusing on that stuff, rather than the flamboyancy of a peacock's tail. But Mabel had never heard of Darwin, nor Richard Dawkins come to mention it, and so she didn't know that evolution lacked that sort of focus. Evolution just was, just like the words that were now ringing and stinging in her head; just like they '*just' was* too.

She pulled her collar closer and leant into the northerly wind as a gust played lustfully with her coat. Unused to the rub of material on her knees, she paused to straighten her calf length skirt and felt a wash of relief. Well that was something at least. Unruly coat flaps weren't a problem today. For there was nothing hidden underneath that could shock; only a Doris Day skirt, one of Dwayne's favourites that he was too stubborn to admit was too small, and a pair of fifteen denier tights. No one was going to raise an eyebrow at that.

The thought was briefly comforting, but then she faltered again, oh god - though neither Darwin nor Dawkins were available for comment - this was an alien world that she was planning to join; was she any more ready for it, than it was ready for her?

And as the conundrum rattled around in her brain, a poignant indicator of how reasonable it was to have as a concern suddenly screeched to a halt by her side. Mabel gave her coat belt a final yank back into position and then straightened up, just as John Bentwick's passenger window whirred down.

"Good morning," his country drawl growled, the words stumbling through the open window like a pair of angry bullocks. Mabel clocked the odd look of fury belying the welcome, and frowned.

"Oh, 'ello, I wasn't expecting to see you."

"Obviously," he replied dryly, the daddy of all bulls now appearing and explaining why the youngsters had been on the run.

For a split second, Mabel wondered what he was getting at and then it dawned on her. Prudently, her cheeks wanted to blush, it was what would have been considered de rigueur amongst the politer end of Lower Bushey society, but in Mabel's world, blushing was an unnecessary risk. The devastating clash with whatever she was about to take off usually negated the need for maidenly modesty. So, instinctively, she chose to elevate an eyebrow instead.

"And what is that supposed to mean exactly?" she huffed, as the beautifully plucked caterpillar rose an extra millimetre for good measure.

Both of John's fuzzy little beasties lifted in surprise. It was clearly not the response he'd been expecting.

"W... w... well," he stammered, "you'd 'ave w-w-waved, or something, if yer 'ad been expecting to see me. W-w-wouldn't yer?"

"Well maybe I would, maybe I wouldn't," Mabel bit back, furious now at his judgemental misunderstanding. "But I wouldn't 'ave jumped to any conclusions, that's for sure."

"Well, quite. Err…" he tried, but Mabel flashed him a livid look. As innocuous as the phrase was, it had now become an unnecessary point of triangulation in the conversation.

"Look," she humphed, and clumped her hands onto her hips as she shifted her weight onto the other leg. "What do you want?"

"I...I...I..."

"Come on, spit it out," she challenged impatiently and hardened her stare. "I 'aven't got all day. In fact," she then stressed, looking theatrically at her watch, "I'm late for my interview. So, if you don't mind."

His face fell. "Well if you're going to be like that..."

John paused, clearly wanting to be contradicted. But when she simply shrugged, he flushed, looking awkwardly at the steering wheel as if searching for inspiration, and then sighed. "Look I was going to offer you a lift," he added, crestfallen. "I 'ad remembered you 'ad an interview, and I thought yer might want a ride into town. 'Ave one thing less to worry about."

A puppyish look of hope crawled across his features as he said it, the grumpiness of but a minute before forgotten, and despite herself Mabel felt her anger wane too. She hadn't expected this. Not in a million years; a touch of thoughtful kindness.

"Well, alright," she conceded and opened the passenger door. "I'll let you give me a lift if you say you're sorry."

"What for?" he exclaimed.

"For thinking that I was up to no good with old Titzfumble, that's what for!"

"I never!"

"You did!"

"I never," he repeated, but the oomph had left his words.

She huffed with satisfaction and climbed up next to him, secretly relieved not to have to get the bus. John gave her a grateful smile and extended his arm to release the handbrake.

It was just at this moment, however, that either fate, god or Dawkins, whom ever had the greatest sway, decided to stick their oar in. No one would be surprised to learn that such a trio could put a cat amongst the pigeons, but in this instance it was the other way round. As Mabel mentally waved adios to public transport, a pigeon suddenly flew down, landed on the road a few metres in front of them, and saw off a meek looking puss instead.

Percy eyed the mog smugly as it trotted nervously away, and then turned his attention to a far more interesting selection of crumbs on the ground. Oblivious of his precarious position, he started to peck away and didn't hear John Bentwick swear. He also didn't pay attention to the mumble of, "I'm going to get you, you little bugger!" and he certainly didn't twig the full meaning of the three litre engine revving aggressively behind him.

Mabel looked at John, appalled.

"I 'ope you're not planning what I think you're planning," she gasped, glaring furiously at him as she said it. John glanced back briefly, glassy eyed, and then turned his head to the front once more. "You'd better bloody not be..." she added.

But it was to no avail.

With a final growl of the engine, the farmer adjusted his fingers on the steering wheel, and then pushed his foot down on the accelerator. The 4x4 lurched forward and Mabel's torso plunged back into her seat and her eyes widened with surprise. This bastard was actually going to do it. Not satisfied with bullying sheep from dawn till dusk, he was now turning to pick on smaller avian prey too.

Well! She wasn't going to have that.

Whilst his eyes were focussed on their quarry, she leant across, grabbed the handbrake, and yanked it with all her might. As the ratchet clicked, the Land Rover pitched in surprise, along with the farmer's eyebrows, and the tyres suddenly screeched to a halt.

Percy looked up and eyed the metal box looming his way. Mild suspicion swiftly mutated into overwhelming awe. He'd seen it all before, of course, people arguing; farmers swearing; Father Christmas displaying his wares to unsuspecting shoppers in the car park of M&S, but never, in all his target hunting days, had he seen a woman work with such a hand action as that. She knew what she was doing. She was his kind of bird.

Keen to get a closer look, he stretched his wings to hoist his heavy body up to bonnet level and deposited himself on top of the engine with a clunk. As the tinkle of eight pigeon toes sounded on the metal, John's passenger door slammed shut, and all ten of Mabel's leather shoed 'little piggies' hit the tarmac. By the time Percy had realised what was going on, she was already storming off up the road, reverting to Shanks' pony and the bus to get to her interview.

Regrets began to swim around in Mabel's head before she'd even turned the first corner. But she stolidly ignored the great big ugly beast of a vehicle as it steamed past her a few seconds later. She smelt the bitter stench of diesel as it sped by, and soon began to taste the bitter tang of overly-hasty action.

No one had ever anticipated her needs like that. He'd remembered she had an interview; he'd planned how to help her; and he'd then tried to see it through. What had she offered him in return? Not even the tiniest bit of faith. People did things for all sorts of reasons, it wasn't always clear why, but what appeared to be a poor defenceless pigeon to her could easily have just been vermin to him, so who was she to judge? Blinkered judgement was the bane of human existence; ignorance was only bliss to the ignorant. She ought to have known it really; Dwayne had taught her that lesson long ago.

As Mabel arrived in Cockerby and clambered off the bus, she concluded she should perhaps give John a chance to explain at least. But only if he called her first…

* * *

Mabel read the job specification with a sinking heart, as she waited to be called for interview. She'd have no problem winging it, saying all the right things and waxing lyrical about administration and paperwork, but what would happen then? She'd have a respectable occupation, but not exactly one that people admired. She'd have a job that paid the rent, but not one that inspired respect. She could already picture Ashley's disdainful expression as she told people what her mother did for a living. At least, at the moment, they could justify making things up, for in some mad way, people understood that kind of lie. But to tell a great big porkie pie just because one didn't want to admit to being an administrator; that was different. People secretly looked down on you for that; was this really what she wanted to do?

A familiar voice filtered through from the public facing section of the office. Mabel looked up.

Hmm, she thought ruefully. With Dwayne by her side, she'd probably never get the chance to worry about it anyway.

"I only want to wish her good luck, sweetheart, that's all," sidled through the gap in the partition. "Tell her Dawn, is here. I'm her best friend so she'll be thrilled to see me. I won't be long, I promise."

Dwayne's sickly sweet, overtly feminine voice tinkled in Mabel's ears like the jangle of a broken Christmas bauble, and warned her that he was in full drag. Probably daytime wear, so on the acceptable side, but caricatured all the same. He meant well.

"Darling, that lovely receptionist has let me slip back here quickly just to wish you good luck," he cooed, and bent across to give her a peck on the cheek. "I didn't get a chance before you and Ash left, and thought we could perhaps grab a coffee afterwards for a debrief. By the way," he then added, always one to be easily distracted, "did you see that woman's lipstick? Ooooh, I want it."

Mabel sat back and took in the full Jackie'O' regalia. He'd gone properly to town today; no wonder it had taken him so long to get ready.

"Thank you," she replied dryly, and then passed him the job spec in her hand. "But I'm not sure I want the position now anyway."

Dwayne took it and cast his critical eye over the text. Unsurprised, she watched him wince, sniff, apply another coating of powder unnecessarily to his face, check his hair, bite his lip, and only then finally wrinkle his nose.

"Well I can see why they chose to interview you," he concluded, returning the sheet to her and sitting down. "You never said it was for the post of 'Removals Executive.'"

She was about to nod resignedly, when the sound of a deeply weathered farmerishly masculine voice sounded through from the front. Dwayne heard it first and smirked; Mabel stuck an unladylike finger up at him.

"I only want to wish 'er good luck, yer see," rumbled across from the front door. "Didn't get a chance earlier, at the school I mean. Oh bugger, look, I just want to wish 'er good luck!"

The click of the heels of the *lovely* receptionist sounded on the faux marble floor, and then deadened as she left the sanctuary of the plush public area and plunged behind the scenes to the murky section where Mabel and Dwayne were waiting.

"You've got *another* visitor," she announced brusquely, clearly peeved at having to play hostess to the competition. And then raised her eyebrows as if to say, 'No I can't see why he's come to see you either, but do you want the bugger to come through, or not?' Dwayne bristled on Mabel's behalf.

"That lipstick's lost its gloss, I think," he mumbled, and Mabel shot him a warning look. He shrugged an indifferent apology and glanced away.

"Send him through," Mabel sighed, and then put her hand up to stop Dwayne from saying anything more. "Don't," she ordered. "Please don't; just keep your gob shut."

John Bentwick appeared at the doorway with his hat hanging limply in his hand, his large frame almost filling the gap. Mabel noted his awkwardness, and watched with mixed feelings as it grew once he'd spotted Dawn behind her. He cleared his throat.

"I just wanted to check you'd got 'ere in time," he mumbled, and then licked his lips nervously as his gaze darted between her and her friend.

Mabel looked at him, irritated by his honky-tonk naiveté and, despite her earlier decision, felt an invisible devil on her shoulder suddenly chortle with wicked glee.

"Well," she snapped, before she knew what she was saying, "as you can see, I have got here in time. So job done, and off you jolly well hop." The little imp chuckled away.

Mabel froze. The words had jumped out before she could stop them, well articulated and aitches clearly huffed. They had sounded *so* absolutely classily fantastic she could, in fact, have been going for a job at Buckingham Palace. The only problem was that she wasn't, and they weren't actually the words she had meant to say. What she had meant to communicate was, 'Thank you'. From the bottom of her heart, she had wanted to give him a big smile, and ask if he was able to hang around until her interview was over, so they could go for a coffee. She had wanted to apologise for being such a grumpy cow and show gratitude for his concern. Yes, all those wonderful ideas had lined up politely in true British fashion, chatting amongst themselves and happily awaiting their turn, only to find they were usurped by a queue jumping quip that made even Dwayne step back in surprise.

With the distraction of the interview hanging over her, she'd obviously not realised quite how angry she still was.

John Bentwick's mouth opened, but then shut when it realised that the action was premature; his brain had not yet prepared a response. A couple of seconds ticked by, and it appeared as though it was about to have another go, when the door to the inner sanctum opened and Mr Snouterton walked through. John's jaw closed for the second time, without having made a sound.

"Ah, Mr Bentwick, how lovely to see you again," Snouterton drawled with the confidence of the middle-aged, and then allowed a frown to crease his sallow face. "I didn't realise you have an appointment."

"I don't," John muttered, and looked as though he was going to have a stab at a few more words, but Snouterton overrode him.

"Ah, jolly good," the insurance broker assured him vacuously. "I was worried, for a second, that there were still some loose ends we needed to tie up. Well, good day to you," he then concluded, and turned next to Dwayne.

Mabel noted the look of surprise that flitted across his grey features and waited.

"Ms. Milner?" he asked, glancing back at the job application in his hand, which included Mabel's mug shot.

Dwayne smirked and shook his head. "Absolutely not," he replied, and pointed across at Mabel, just in case Snouterton wasn't convinced. "Mr Bentwick and I came to wish Ms Milner good luck, that's all."

He then winked at Snouterton, just for good measure, and let the matter rest.

Snouterton checked the photo one more time, and turned to look at Mabel with enhanced appreciation.

"Ah, you have a fan club, Ms. Milner," he said warmly, and held his hand out to her for a welcoming shake. "And it's just increased its membership by one."

Out of the corner of her eye, Mabel spotted John's shoulders bristle.

"Oh! Thank you" she mumbled awkwardly, and the farmer's face fell further. The insurance broker grinned.

"I'm Stanley Snouterton," he announced and passed her his business card. "But please, just call me Stan." She looked at it; it said; *Stan K. Snouterton FCII, MBA, BA Hons, FSA & FSB*, but her eyes only got as far as the end of his surname; the rest looked like the typist had been distracted by a phone call in the middle of doing the job. She put it in her pocket.

"Now, would you like to come through?" he offered, and stood aside to let Mabel pass by.

She nodded, feeling a sickening lump form in her throat, and took one last look at Dwayne before heading through. Until just now, she hadn't actually thought about what she'd be doing day to day here; the imperative had just been to get the job. As far as she was concerned it had always been other people's discriminatory judgement that had held her back, not her lack of ability. Suddenly now though, she wasn't quite so sure.

"Oh well," she muttered under her breath. "*Carpe Diem.* Isn't that what they say?" And flashed a final look behind her.

John Bentwick bristled for a second time, but she ignored him and headed instead into the corridor beyond. The last thing that followed her through the doorway was the sound of Dwayne's dubious translation.

"S-E-E-S," he spelt, letter by letter, to John, "sees the day. I believe that's what it stands for, but it doesn't make any sense to me either."

* * *

The first thing that struck Mabel, as she followed Snouterton into the interview room, was the claustrophobic smell. It wasn't stale, sweaty and alcoholically fumigated in the way that she was used to, but it was over-breathed all the same. She glanced around morosely and spotted that the place had no windows. Familiar territory perhaps, but normally there'd have been multi-coloured lights pumping away to a pelvic beat rather than the fluorescent strip on the ceiling that there was now. It didn't inspire.

She continued her assessment with a sinking heart. The front entrance to the building, the public facing aspect, had been spotlessly marbleised serenity. But this back section, the bit cut off from all but the most unfortunate, was spotlessly polymerised plastic death. Three of the four walls were covered in floor to ceiling shelving, each with what looked like row upon row of eyes staring back at her. Mabel felt her spine shiver, and then realised that every tiny unblinking iris was actually the finger hole of a lever arch file. This is exactly what hell looks like, she thought glumly; it's a premonition.

As this damning realisation sank in, Ricky Ribley and Troilus Trotter shuffled in and introduced themselves. Expecting a trident to appear at any moment, her eyes flicked nervously between them, taking in their greying pudding bowl haircuts, blended pantone-neutral pallor, and previous season's M&S suits.

Where does one man end and the next one begin? she wondered. Would playing spot-the-difference solve the problem? Probably not, and as quickly as it had flared, the fear of flames, fiends, and little red beasts with tails disappeared in a puff of freezing fog only to be replaced by gloom.

Troubled, Mabel walked across to the table and steadied its wobble as she sat down. Determinedly shoving aside her doubts, she waited for Ribley, Trotter and Snouterton to join her. The interview began.

Stan K. kicked things off.

"Could you just confirm your title please, *Ms* Milner?" he asked, pen held poised over a multi-coloured triplicate form.

Mabel looked at it and cautiously confirmed her single status. But as she gave her answer, the corners of his mouth turned upwards and before too long it was clear that Cockerby's answer to Dickensian small business entrepreneurship had actually only got as far as page one of the interviewing manual. Mabel surreptitiously edged her skirt up her thigh, and so things progressed.

They were unanimously impressed that she knew her name, and commended her with enthusiasm as they leered at her chest. Then whilst Stan K. eagerly took notes, Troilus delighted in her ability to quote her date of birth and Ricky marvelled at how brilliantly she could rattle off her address. It seemed for several minutes that Mabel couldn't put a foot wrong, but then Stan K. went and blew it.

"Well, there's one final question we need to ask, Ms. Milner," he said in an apologetic tone, and flicked a nervous look across at his colleagues. Mabel tensed. "You mention in your application that you are currently a Removals Executive," he mumbled, and her blood ran cold. Without thinking, Mabel pulled the hem of her skirt back over her knees and held her breath. "Clothing Division," he then added, and looked at her expectantly.

Mabel bit her lip. She now felt back on familiar territory, but it wasn't where she wanted to be.

"Well the thing is, Ms Milner" Troilus continued quickly taking over from Stan, who seemed to have lost his nerve, "we expect that you've excelled in that role with your current employers, but were wondering if you'd be prepared to extend the services you offer?"

Every muscle in her buttocks froze. She was stuck, wasn't she? Stuck between a rock and a pistol shaped hard place. Her instincts screamed to stand up indignantly, proclaim that she had never been a prostitute, and tell them where they could poke it; although that bit would probably require clarification.

But to Mabel's infinite fortune, Ricky intervened before she had a chance to say a word.

"Well the thing is, Ms Milner, having spoken with you at length," he coughed as he said it, clearly aware of the absurdity of the statement but not prepared to drop the facade quite yet. "We'd like to know your thoughts on extending your duties beyond wardrobes, and applying your significant experience in the removals industry to the remit of *all* household contents as well."

The words now said, he sat back with relief exhausted, and three pairs of eyes looked at her shining with expectant hope. Mabel's brain whirred. The final section of their 'proposal' appeared to be bringing things back more into line with what she'd been hoping, but it had to be said, she still couldn't quite square the ever undulating circles of agricultural insurance with the concept of household removals.

"Household contents?" she managed, and then petered out.

Stan K. Snouterton winced.

"I know," he confessed. "I expect it's not been your bag up until now, some of it rather mundane. But the thing is, Ms. Milner, when your CV arrived we really took it as a sign." He paused, looking at his colleagues in turn to gain encouragement. Each nodded and he carried on. "You see, we've decided to diversify into house removals protection." He looked crestfallen as he said it, as though the bottom had fallen out of his world; to have to admit that this was what they'd been brought to. Ricky picked up the baton once more and Mabel turned to look at him.

"The uncomfortable truth is this, Ms. Milner. A great many of our farming customers are pulling out of agriculture altogether and converting instead to five star holiday retreats, conference centres, or selling to Wimpy Homes. We've lost so many quotes this year to commercial competitors because they've insured our customers' house moves, that we really have no choice; we have to stem the flow. If we offer removals insurance, we reckon we'll be saved, and you, Ms Milner, with your extensive knowledge and experience of what can go wrong in that industry, *you* could be our saviour."

* * *

"Oooh, darling, how did it go?" Dwayne asked, as soon as she reappeared in the real world. The receptionist looked up too as he said it, obviously intrigued.

Mabel clocked her and tried a humble grin. It didn't make sense to cultivate enemies yet; although she wasn't sure how to answer the question anyway. On the one hand, everything had appeared to be tickety-boo, successful beyond her wildest dreams. On the other hand however, she was quite possibly about to take over responsibility for saving a business she knew absolutely nothing about. It felt as though she would soon be required to wear pants on the outside of her clothes, when she wasn't even used to wearing pants underneath them.

"Oh, you know what interviews are like, 'don't call us, we'll call you'" she managed as casually as she could, and checked the receptionist once again. If she was going to have to deal with L'Oreal's primary method of promoting orange as the new brown, she didn't want the woman preparing a counter attack. Miss Loppylips looked away and Mabel moved her thoughts on. "But where is he? Has he gone?" she then asked, knowing that it would act as a useful red herring.

Dwayne's smile faltered just a smidge, but Mabel spotted it and went on alert. Something fishy was going on.

"Who, darling?" he asked, but Mabel wasn't fooled. Her eyes narrowed.

"D..."

"Oh, what? Your farmer friend? John?"

"Yes him."

"Ah, well yes, I've done you a favour there. Really I have. Absolute belter of a favour, actually. You'll be thanking me ..." he added and Mabel knew that he had moved into distraction mode. "Really I have." he repeated no more convincingly than the first time.

"Really?" Mabel raised a pencil thin eyebrow. "D., what have you done?"

Dwayne's nose wrinkled.

"I've got him off your back, that's what I've done," he replied and sniffed decisively, probably more to convince himself than for any other reason. It did the trick and he continued. "It was quite obvious when he turned up this morning that you didn't want anything to do with him. So I got him off your back, didn't I? I told him you were working on Thursday."

"But I don't want him off my back!"

"But you said…"

"Oh, I know what I said," she cried in frustration. "But. But..." and then suddenly her forehead creased. "But I'm not working on Thursday!" Her frown deepened. Dwayne stretched a false grin across his lips and took a step back. Mabel cocked her head to the side.

"And what the hell has Thursday got to do with anything anyway?" she asked, and Dwayne made a dash for the door.

Chapter Eight

John watched Mabel disappear off to her interview with a heavy heart. As the door closed behind her, his poor farming brain struggled to work out what had happened that morning, and came up wanting.

After their disastrous exchange at the school, he'd driven the muddy lanes for a while, eventually heading across to his pal Roger and what he'd hoped would be a flock of painted arses. He'd driven hard, pushing the Land Rover to its limits and scaring the living daylights out of a fair few verges on the way, whilst his anger had oscillated between hairless headmasters, pointless pigeons, and women with independent minds.

For starters, how did Derek do it? What with Sandra Lovelock muttering the man's name to herself the day before, and then Mabel's interest today, the bastard seemed to be a fanny magnet, and yet Derek had never struck him as a particularly lust-ridden or even vaguely attractive man before. Surely that wife of his was enough to put one off women for life! Yes, it really defeated him. Not even Roger was able to draw the opposite sex in the way that Derek could; which at this moment was particularly galling, bearing in mind there hadn't been a painted backside in sight when John had arrived at the tupping paddock.

But that was just an aside. The 'thing' that was bothering him more than anything else, and which had consumed *all* his thoughts for the last twelve hours, was now in the process of disappearing off with a snivelling snout who was giving her buttocks a thorough inspection. The man's lascivious look had made John's hackles rise. Those buns weren't for the likes of Stan K. Snouterton. No! Those buns were for him, in a manner of speaking, he hoped. One day, maybe...

An unwelcome voice interrupted his thoughts and drew him back to the present.

"S-E-E-S," Dawn spelt out slowly, and then repeated it for good measure. "Sees the day."

John sighed. In truth, he wasn't aware of anything worth 'seeing' in his day now. And to be prompted to peer a bit harder at his latest monumental cock up was not something his brain was particularly receptive to.

"Oh, I don't get this Latin lark," he lamented, and gave his chin a good scratch. "It means nothing to me, I mean, why can't they just speak English like what I do? You don't 'ave to go all fancy just to get yer message across, do yer?"

It was an appeal to no one in particular, but he felt better for expressing the opinion anyway. Hearing the words of a dead, if educationally elite, language was only serving to add salt to his wounded ego, and it was a sensation he had no idea how to tackle. One had salve for a horse; liniment for a sheep and possibly vegetable oil for a pig with dandruff, but for a broken heart? He knew not what there was.

Dawn grabbed his arm and made him jump.

"Here," she said, and gave his bicep a supportive squeeze, "don't take what Mabe says too seriously. She just can't spot a good thing when she sees it," she added, and followed it up with a wink.

John watched the heavy black eyelashes dip down in a knowing sweep and cleared his throat.

"Well, quite," he managed, just, but in doing so then realised how much like that bugger Fitztumbleton he sounded and coughed for a second time. Was this what things were coming to? he mused morosely. Was he cloning himself on a man he'd not have waved a droopy wheat stalk at a year before? It wasn't good, was it? It wasn't what Roger would be looking to for inspiration, and it wasn't going to pull a top notch stunner like Mabel either. "I'm afraid I don't understand anything about women," he confessed, and felt his heart sink to the bottom of his rubber soled boots. "I think she's probably better off without me, really. I expect she wants a man of position, doesn't she? A man of status." Like a headmaster, he thought, but chose not to voice that bit. Even to his own lugholes it sounded pathetic.

The squeeze on his arm tightened.

"I'm a very good listener, you know," whispered in his ear, and it was only then that John realised quite how close Dawn had got. A waft of musky perfume sauntered up his nose and made him sneeze. Through great long lashes, she looked back at him with concerned eyes, the caked on makeup just allowing a sympathetic expression to escape, and then pulled a hankie out of her handbag and passed it across. "Perhaps I can help?"

John took the offering and blew his nose. After a second good blow, he frowned.

"Really?" slipped out incredulously before he could stop it, and he handed back the tissue without thinking. A pair of manicured fingernails pinched it between their tips and let it fall to the floor.

"Oh absolutely," she muttered, unfazed. "I'm definitely sure I can help."

John looked at the scrunched up tissue and sniffed. "Well, thank you, but I'm sure that won't be necessary." He said it more to satisfy himself than to placate his listener, who was now just staring at him with a benign smile spread across her chops; but it didn't work.

Two long lingering seconds sauntered past before Dawn then drew in a deep breath and reached across to pull a stray hair away from his eyes.

"No really," she said finally, and ran her tongue across her lips. "I do know Mabe very well. She shares her innermost secrets with me," she added, and lifted her eyebrows knowingly.

John swallowed hard. The expression on the woman's face was disconcerting enough as it was, but how many secrets could a Removals Executive possibly have? Of course, there had to be the odd amusing work anecdote. And who knew what manner of things people left behind when they moved house. But with a day job, and a child to look after, surely poor Mabel had been starved of the excitement of 'country pursuits' for months, if not years. Her life could only have been one relentlessly dull day after another. Which, when considered from that angle, should have made catching her eye plain sailing, shouldn't it? Simple. A breeze. In fact, absolutely anything could have been possible, but he had not expected the touch and go nightmare this was turning out to be.

Oh god, he thought. I'm up a creek without a paddle, aren't I? I'm out of my depth. The dashing cut of a headmaster's jib is commanding her attention and taking the wind right out of my sails. I'm going to have to try a different tack, or I'll be left high and dry.

"Well, what can I say?" he sighed heavily, now convinced that he'd reached the bitter end. His mind struggled for an answer, and his lips rebelliously considered the question instead and continued to move silently of their own accord. *Although I 'ad been 'oping she'd be free on Thursday night,* they mouthed, unable to connect with sound whilst the concept of the particular 'Thursday' to which they were referring filled the void in his brain with the sheer magnitude of its, now unfulfilled, 'Thursdayness'.

"She's working on Thursday," landed unexpectedly in his ears, and dragged him from his thoughts. He frowned.

"I'm sorry, what did you say?" he asked, astonished.

Dawn smiled.

"She's working on Thursday."

His forehead wrinkled further.

"I read your lips," she then added, and winked again.

"Oh." he muttered, taking in the information and heaving a very deep sigh. I can't even *not* say something properly, he reflected gloomily. Things had definitely reached rock bottom. "Well, I'd only wanted to ask 'er if she'd like to accompany me on a meal out with this Ofsted inspector, but I expect these officious types prefer to keep to themselves when they're working anyway. It 'ad only been an idea."

"I'm free though," Dawn offered, and beamed a lusciously lipped smile back at him. "And I'm just mad about education."

John nodded, wondering who had mentioned anything about paying, and tried a "That's nice," whilst he contemplated whether she was actually just mad.

It wasn't a thought that had time to hang around, however, for as he was about to say his goodbyes, his mobile rang. He looked at Dawn for a couple of seconds before it hit him that it wasn't hers, and then groped about in his pockets and pulled his out. Derek's conscientious tones met his ear. John's hackles shot up; quivered furiously for a few seconds, and then forgot about their mission as the conversation progressed.

Derek explained that he had called as soon as he could, but only after he'd checked things with the local authority. He said John wasn't to worry; everything was under control and he was now simply phoning because, as Chair of Governors, he felt John ought to know that a) the plumber was still yet to arrive, and b) the school was temporarily without a janitor.

John bore the news calmly. It was a universal law that an inverse relationship existed between plumbers and the concept of time. However, the direct link between janitors and the concept of 'temporarily without' was not one he had heard of before. Derek swiftly explained what had happened and they both agreed that, bearing in mind the impending inspection, this was turning into a rotten week. It was a tenuous truce between them and as he finished the call he gave his nose a scratch.

"So Thursday's sorted then?" Dawn stated, and smiled as he looked vacantly back at her. "The only thing I need to know now then, is whether you prefer lilac or pink?"

He couldn't actually say he preferred either, but nodded anyway and plumped for pink, mainly because it was a shorter word, but not forgetting that it also sounded a lot like stink; and he liked pigs.

Which then reminded him; he was needed elsewhere.

* * *

There were many who had never acknowledged the existence of Cockerby's law enforcement service, full stop.

There were then a few, those in most frequent contact with police officers, as well as members of the neighbourhood watch, who believed it suffered from delusions of grandeur, hogging the town's only listed building as it did.

And then finally there were a handful; two or three at most with shaved hair, braces, and turned up jeans, who stated emphatically, in accents short of a consonant or two, that the police station itself was a symbol of the tyranny of a despotic minority and an over-used tool of the fascist oppressors that plague our country.

On whichever side of the fence one sat, however, there was no disputing that the building had definitely seen better days. Its religiously gothic entrance, ancient flag stones and arched doorway made it both an unlikely looking purveyor of reasoned rational opinions, as well as something akin to a Bram Stoker piss-take without the bats. Mind you, that wasn't to say that there hadn't been bats at one time, but simply that the bats had been re-homed at much expense to the tax payer. And it also wasn't to say that their lack of presence was not missed, but simply that the cobwebs, unkempt look, and scent of eau de toilet confirmed that much piss-taking had still continued over the years.

John sniffed, relishing the familiar farmyard smell, and looked up at the gable clock. It was five past eleven; or at least possibly so. Someone with a sense of humour had snapped off the end of the minute hand to make it equal in length to that of the hour hand; one, which meant it may have been five to one; but that didn't feel right. John's body responded to the passing of time in all manner of strange ways, but the one thing he was certain of was when it was nearing time to eat. He also knew when it was six o'clock in the morning, for his bowels told him so, but that was by-the-by. For now, however, he was sure it was elevenses for the less demanding gurgle in his stomach confirmed it, and although Bob was probably still being questioned, it wouldn't harm to provide the bloke with a little moral support.

The officer at the front desk greeted John with an indifferent scowl and took a sip of his tea. The apathetic sniff that then erupted after the casual partaking of said refreshment did nothing but emphasise the difference between their worlds. For John, a cup of tea was something to savour; something that denoted a break from the sweat of the day; something that put him at one with himself when he was at sixes and sevens elsewhere. For Officer Groundnut, however, a cup of tea just, well, it just was. Whether it was the fluid or the container that was more important, it was hard to tell, but the mug itself was as much an extension to his hand as a baton was to that of a conductor's. Not an explanation, discussion or order was proffered without the said vessel clarifying the situation. And let it not be mooted that a single drop was ever spilled.

Groundnut eyed him suspiciously and then took another gulp before speaking.

"Yesssssa." Not a man of many words, clearly. But it seemed to convey exactly what he wanted to say, as it lifted in tone at the end, along with his cup, and he left it at that.

John frowned. Was the man asking him a question? Or was he answering the one John had not realised he may have inadvertently mumbled without knowing? Seeing as everyone appeared to have become a bloody lip reader these days, he hedged his bets incorrectly on it being the latter.

"Really?" tumbled out, although he just managed to keep the surprise under control. "Blimey," he then continued, the control already beginning to slip. "I didn't think yer'd let me, I 'ave to say. He was saying only this morning 'ow 'e was looking forward to getting it just right for the kids."

Unfortunately, his efforts were rewarded with another noisy slurp, which was then followed by a cynically raised eyebrow. The mug tipped to the side as Groundnut did it; a beautifully coy little movement.

"Is that right, sir?" the officer asked, as he swallowed the contents in his mouth, his eyes narrowing. "And to whom would you be referring, sir? Could it possibly be the gentleman currently helping us with our enquiries into the FC Flasher?" Groundnut reviewed the contents of his cup and breathed in deeply.

"Froskin!" he then cried, not bothering to turn to look behind him, as the lift of the vessel was all that was required. A call issued from the back in response. "You might want to take a statement from this gentleman," he said, and then turned back to look at John with an amused glint in his eye. "But tell me about this, er, discussion that you had this morning, sir," he muttered smirking, the hot steaming cuppa now sliding forward across the counter, eager to stay involved. "Was it over the breakfast table, sir?"

* * *

There were many things that John had had to consider already that day, but what breakfast had to do with any of them, he didn't know.

Why he'd been given his own personal waiting room before they sat down for a chat, he also didn't know.

Why someone had made a joke about happy mariners; had left him completely flummoxed.

Though why he'd not been offered a coffee or a biscuit he had at least been able to put down to government cutbacks.

But when someone had finally arrived for a natter, they'd certainly asked some bloody odd questions.

Do you live with Bob Cartright?

Do you know where Bob was last night?

Do you like dressing up too, sailor boy?

Very odd questions, now he came to think of it. Although at least the answers had been easy enough: No; no; and yer what?

That part of the discussion hadn't taken long and, as he'd already ascertained that these policemen were men of few words, it hadn't been an issue. By the end of the short exchange, he wouldn't have gone as far as to say that there had been a meeting of minds, but they'd certainly got the message.

"So, sir," Plod number one now asked as he got up to leave, "when the sun is over the yard arm, do you find yourself getting six sheets to the wind?"

Plod number two bit his lip. "Do you keel over?" the second one posed, and couldn't suppress a chuckle.

John looked at them quizzically. The words were making little bloody sense, but the tone of their voices had put him on alert. Was this a shot across his bows? he wondered. Were they suggesting it was sink or swim? He couldn't fathom what they were getting at but, he decided, he'd best give these fellas a wide berth in future.

"I don't drink much, as a matter of fact," he replied dryly. "I'm pooped in the morning if I do, and I 'ave to get up early seeing as I'm a..."

"Uphill gardener, sir?"

John felt his blood pressure shoot.

"No!" he replied indignantly, insulted to the core that it could ever be inferred that he was interested in domestic horticulture. "I'm a farmer, and I prefer level ground, if yer must know. Now, is Bob free to come with me or not?"

Plod number one cleared his throat.

"Yes, sir, Mr Cartright is free to come with whomever he wishes as long as it's legal."

"Mr Cartright is free to set sail," number two added, and they both sniggered out of the room.

* * *

John sat in the station entrance for another hour whilst he waited. This wasn't the day he'd planned. Mind you, he pondered philosophically, this probably wasn't the day that Bob had planned either. He'd seen this type of thing happen in farming of course, you think everything

141

is sorted, and then your favourite ewe goes and gets foot rot without a word of warning. But that was how it was in farming. You were always at the mercy of nature. Today, however, was different. The recent events were not something that could have been predicted in any way. Bob's day, or even week, was currently being affected by the behaviour of an unknown individual who was *still* at large gratifying their desires. It wasn't fair, he decided finally. The poor bloke must feel completely at sea.

Bob eventually appeared between two uniforms, a haggard but relieved look on his face.

"You're a solid man, John, and don't let anyone tell you otherwise. Hard as nails, but a good 'un," he offered gratefully, and extended his arm to shake hands.

John took it, and only then spotted the two coppers swapping looks. It wasn't often said he was the world's best reader of expressions, but after a compliment like that he was prepared to bet that they were looks of respect and high esteem accompanied by raised eyebrows of reverence.

"Well, you're not the first to say I'm 'ard as nails," he replied smugly to his pal. "There are a few sheep out there that would agree with yer, an all," he added for good measure, and smiled a roughty-toughty smile to go with his little joke.

The looks of veneration on the officers' faces deepened, as their eyes widened with awe. John felt he'd won them over.

"Well shall we head off then, Bob?" he suggested, and Bob nodded, but then faltered. He flicked an uncertain look at Officer Groundnut, who was still standing behind the front desk.

"They've *recommended,*" he whispered, and lifted the two main fingers on each hand to signal inverted commas, "that I don't go out at night for a while… or not until this mess is cleared up, at least. So I don't suppose I'll be allowed back to work until then, eh?"

John shrugged. It was awkward. Bob was right. He'd had a quick chat with Derek on the phone whilst he'd been waiting and really, until the caretaker had been fully excluded from their enquiries - and Derek was absolutely sure he would be, wouldn't he? - It was prudent for Bob not to be on site. Parents were touchy about this sort of thing apparently, and for some reason, a little "alleged" revealing of one's parts was not considered acceptable behaviour. John had wavered on that bit, as far as he was concerned parts were natural, nothing to be ashamed of. But, he did agree that to get them out in this weather one had to be barking mad, and to have an insane caretaker on the premises would probably break some policy or other. The decision had thus been made.

"No, you're right, Bob, I'm afraid. Probably best to lie low for a while until this is all sorted out. They'll catch the daft bugger 'oos doing it soon, I'm sure."

Officer Groundnut coughed in the background and the caretaker's face fell.

John felt for the man. Bob lived alone, for he didn't have a missus or anything, and there wasn't much to his life outside of the school. In fact, when it came to it, John wasn't even sure that Bob had a hobby to tide him through the difficult days ahead. And then it suddenly struck him that the man needed cheering up. He needs to see that there is hope, he thought. He needs to be shown that life does still have more to offer and that it's not all bad.

Well there was only one thing that John knew to do when presented with a challenge like that. He cleared his throat momentously.

"I know what'll give yer a bit of a boost, Bob," he announced. And as he said it, a certain mug on the other side of the room leant closer across the desk. "Would yer like to meet my ram?"

The clunk of pottery chinked. "Oh you bugger," accompanied the noise. "You've made me spill my tea!"

* * *

"Oi, John, can you keep a secret?" Bob looked at him as he said it, breath puffing out into the chilly air. A ewe baaed in the background as Roger approached her with intent, but John felt his stomach twist. He didn't like secrets; they made life complicated. His brain didn't work well enough to be sure that they wouldn't come out when he was in the pub, or something. Secrets put him on edge.

"Not really," he answered honestly, and then noted despondently that Roger had only been chasing down a new clump of grass.

To add to his disappointment, he also found that Bob had not been listening.

"I think Fitztumbleton's wife has left him," the caretaker whispered, and then looked around to check that no one else could hear. The call of a distant sheep met their ears and he seemed to take it as adequate confirmation that they were alone. He continued. "She pissed off with some bugger in a pin stripe suit yesterday. I watched 'em leave together. She gave him a great big snog and then they drove off. So what do you think of that?"

Unusually for John, quite a few thoughts began to mill around in his head. *What on earth is a pin stripe suit?* Was one thought. *How could a horse like that ever manage to attract two men in her life?* Was another. *What was he going to have for tea?* Rudely snuck in, under the radar. And then finally, *'that's why he's chatting up my bird!'* leapt in and snatched the prize.

Oh blimey, he thought with a sickening jolt; it's not that she's into him, it's that *he* is into *her*. No wonder she'd got so angry that morning. He'd got it completely the wrong way round.

He needed to think this through carefully.

Perhaps he should call her. No, perhaps not.

Perhaps he should call her. No, perhaps not.

Perhaps he should call her. No, perhaps not.

And just as the repetitive noise of a pigeon could continue for an unpredictably long time, so the sophisticated debate in John Bentwick's head now began to rage...

Chapter Nine

Sandra looked at her watch. It said 8:37am, Wed. *Titanium. Swiss Made*. She sniffed regretfully, more at the time presented than the questionable provenance of the watch, and realised that Derek was late. Again. That made it twice in two days, which wasn't good, and her heart didn't like where her mind was taking her now either. After the night that she'd just had, there was no doubt that today her sympathies for his plight were somewhat muted.

Visions of women with pert buttocks and fishnet stockings had plagued her dreams. Some had been clad in academic cloaks, whilst others had simply donned a mortar board. But they had all, every single one of them, looked like Mabel Milner, with their long flowing locks, four inch heels, and pinky perky nipples.

As one dream had merged into the next, each one more breast ridden than the one before, their surreal nature had taunted her psyche until eventually Lady Lovelick, Mistress and Minister to the Minions at hand, had had nothing left to compete with but a pair of soggy fried eggs stuck to her chest.

As her eyes had fluttered through REM sleep, Derek had burst each orange disc with a fork, and then both he and Mabel had scooped up the oozing yoke with toasted soldiers and swallowed it down with tea.

Odd, to say the least. And entirely the wrong way round. For it was the submissive who would normally be eaten for breakfast not the dominant; but there was more...

Early on in the course of the night, she had managed to muster a crooning caricature of Tom Jones in the background whilst the traumas of her nightmares had played themselves out. She'd had him singing songs about keeping your hat on, new pussies and devious biblical harlots. And at first it had done what she'd subliminally hoped it would; cheer her up. None of that was unusual, of course, for he quite often appeared in Sandra's dreams. But new problems had developed later when she had been unable to prevent her brain from conjuring up a new Jones incarnation now dressed as a rasher of bacon. Mabel had then proceeded to chase poor Tom around the great big breakfast plate of life, hair and boobs flying everywhere, before finally gobbling him up with what was left of Sandra's eggs.

Well, if one had been looking for a new meaning to be brought to the concept of streaky; that would have done it. The problem was that Sandra hadn't been on that particular quest last night.

It had all been very unsatisfactory, unsettling, and unappetising. And when she'd awoken to find Mr Perkins curled up asleep in the middle of the bed under the duvet, with her own shivering body hovering on the edge of the mattress uncovered, the sense of being an unwanted dried out crust of bread had been hard to shift. No amount of stomping around in jack boots had been able to lift her mood and she'd given up on her bowl of porridge half way through, choosing instead to head morosely back upstairs to get dressed.

Now, having made it into work early, only this time clad in an outfit Rosa Klebb would have killed for, (the austerely grey suit had resonated so strongly with her frame of mind that she'd not been able to resist its ascetic appeal, although she had drawn the line at the flick knife shoes) she cast her eye over the boys' toilets just to check that no new pairs of pants had slipped in overnight.

Her nose wrinkled in disgust.

It appeared that although Sid had made it in eventually to sort things out, his skill set had not extended to dealing with the remains of the eruption that had already taken place. With Bob unavailable, The PTA had, of course, come to the rescue. Endowed with an armoury of cleaning devices that only those with OCD could have, they had descended upon the mess with gusto and left the place smelling like a testing lab for Cillit Bang. It had been a grand result at the time, and the women had headed back to their sterile havens reassured that they had conquered all. But now, with the marketing gloss long gone and the lavender scented overtones gone with it, the unpleasant smell of bleach had begun to reign supreme once more.

Sandra sighed resignedly as she took one last look at the scene of the crime, and then slipped her coat on in anticipation of going outside. If she was honest with herself, she had felt a tad guilty yesterday walking out after school was over, leaving the cleaners to it; but there was only so much her poor battered heart could cope with. The crushing disappointment she'd felt when she'd seen Mabel Milner climb out of Derek's car had been an overwhelming distraction all day, and she had just wanted to get away as soon as she could. Not her finest hour perhaps, but that was yesterday and today was today. With a lousy night under her belt, and a rindless Tom still humming away in her mind in consolation, she suddenly realised she should, could and would rise to the occasion once more.

Comforted by the thought, she did her last coat button up – 'cos, *Baby, it's cold outside* – and headed off to the playground to greet the first of the pupils to arrive.

It was only once she'd closed the front door that she realised things were not as they would normally be. She was quite used to seeing maybe two or three of the keener mothers loitering at this time, but the makings of an angry mob that actually met her eyes stopped her dead in her tracks. Sandra faltered. They were all there, dozens of them, and suddenly she realised that the playground was heaving with a fury and emotion that she'd never seen before.

Stomach-turningly throbbing with it.

She gasped and looked around.

Already, the milling groups appeared to have divided into a double act of warring factions. She was well aware that membership of the two main playground posses was loosely split between urban newcomers, who slouched to the left side of the tarmac, and indigenous agriculturalists, who lolled to the right. There was also usually some sort of I've-not-got-any-mates-yet brigade bridging the gap in the middle, but today they were nowhere to be seen. What had jovially been referred to as the '*thems*' and the '*usses*' for years, had suddenly become a schism that had hewn the village in half.

Sandra focussed first on the group to the left and took in the swaying placards held up on bits of discarded exhaust pipe and guttering. Livid headlines in dripping black paint screamed out their sordid messages. *Tan 'im, Can 'im, Ban 'im,* caught her eye, as one of the more literary offerings, clearly there to appeal to *The Daily Mail* readers amongst them. She sniffed and moved on. *Bits of Bobs? No to knobs!* it yelled, no doubt for those who preferred *The Sun.*

Inwardly at a loss, her gaze swung to the other side to find it offered only a modicum of relief.

In contrast to the tinky townies, the agricultural right had utilised a solid supply of pitchforks and four by two to extend a more subdued, although still imaginative, set of messages. The two most notable to catch her eye screamed; *Bob's no slob. He's the job!* And; *Bobby C, is the man for me!*

The last one in particular caught Sandra's eye, as she'd not been aware that the caretaker had an admirer. But it was still a lone voice in what was otherwise a sea of indignation.

Hmm, she mused cautiously. The atmosphere didn't just *have* an edge, it was *on* the edge. It was as though a sense of solidarity had bound each group together in preparation for something. Although what that something was, she dared not think.

A chant struck up to the left.

"*With his bits on show, Bob must GO!*"

Despite her concerns, Sandra huffed with disapproval. How her students were ever going to learn poetry when presented with stuff like this, she didn't know. It was such a poor play on words; 'bits and bobs'. And what were 'bits' anyway? It was an awfully partial phrase, and one so lacking in entirety that it was certainly not what any flasher would like to be remembered for; of that she was absolutely sure. But there was more...

"*Shut your gob, we love Bob!*" countered from the right. But before Sandra even had a chance to tut, "*Put his dangle through the mangle,*" swiftly came back, and forced her to wince at the new level of sophistication.

Oh my god, they're running out of rhymes, she thought in panic. Their patience will soon have disappeared.

Within seconds, her fears were proved justified. A breakaway group of Bob supporters suddenly edged forward and the resounding thump of their wooden batons began to throb a chunky beat.

The anti-Bobs growled in response and took a step forward to meet them.

The battle lines were drawn.

Sandra licked her lips. This had to be the climax; things couldn't possibly get any worse. But as the cacophony of sound escalated, a beaten up white van suddenly screeched to a halt outside the school gate and blew her hopes to smithereens. As she bit her lip in apprehension, a sweaty overweight man with thinning hair clambered out, and Sandra scanned the words running along one side of the vehicle. She felt her back stiffen. '*Cockerby Chronicle – News and Views for Yous'* it said.

She needed to think fast.

Up until this point the scenario had been manageable, a walk in the park for an expert in minion control such as she. However, with the arrival of this reporter and his mutinous Celtic grammar, the emphasis had now shifted. Diplomacy would be required.

Sandra swallowed; subtlety and tact weren't her strengths. She was better at barking orders than placidly manipulating the press, but knowing this fact and simply bemoaning it wasn't going to help. It was quarter to nine and Derek hadn't yet arrived. Within seconds all hell was going to break loose in a village that would normally consider a crowd of this size to be a fête.

Despite everything she believed in, Sandra Lovelock knew what she needed was a boost. She needed something to give her faith in herself like she'd never had before; something that confirmed that she had done the right thing by staying here all these bloody years.

It was at this moment that Ashley Milner appeared, scuttling anxiously down the road next to her dawdling mother. Sandra's stomach clenched. It wasn't what she'd been asking for, but despite herself, her eyes still sought out Derek's car.

They scanned first one way up the street and then down the other, searching for the familiar blue oval and his lovely adulterous face; but not a single Ford could be seen. Her heart gave a little flutter; this was good news. It meant he *hadn't* been with 'her' last night and it meant that the 'Milner Misses' had come to school by means of their own steam. And it was this tiny nugget of knowledge that provided the much needed edge she'd been looking for.

"Is the 'eadmaster around?" an amused voice sounded behind her, and Sandra spun round to find herself looking the journalist in the eye. "It's just we're doing a piece on the FC Flasher, and I was wondering if I could ask a few questions. Who's in charge?"

"I am," she countered immediately, her nostrils flaring with reinvigorated passion. "But now is not a good time. Can't you see that I have a few things to sort out?"

The man looked across at the group of angry parents pacing up and down in the playground and gave his head a scratch.

"I think you're going to need some 'elp, darlin'," he drawled. "Someone wiv a bit ov experience in crowd control per'aps?"

As the words slipped dismissively out of his mouth, Sandra felt something snap. Such impertinence! What did this oik know about power? What did this silly little man, with his silly little notepad and silly little pen, know about getting people to submit to his will? There was only one thing for it; she was going to have to show him.

"You just watch," she muttered crossly, and strode across to her car and flicked open the boot. As her eyes sought out their quarry, his jeering chuckle rang in her ears and her plan solidified in her mind. What she was contemplating had its risks, but she was positive that it would work. No one would be expecting it; that was for sure.

She leant in towards the back and grabbed what looked like a coiled black snake. "Come on, Natasha," she whispered lovingly to the whip. "Let's show these people what we're made of..." And with a clump, she then slammed the car boot shut and marched to the middle of the road.

Rigid with composure, Sandra Lovelock turned to face her rowdy audience, ready to meet her fate. My time has finally come, she thought, as her internal persona shifted inside; this is my moment of glory. And with that final deliberation, the Mistress and Minister to the Minions at hand breathed in deeply, pulled her arm back, and heaved her trusty love snake into a breathtaking swirling swoop.

Its crack electrified the air.

The ear splitting snap echoed off the walls of the houses and reverberated in reverential respect to its indomitable creator; the woman with the whip. Lady Lovelick revelled in the sound. And only once when she was absolutely sure of its perfection, did she then allow her alter ego to open her eyes once more.

Almost as one, the voices in the playground had hushed to a bemused silence. Sandra looked at the faces, noting the wondrous expressions with satisfaction, and finally let the breath slip out of her lungs.

"Well that did it," Mabel's amused voice filtered across, and Sandra caught herself begrudgingly accepting the compliment. She straightened her jacket and finished things up with a nod. It was time to wrap this fiasco up.

"Mrs Milner!" she called across. Mabel looked up in surprise. "Would you mind collecting those placards please? Not the sort of reading matter we would like our pupils exposed to."

As Mabel nodded obediently, a few of the embarrassed faces began to look around, expressions of shame and sudden doubt now casting a shadow across their features. Several of Bob's supporters started to give Mabel a hand too and within a couple of minutes, what had been a gaudy gobby crowd had suddenly become a motley collection of meek and mild mothers once more.

The journalist looked across at Sandra in awe.

"What's yer name, love?" he asked, notebook and pen at the ready.

"It's Love*lock*, actually," she corrected, and he looked quizzically back at her. "My name," she sighed. "My name is Sandra Lovelock. I'm the senior teacher in this school."

He scribbled madly on his pad.

"Ok, well could we 'ave a photo, Ms Lovelace?" he asked. "You know, '*Daring Teacher Tackles Mob Single Handed*', that type of thing. Or maybe," he then mused, as if carefully weighing up the possibilities, "'ow's about, *Bushey Babe Cracks The Whip."?* He raised an appreciative eyebrow as he said it, looking into the distance as if picturing the headline in his mind, but then glanced back at Sandra. "Or perhaps not," he added, taking in her outfit of choice.

Sandra bristled, "I am not from Lower Bushey," she spat crossly, and started to coil Natasha back into a nice neat ring. "I only work here."

"Fair enough," he conceded, clearly not sold on his second idea anyway. "Maybe we should just stick to '*Flasher's Trashers*'' - *Fifty Lashes* then!"

* * *

It stuck in the craw to do it, but Sandra managed. She thanked Mabel for her help, as the two of them headed towards the front door laden with placards, and even achieved what she hoped was a smile.

Actually, if it hadn't been for Ashley by the woman's side earlier, Sandra wasn't sure she'd have recognised her at a distance. She hadn't really twigged why at first, it was just that Ms Milner had seemed to be looking so much more - what was it? Countrified today? - but now that she had spotted the fawn trench coat had been set aside to make way for a more Lower Bushey style Barbour, it had started to make sense. Mabel was also in jeans, something she'd not seen the woman wear in all the three weeks she'd known her, and the outfit had been finished off with a carefully chosen pair of pink and white wellies to boot. Not pulling gear exactly, and definitely not a winning combination for the metro man of Sandra's dreams. On balance, Sandra concluded, it boded well.

She was about to thank her ex-nemesis for the second time, when she caught sight of a tiny scruffy beasty of a boy scampering across to the entrance. All three of them reached the front door at the same time and, as the sorry excuse for a school uniform squeaked to be let in, Sandra turned to Mabel once more.

"Thank you again, Ms Milner. I don't know what I'd have done if you'd not turned up late when you did." Ok, her magnanimity could only stretch so far, but there was no reason why she couldn't add a little remonstration whilst she offered words of appreciation. She continued. "If you wouldn't mind just taking that stuff through to the staff room, I need to speak with Peter Drayton briefly; alone."

Mabel nodded amiably, waited for Sandra to punch in the entry code, and then clattered her way into the building, dragging the equivalent of Bob's '*This is your life*' crib notes behind her. Sandra waited for her to disappear and then turned to Peter.

It didn't take long for the scene to register in all its gory glory. At most, only two senses were required, but the scratches, the twigs, the leaves and the smell would all, no doubt, add texture to what she was sure would fast become a very tedious tale.

"I'm sorry I'm late, Miss Lovelock," Peter mumbled, and looked down awkwardly at his shoes. "My mum told me to walk across the fields this morning as we was running out of time."

"We *were* running out of time," Sandra corrected automatically, before realising that the crux of it was actually that he'd just walked through a meadow full of cows. Not only did the insight explain the aromatic scents now wafting from his footwear, but it also put the spot light on something else far more significant; namely that the field had no fence and no gate along their boundary. In fact, it had no entrance to the school whatsoever. She frowned. "So tell me, Peter, how did you get through the hedge?"

The question was more rhetorical than she'd intended, but the cynicism was lost on the young boy. Sandra prepared herself.

"Well you know where Billy Barber pushed me in the other day?" he asked, and Sandra nodded, remembering all too well how she'd had to drag the two of them out, fighting and kicking. "Well, I just made the 'ole a bit bigger and walked through, it were easy, Miss. The only thing is though," he added, wrinkling his nose in childish dismay, "I must 'ave done me finger in again, 'cos I 'urt to buggery all over." And with that he proceeded to demonstrate his theory by prodding himself wherever a scratch or a bruise could be seen.

* * *

It was only as she began to set out the lesson objective to her class that Sandra heard Derek arrive. Actually, it was more appropriate to say that she heard Mrs McFreece discussing the matter of his late appearance with him. But it was clear, either way, that he was a spent man, for his meek, somewhat pathetic response to the diatribe did nothing but emphasise how bad things had now got.

Her distraught heart fluttered on his behalf.

Once the admonishment was over, Sandra next heard him receive a perfunctory synopsis of what had occurred in the playground that morning, her commanding control getting but the briefest of mentions, after which he was then presented with a list of Ofsted tasks and dismissed. Within seconds, she heard his door close quietly and knew he had retreated to the sanctuary of his office.

Now, her distraught heart fluttered on her own behalf. This was what she'd been waiting for.

Sandra struggled through her algebra lesson, masterfully keeping her sarcasm at bay as Peter Drayton grappled with the concept of letters occurring in both mathematics and literacy, and clung to the knowledge that the mid morning recess was close by. The first moment she was free, she dipped out of the break-time coffee round, and headed through to Derek's office.

She paused briefly before knocking; bracing herself with a deep breath.

"Mr Fitztumbleton?" she tried, and then found to her relief that she did still have the strength to go on. "Could I have a word?"

Derek looked up as she walked in, his disconsolate face initially chequered with what she assumed were lines of exhaustion and stress, until she spotted an additional factor had also come into play; fear.

How very odd. Fear was an emotion she was accustomed to seeing, but it was strangely out of place here. There was no doubt that it had been an inordinately long list of tasks The Fridge had given him earlier, but not one that was insurmountable. There was no need for him to be frightened.

Derek broke her train of thought.

"Cumberland sausages?" he asked, his face remaining otherwise at a standstill. Sandra twitched her head to the side and frowned. "Well, it's a word, isn't it?" he explained. "Actually it's two words, but I'm feeling generous today and I know you're into your cooking," he then added, as though it was meant to be some sort of joke that neither of them was prepared to find funny. "Well, quite," he muttered finally in more familiar fashion, and Sandra felt herself relax.

"Well that's, er, very culinary of you, Mr Fitztumbleton, thank you," she said, trying to get things back on track. "But actually there are a few other bits I'd like to chat about first, and whilst I don't want to add to your burden today, they do need sorting before the inspector arrives tomorrow."

As she hoped, the mention of the imminent visit instantly had an effect; though not quite as anticipated.

A frown would have been understandable; a shrug courageously cavalier. However the filling up with tears that actually proceeded to occur had not been on her radar at all.

Sandra spotted the moisture forming and the dominatrix in her tried to cut in. She'd seen it many, many, many times before when a severe dose of gratitude had welled up in a subordinate's eyes. But this was different. Her instincts were telling her that the salty pools collecting within Derek's lashes had an alternative cause, and she shifted from one foot to the other uncomfortably. Worst case scenario, this was an unfortunate response to some sort of independent thought, a tricky thing at any time, and it could now go one of two ways. She waited with trepidation.

"You might as well know," Derek mumbled and reached across to grab a tissue to blow his nose. "You'll find out soon enough anyway, and I'd prefer that you heard it from me rather than via the village tom toms."

Sandra felt her heart swell; it was heading in the right direction.

"Miranda has left me," he sighed, and swallowed hard. "She's..."

Without thinking, Sandra reached out and put her hand on his shoulder.

"Derek," she whispered, hardly believing herself capable of such a gentle sound. He too looked astonished, but managed to remain mute. "I already know," she then said softly, and lifted her index finger to her lips as if to say 'hush', before trying a brief smile.

As her lips began to stretch, his eyes widened in horror and he recoiled back into his chair. Begrudgingly, Sandra straightened her mouth again, and as his shoulders began to relax, she silently cursed her wretched face.

"What do you mean, you already know?" he whispered back.

She sighed.

"I'm afraid I saw her on Monday dropping off a letter and then getting into a... a... disgustingly vulgar car, if I may say, and driving off with some awful man who looked like..." Suddenly, she was lost for words. To say that the man had looked like he was stinking rich, worked in The City, and would know how to show a girl a good time wasn't what he would want to hear.

"Looked like what?" he gasped, and Sandra realised she had no choice but to plough on.

"Well, quite frankly, he looked like a complete w-w-swanker."

"I think you mean banker, Miss Lovelock," he muttered, but she interrupted him before he could go any further.

"No, Mr Fitztumbleton, believe me, I know exactly what I mean."

Inside, Sandra felt exhausted. It went against the grain to be so light hearted and, even though it was quite clear that the situation absolutely demanded it, she was shattered.

"But I'd like to help you if I can," she added finally, desperate to move things around to what she really wanted to ask him and get this conversation wrapped up. "And I was wondering if we should work through the school policies later on today?"

It was a trump card. His shoulders sagged with relief.

"They do need a final check. I confess they've been sitting on my kitchen table for two days now and I haven't even looked at them."

"Well, why don't we go through them together? Two pairs of eyes are better than one, as they say," she tagged on, surreptitiously crossing her fingers behind her back. "And I could make us a snack at mine, if it would help."

It was clearly a tempting offer, but as Derek started to nod, an unwelcome voice then landed in both their ears and destroyed the golden moment.

"Mr Fitztumbleton," The Fridge said frostily, having arrived in silently glacial fashion, sporting a suspicious look in her eye. "You asked me to remind you about the scarecrows. Oh my god!" she then exclaimed, and as she said it, her jaw dropped in astonishment. Derek's head jerked up.

"What on earth is wrong, Mrs McFreece?"

"Did you hear what I just heard?" she asked, her worried face now glancing from one person to the other, pleading with them to agree. Derek shook his head and Sandra watched a shiver visibly wobble across the woman's shoulders. "B-b-but," she stuttered finally, "I'm sure that was the sound of a cow mooing in our playground."

Chapter Ten

John's mobile rang just as he was about to reward Roger with a solid kicking in the tenders. The timing was good for both of them. Given the briefest of moments to change his mind, he concluded that it wasn't in his interest to have a de-testiculated ram, and deep down he knew that he would simply have to accept that Roger was Roger, and would only 'roger' when he was ready; patience was a virtue. All good things come to those who waited, notwithstanding the fact that 'coming' was currently an unrepresentative word, and the fat lady wasn't singing yet. Well not for Roger's scrotum anyway, although she may well have been belting out a requiem for Derek Fitztumbleton's sanity.

He listened to the distressed tones of the headmaster and felt his hackles rise. On balance, despite the fortuitous timing of the call, Derek was not a person he wished to talk to right now. The sleepless night he'd just had, where counting sheep had done nothing but emphasise Roger's disinterest in reproduction, was not one he cared to repeat. Stuck in a semi-conscious state, Mabel's furious face had floated in front of his eyes, whilst her odd little friend had lifted a coy but expectant eyebrow; again, and again, and again. And the Latin incantations chanting in the background had done little to help. Eventually, in the darkness of the early hours, when repetition of *seize the day* had all but seized his mind, he'd buried his face in his pillow and begged for daylight to come.

When morning had finally arrived, the breaking of the *dawn* had brought with it an ambivalent set of feelings towards the word. But he had decided, at least, to try with Mabel one more time.

The insistent warble in his ear broke his chain of thought.

"Well how long until you can get here?" Derek pleaded, and John shoved his misgivings aside and took a very deep breath.

"I'll be there when I'm there," he replied, believing that honesty was the best policy and secretly unsure of what good he could do once he'd arrived anyway. It was true that he had a reputation for ruminants, however cattle really weren't his thing. But, as he explained this salient fact to Derek, he soon realised that his efforts would go unrewarded. As far as Fitztumbleton was concerned, the animals currently wandering the wastelands of the school playground - grazed upon open grass - like many farm animals did; had a leg at each corner, like many farm animals did. And, well, that was all there was to it.

A rather simplistic view? Yes. Overly urban? Certainly. Relevant in any way? Virtually not at all. But what did that matter to one who would never understand?

Bloody townies, John thought to himself, and aimed a kick at an evil looking molehill instead. His instinctive reaction was to tell Derek to sod off, but a little voice was harking that Mabel's child was at the school, and he realised he'd have to ignore his better judgement and agree to help them out.

Roger's eyes followed him as he walked off, and then flicked away to view a particularly tasty looking tuft of grass instead. There was nothing quite like a good chew on the cud, he mused; although it was possible that there were better things and he just couldn't remember what they were. And with that ponderous thought, he lowered his head to take one last mouthful of his current patch, just as a ewe spotted the new clump too and made a beeline for it with a saucy ovine waddle.

Roger watched the sway of her hips in fascination and instinctively took a sniff.

Good Lord that smelt good!

He straightened up and tried again.

Yes, he'd definitely been right the first time, and not only was it surprisingly good, but so much so that it was now tapping into an innate urge to be warm, moist and hard.

His nostrils quivered for a third time, and this time, to his surprise, something altogether different happened. As the air shot up his nose, her fertile pheromones hit him like a combine harvester, and before he knew what was going on, his lip was curling like a good 'un and recollections of all that he'd forgotten began to tumble in.

Suddenly it was all making sense. It wasn't grass he wanted. It was ass! And with this new item now on the agenda, plus an extra leg in tow, he barged his way across in a bid to stake his claim.

Already heading away from this touching love scene, John never had the opportunity to take heart in his ram's interest in the opposite sex. Mind you, it was probably for the best. For it meant that he also didn't despair as the beleaguered ewe took exception to the encroachment on her meal, and head butted Roger's over-sized scrotum with all the nous that she had.

* * *

John pulled up near the school, parked a few yards along the road so as not to scare the buggers into a stampede, and took a good look.

Limousin; a righty pesky breed. But there were only eight of them; a manageable number even if they were looking a little disgruntled now.

He leant across to the passenger seat, grabbed his cap, and put it on to think.

People often underestimated the intelligence of these animals, but he could see that they were already trying to take control of their habitat. As far as any rational beefy brain was concerned, there could only be one reason for there being no grass in the corral in which they were penned, and that was the barren nature of the ground. With such a premise in mind, a meat head had no option, therefore, but to deduce that fertiliser was the solution.

They knew that. He knew that. And, no doubt, Derek Fitztumbleton and his teachers regularly taught such concepts to their pupils. So one could only stand back and admire how rapidly these particular eight beasts had taken meaningful action to commence the metamorphosis they now planned.

John got out of his Land Rover and quietly shut the door. The acidic aroma of fresh droppings wafted up his nostrils and he wrinkled his nose in distaste. Bloody cattle; so similar to lightening, they couldn't see it in their hearts to strike at the same place twice; already it was quite a mess.

He cast his glance across the freckled scene and spotted Derek's anxious face peering through the glass panel in the front door. The man's eyes were flicking from one side to the other, fearfully. *Yer'd think this were a pack of bloody wolves*, John mused, carefully disregarding the fact that he'd still ensured there was a fence between him and them too, and without thinking, a condemnatory huff slipped from his lungs. One of the bullocks raised its head and bellowed back. As it roared, a tail lifted at the other end and deposited another dose of fertiliser just for good measure, before it bellowed again.

"Oh, put a sock in it. Both ends," John barked, and braced himself to go in. Despite his dislike of these animals, it wouldn't do for Derek to see him falter. Someone had to stand strong.

He set off across the playground knowing eight pairs of eyes were watching, if not with interest then at least for entertainment, and managed to get half way before a trio of heifers blocked his path and refused to budge. John humphed and stepped to the side. This breed were so bumped up with attitude, he suspected even an invasion of their personal space would not force them to submit to his will.

He reached the school entrance buoyed by his irritation and waited for Derek to undo the latch. A quick last glance behind confirmed that his escape route had already closed off, and he turned back to face the door, keener than ever to get inside.

To his dismay, Derek hadn't moved.

"Well are yer going to open up?"

It wasn't an unreasonable question, he thought, but Derek simply blinked in reply. John frowned, suppressing his discomfort, and tried a different tack. "Well do yer want me to leave these buggers to you then, or shall we 'ave a chat first?"

It had the desired effect.

Derek quickly unlocked the door, pulled the farmer inside, and then slammed it shut behind him.

"Should we evacuate the school?" he asked immediately, hopping from one foot to the other. John scowled.

"There are only eight of them, Mr Fitztumbleton, and they seem to be in a good mood. At the moment," he then added, not wanting to share the full repertoire of thoughts currently angling for a headline in his mind. "I don't think we need alert the children. It will only take a short while to move 'em on."

Sandra Lovelock's voice snapped loudly somewhere deep within the bowels of the building, berating Billy Barber for calling Peter Drayton a 'knob', but Derek barely budged.

"But can you deal with them?" he asked, wide eyed with terror instead.

John looked at him and ran a finger along his shirt collar before answering.

"Well do yer know 'ow they got in 'ere in the first place?"

At last, Derek's eyes lost their haunted look and he pointed behind him to the back of the school. "There's a hole in the hedge, which must be the size of ..." he paused, clearly waiting for inspiration, and then carried on. "Well," he sighed finally, "it must be the size of a cow I suppose."

John took a deep breath. He was no more a fan of this species than Derek, but a few things needed to be sorted before they moved on; life was like that. It was important to get the details correct.

"They're not called cows, Mr Fitztumbleton, they're called cattle. Before we start we should at least get the terminology right. When yer refer to cows, yer is usually referring to the female gender, and as yer can quite clearly see," he turned to look outside again as he said it, "we 'ave both sexes 'ere this morning."

He watched Derek's eyes flick obediently to peer through the window, and felt a smidgeon of pride. That had been quite a good little speech, he thought. It had sounded rather knowledgeable, perhaps even academic.

But sadly, Derek's understanding of the difference between bullocks and heifers was academic too.

"To be honest, Mr Bentwick, I don't really care if they are hermaphroditic bison, I just want them out of my playground."

And as he said it, an inquisitive heifer lumbered up and gave them a good staring at through the window. Unimpressed with Derek's ridiculous expression, she then proceeded to lick the glass, her tongue and nose leaving great big smeary smudges all across the pane. The headmaster winced.

"Can you get him away?" he pleaded, and John sighed with consternation.

"That's a heifer, Mr Fitztumbleton. He is a she, so to speak. You can tell because..."

"Well, quite," Derek interrupted impatiently. "But can you get rid of *them* before *they* do any more damage?"

As the words slipped out of his mouth, the crash of the Wendy house roof suddenly clattered in their ears. John spun round to catch the largest of the brutes already having a go at the roofing felt now that it was exposed. They're going to get bored soon, he thought to himself. What with no grass to eat, and little else to do, a shed would only be the start of it. He needed to get this sorted quickly.

"Show me this 'ole in yer 'edge then," he sighed grudgingly. "I'll work out what to do."

The panic stricken ruts on the Head's face eased and he led John silently past rows of cloak pegs and through to the rear play area. As they walked back out into the cold fresh air, for a split second John felt his stomach lurch. The last time he'd stepped foot on a playing field had been at Cockerby College twenty years before; and he'd only done it then to get to the other side. Sport had never been his thing; all that running around with balls and stuff. There was only one use for the word 'balls', as far as he was concerned, and it didn't have anything to do with sport. Experience was showing that it also had little to with Roger, but that was another matter.

He stared across the expanse of patchy grass and straightened the flat cap on his head. There wasn't a huge amount of ground to cover, but it still wasn't going to be easy. He let his glance move across to the far left corner and noted wryly that it, at least, offered a tiny bit more promise. A pool of autumn rain had collected in the crook of the hedge's arms, which, if he'd read this herd right, could possibly prove useful; for they wouldn't want to get bogged down over there. He stored this valuable piece of knowledge away and let his gaze move on.

As his eyes surveyed the landscape, however, the right side of his face began to burn. Sizzle, sizzle, it went. *You know you want to look over there, really* his farmer's sixth sense sputtered. Until finally, as the sautéed transmission crescendoed, he gave in and looked across to the other half of the field.

Hmmm, that would do it. Something was staring at him.

Lots of somethings.

Derek shuffled awkwardly behind him, and as John tried to fathom what these 'somethings' actually were, an "Oh my god, I'd forgotten all about the scarecrows," simpered from the headmaster's lips. "Miss Lovelock will have a field day."

At that moment, a gust of wind added its tuppence worth and helpfully blew the tinkle of rusting cans their way.

John stared at the football-shaped faces gazing vacantly back and gave his nose a scratch. It was an odd scene. To his mind, the winner of that summer's competition looked like a right cocky little bugger, brandishing his foil crown, whilst the rest paid homage.

Yet it was still an educational little scene. Dressed in everything from football kit to fairy dresses with wings, the scarecrows had scientifically proven that nylon beat cotton with respect to withstanding the weather. The PTA had no doubt taken extensive notes.

As John glared at the motley group, the seed of an idea germinated and grew.

"I think I'm going to need your 'elp, Mr Fitztumbleton," he said. But as the word *'elp* left his lips, Derek's face turned white. Disconcerted, the farmer ploughed on. "'Ow many of them scarecrows are there then?"

Derek looked at him vaguely and shrugged.

"Err... I don't know, twenty?"

John paused and then nodded. "Well that should be enough for our purposes. Now this is what I need yer to do..."

As he began to outline his plan, the remaining hint of pallor clinging onto Derek's face slipped away. Having explained things, John stopped talking and looked at him. "Are yer alright, Mr Fitztumbleton?" he asked. "'Cos yer look like yer've seen a ghost."

But Derek didn't reply. His brain appeared to have gone into stasis. Nothing moved except his mouth, which opened briefly, shut, opened again and then finally stayed where it was as if clinging onto the last syllable of 'moo' forever.

John Bentwick frowned and raised his eyes to the heavens for inspiration. "I don't need yer to talk to 'em, Derek," he muttered, at a loss. "I just need yer to do what yer told."

* * *

As soon as Derek had grasped that he wasn't required to go anywhere near a cow, the panic in his face simmered down. Once instructed, it didn't take long for him to then follow John's directions, whilst the farmer got on with ushering the cattle into a corner of the playground on the other side of the school.

John stood back and rubbed his chin thoughtfully. He wished he had his collie with him, but these animals didn't like dogs and were unpredictable at the best of times. The only option really was to channel them down to the lower field himself.

He waited for Derek's signal, a petrified face appearing at the front door, and took one final look around. What he needed now was the ring leader; every group had one, it was just a matter of singling them out. He cast his eye across several long-lashed, disinterested faces, and then found the one he'd been looking for. Bloody typical. He should have known it would be the biggest of the lot; and the bugger had been eyeing him the whole time.

He watched the animal register the attention with a twitch of its ear and marched decisively up to it.

"Come on, Fred," he growled, and slapped the brute on its rump to get it on the move.

Fred snorted, whether because of the blow or the ridiculous name it was hard to say, and swished his crusty tail from one side to the other to signal his disgust.

John was unperturbed. He'd expected this and already had another slap waiting in the wings. As the sound reverberated through the air for a second time, the bullock's legs jerked into action before his brain had a chance to challenge the idea, and the rest of the herd started to tag along.

He watched them saunter down the path at the side of the school, one by one, and then trailed after them into the open expanse at the back.

Derek had followed his instructions precisely, as any petrified cow hand should, and the product of his labours was now laid out for the farmer to see.

John looked at it with apprehension. Two converging lines of scarecrows were welcoming him and his wards, drawing them into their tapering arms to a point at the bottom of the field. Like a funnel, they were pulling his eye down to the gap in the hedge and what he hoped would be the cattle's exit from the school site.

For want of a better idea, it was the makings of a plan. He set off.

Things started off well, for the newly dubbed Frederick seemed prepared to carry the mantle of responsibility with equanimity. His lumbering stride took them, one step after another, down towards the apex of the channel and on to the gaping hole at the bottom. John's eyes followed him, almost hypnotised by the rhythm of the pace, and a sense of satisfaction began to grow.

But it was short lived.

Disaster could have struck in many ways, but for it to appear in the guise of a mouth-watering clump of greenery was not something the farmer had considered. John watched in horror as success swiftly mutated into looming failure.

Any other day, Fred stopping to have a chomp wouldn't have been a problem, for any other field could have accommodated him and his pals without issue.

But today *wasn't* like any other day.

The school playing field *wasn't* like any other field. And two converging lines of scarecrows *were*, as one would expect, just like any other pair of converging lines of scarecrows.

In essence, they constituted a cattle guidance system that was based on a cone with no material sides.

In a nutshell, it was a system that required an understanding of dot-to-dot such that a row of toothless grins could suggest a subliminal fence.

In reality, a bovine brain didn't work that way.

Fred stopped walking and lowered his head to commence his snack. There was just enough room for Frederick Mark II and a pair of Frederickas to sidle up beside him. But thereafter, the four remaining namesakes found they had run out of space, and their only option was to search out their own little cafeteria elsewhere.

John froze. If he moved to the right too quickly, the break-away gastronomes were likely to head further off, and he'd have two groups to round up. If he moved to the left, he was going to get bogged down in the muddy quagmire.

Frederick Mark I, was his only option.

He crept along the edge of the right hand line of scarecrows and stopped at a Peter Crouch lookalike standing proud next to his prey. Peering up at its algaefied face, John realised that it was the tallest and raised an eyebrow. At this point, he was prepared to accept any silver lining, for the only plan he had was to sway the pole one way, whilst he leant to the other, so it would look like two human beings were suddenly on the case. It wasn't much of a plan, and may well have been laughed at in a parallel dimension where the universe looked more critically upon the concept of buy-one-get-one-free. As it was though, John wasn't in that distant land, and there was no one around to tell him to bog off.

He grasped the scarecrow by the waist and gave it a yank. Oh, what a satisfying, firm action it was; so masterful and manly, so in control, and yet, it soon appeared, also so 'over the top'. Given the sodden nature of the ground, he quickly realised he'd added too much oomph, and the football head suddenly pinged off the end. As the grinning orb whistled through the air, his eyes followed its arc and then watched it slap Frederick briskly across the backside.

Fred's head jerked up. That wasn't the first time someone had done that to him today. He turned in the direction of the source, and caught himself thinking, just as a late-flying baseball cap whopped him on the nose, 'Knock it on the 'ead, son!'

The bullock ran a disgruntled tongue across his lips and surveyed John through his lashes. Ermintrude may well have been a dim and distant ancestral echo, but still the attraction of a twizzling flower drew him. This playing field was beginning to get on his nerves, not only had he now found that it was, in reality, *just* another grubby patch of grass, but there wasn't a splash of colour to be seen either; not even a bit of cow parsley. He'd led his cronies across the great divide with the promise of such hope, and now it looked as though he'd made a very big mistake.

Fred felt the cloak of responsibility weighing heavily on his withers and looked longingly towards his original home. Such luscious grass it had, so much thicker, greener and better it looked; just how grass was meant to look from the other side. In fact, what on earth had he been thinking of?

Suddenly, his mind was made up. There was no time like the present; one had to take these opportunities when they were offered, and learn by one's mistakes. So with a disgusted belch, he gave the sports field a final derisory glance, and then sidled back through the gap in the hedge like a character from The Magic Roundabout.

John tracked the others with his gaze as they obediently followed suit. Within a minute, the last rump had disappeared, and all that remained was the twittering of birds, a splattering of cowpats, and the original gaping hole.

He stared at it with consternation. Holes in fences were easy to deal with, for you simply patched them up with more wood. Holes in hedges, however, were an entirely didn't matter, for they didn't exist on their own. They were sociable entities that liked to gather in groups; where one found one hole, the rest of its family was usually close by. But, to Derek Fitztumbleton's good fortune, a farmer knew about these quirks, and being a man accustomed to making use of what was to hand, John shoved his concerns aside, grabbed his headless helper in his hand, and yanked 'him' fully out of the ground.

"You'll stand guard whilst we sort out something more long term, won't yer, mate?" he muttered, and marched over to the gap not expecting a reply.

A single solid thrust pushed the scarecrow firmly into place, its arms reaching across from one side of the breach to the other. John stood back to admire his handiwork and then wondered if the Tottenham away-kit looked rather out of kilter. It's missing something, he thought, and then realised what it was; its head. A quick search located the football, and he stuck it back where it belonged. There, he thought finally; that's better. At least it could see where it was going now; a team like that needed all the help it could get.

* * *

"So do yer think that Pat can give yer an 'and again then?" John asked Derek, as the two of them surveyed the mess in the front playground.

Derek frowned. "Who's Pat? Do I know her? Or is it a him?" he then quickly asked, looking slightly askance.

John's forehead wrinkled too. "Oh, you know, Pat," he urged. "You're always telling me about Pat. P-A-T," he then spelt out, just for good measure.

Derek peered back. "Are you sure you don't mean the PTA?"

John's smile broadened. "Yes, that's exactly who I mean, and now you know who I'm talking about, do yer think that this '*The* Pat' can give yer an 'and before tomorrow's visit?"

Derek sighed and raised his eyebrows.

"Well I suspect that the PTA will be falling over to redeem themselves after their performance this morning. So we can but ask, Mr Bentwick, I suppose we can but ask."

"And talking about tomorrow's visit," John interrupted, pleased that he had now found an appropriate way to raise a subject that had been playing on his mind. "What do yer say to us inviting this inspector out for a meal in the evening? Yer know, wine 'im and dine 'im. Show 'im that us country folk are as civilised as the rest of 'em."

Derek's face collapsed back into a scowl. He obviously struggled with the concept himself.

"I don't think that's how things work, to be honest, John," he said. "I don't think that they are supposed to fraternise with the enemy. It leaves them open to accusations of bribery."

"Oh but we can but ask, Mr Fitztumbleton." John cut in, keen to ingratiate himself through mimicry now that his plan was within reach. "As yer ever so wisely say, I suppose we can but ask."

* * *

Derek was a rum one, John thought, as he walked away from the school and on towards the Co-Op; but he'd be able to set the man straight tomorrow. What with Mabel on his arm as his partner, the headmaster would have to get the message then, wouldn't he? Hands off, she's mine, and that was all there was to it.

Encouraged, he picked up his pace, unaware that he was being watched.

From a levitated position on top of the school roof, Percy tracked the farmer with the trained eye of an expert, and noted the man's little skip of happiness with indifference as he set off. With a well timed swoop, he dipped down silently, deposited a gift on his persecutor's shoulder, and then flapped off, content. Boy, oh boy! There was nothing like lightening the load to ensure that revenge was perfectly wrought. Nobody tried to run him down and got away with it. He had a reputation to protect.

As John reached the shop door, he stood aside to let a lady come out and frowned as she gave him a quizzical look.

"Good day," he tried, but she just glanced at his shoulder for a second time, before scuttling off.

He followed her with his eyes, perplexed, but then felt his stomach rumble and headed into the store with other things on his mind. A pork pie was a far more constructive topic for his mental resources at that moment. Well, that and a cup of tea.

The door swung shut behind him and he was about to make his way across to the refrigeration unit when suddenly his heart skipped a beat.

Oh my, it was a glorious sight.

Mabel was there, looking breath-taking in a pair of pink and white wellies, staring at a custard tart whilst standing between the freshly baked muffins and a precariously piled stack of crumpets. A quick and wistful visualization of her standing there in *just* her pink and white wellies sent a shiver down his spine.

"Yer not in work today?" he asked jovially, disconcerted by the tension growing in his trousers and wanting to focus on something less arousing. "Does that mean yer got the job then? I 'ope so, 'cos I did try to put a good word in for yer."

For a split second, Mabel looked confused.

"Oh, err... I took a day off," she explained hastily. "I thought that two days off in a row would look less suspicious than one. How's Roger?"

John nodded, hoping that it would appear that he understood what she was getting at, although having always worked for himself and never had a day off, her strategy was, in truth, lost on him. He stood aside to let an elderly woman slip past to reach the bread shelf, and then returned to considering her question.

"Oh, Roger's no different, to be honest. Still more interested in 'imself than any of them ewes. I don't think 'es grasped what that great big ball bag is for yet."

The blue rinser's jaw dropped as he said it, and she put the pack of currant buns back down and waddled off as quickly as she could. John's gaze followed her to the tinned vegetable counter, relieved that the accompaniment to his own lesser ball bag had started to simmer down, and then cleared his throat.

"Anyway," he tried, more for the sake of conversation than anything else, "'ow's yer friend?"

It was the wrong subject to choose. Mabel's eyes narrowed.

"Looking forward to Thursday, apparently," she hissed, and put the box of custard tarts back on the shelf. John listened to the crinkle of the wrapper, such a homely sound at other times, and realised that today for some reason it jarred.

"Oh that's nice," he began, wanting to add *'why's that then?'* but Mabel didn't give him a chance.

"I expect it is," she spat. "Not that I'm supposed to know anything about you taking my best friend out though, eh? You. Bloody. *Arse!*"

The grey haired granny dropped a can of mushy peas and John took an involuntary step backwards.

"Yer what?" he gasped. "Thursday was never meant to be a surprise or anything, I just 'adn't got to speaking to yer yet, that's all."

"Well, quite," Mabel managed, and then huffed with annoyance as they glared across at each other, clearly aware of whom she had just aped.

A second of silence hung heavy between them, only to be broken by the clatter of her shopping basket as it fell to the floor. Mabel looked down, sneered, and then shoved it to the side with her beautifully booted foot.

"Well, I'm afraid you'll have to excuse me," she finished off. "I've got better things to do than waste my time in here. Oh, but by the way," she then added quickly, as she turned on her rubber wedged heel, "it looks like that pigeon has got his own back on you." And with that, she pointed at his shoulder, laughed with cruel mirth, and then marched out of the shop.

Chapter Eleven

Mabel imagined the dismal shuffle of John Bentwick's stare sidling up behind her and carried on marching, one foot in front of the other, back through the shop. That's right, Mister, she thought; look and grieve. See what you've dismissed, and take one last peek at what you could have had; 'cos nobody treats me like that. *Nobody!*

And with the memory of his bumbling excuses still fresh in her mind, she chucked a mental *Good Riddance!* in for good measure.

Easy come, easy go; that was the mantra. That was how it had always been, so there was no reason why things should have changed just because they'd moved out to the country. Lower Bushey didn't owe her anything, did it? She had no call on its magnanimity, and, equally so, nor did she owe it anything either.

Really, she concluded as each pink-hearted boot strode purposefully towards the door, if close shaves were judged on a Remington scale for near misses, this was definitely one for Shaun the sheep.

Goodness, what a strong stiff-upper-lip set of thoughts they were that tumbled through her mind as she reached the exit, real I-will-survivors. Exceptional concepts, in fact, for helping her turn her back on the only thing that had caught her eye in recent times; bar one tincy wincy snag, of course.

Because that that was all they were still; mere thoughts.

They'd not yet been promoted to the status of proper feelings and, as a result, remained wholly unconvincing despite being an appealing set of gits.

It was a bloody pain in the arse!

Annoyed at being such a sentimental whim-wham, Mabel gave the Co-Op door an extra hard nudge and winced as it banged against the doorstop. Not noticing the person following her out, a frosty Gaelic lilt butted in on her moment of self flagellation and stopped her in her tracks.

"Oh good morning, Mrs Milner," it said, just as the edge of the door swung back and caught Mabel on the side of the cheek. She lifted her hand and disconsolately rubbed what would soon require a double layer of foundation. Mrs McFreece continued, "I'm just stocking up on supplies for tomorrow when the inspectors arrive. I've bought some nice chocolate biscuits to give them with their coffee," the woman explained, oblivious of Mabel's plight, "and some garibaldi too, of course. You can't have a cup of tea without a garibaldi, can you?"

The words gabbled out of The Fridge's mouth at a rate of knots, undulating with the consummate fervour of a covert biscuit expert. It was clear that the woman was very excited. Mabel shook her head obediently before realising, a second too late, that it was the wrong thing to do, Mrs McFreece stretched her mouth into something akin to a smile and a shudder rattled down Mabel's spine.

"I thought it was you," the frosty one carried on, her lips contorting further into the upturned grimace. "I could hear someone speaking to that... that... farmer person." And at this point, The Fridge's mouth then curled back down with disdain and the status quo returned. Mabel felt herself relax, just slightly, "Oh, he's a right one, that one," McFreece whispered finally. "Always going on about his bloody ram. You'd think the bugger had balls made of gold!"

How Mabel held her poise at the insight she didn't know. Despite it being The Fridge, astute words of wisdom were, at the end of the day, still astute words of wisdom and not to be disagreed with, for she too had had just about enough of Roger and his scrotal circumference to last a lifetime.

"You should try an evening of it." she suggested instead, and her companion looked back at her in horror.

"Good lord, no!" Mrs McFreece exclaimed. "I couldn't do a whole evening of it, it would drive me mad, all that talk about sheep and what not. I reckon I'd have bad dreams after a night out with that man. You know what, Mrs Milner..." she now said, leaning forward, and as she moved closer, Mabel caught a whiff of stale-coffee issuing from her breath and wondered if she really wanted to find out something that she probably already knew. "I hate kids," the woman confided, and Mabel commended herself on being proved right. "But give me an evening with your daughter any day of the week, rather than one minute with that boar."

The weighty significance of the words landed in her ears. They were probably supposed to be illustrative of something meaningful, and as Mabel was about to clarify whether reference was being made to 'boar' or 'bore', out of nowhere, a pang of defensiveness on John Bentwick's behalf suddenly twinged.

Reference either way wasn't nice, was it? And to not be present to defend oneself, well that made it even more unpleasant. As a friend of hers, John deserved better than that; he was a good man.

Mabel suddenly found herself frowning. It was quite an extraordinary mix of emotions to feel, pride and prejudice, and certainly not something she'd been expecting.

"Oh, by the way," The Fridge added on a final note, oblivious to the torrent of emotion that she'd just elicited. "I expect Mr Fitztumbleton will be calling you later today, Mrs Milner. He needs to fast-track some paperwork for getting Ashley onto our Gifted and Talented scheme before the inspectors arrive tomorrow."

Still distracted, Mabel muttered something about popping in later to speak with him, and to her astonishment Mrs McFreece's eyes instantly glowed with appreciation.

"Oh, that would be grand, Mrs Milner. Absolutely grand."

* * *

Mabel assessed the dot-to-dot cow pat design decorating the front playground, and supposed that it would have looked for all the world like a rabbit humping a pizza, were the dots to have been joined together.

Which reminded her; Dominos would do for supper later.

As the picture of pepperoni with mushrooms and anchovies hovered invitingly in her mind, the shrill sound of well-to-do-women-at-work warbled from behind the main building and wheedled its way in. She cocked her head to listen harder. From the bits being proffered by the more strident voices, it seemed that a flurry of manure-based activity was taking place. Mabel supposed that her rabbit pal here at the front had a warren's worth of mates joining in the gang bang elsewhere.

Perhaps the pizza place was running a special offer.

She chuckled to herself and opened the school gate just as a loud, probably feminine, voice confirmed her theory.

"I tell you what, Priscilla, give me a barrow load to take home," the well spoken, undoubtedly stout, mother snorted. "Jonty can have it for his veg patch."

"But you have to let it rot down first, Sacrementa," Priscilla's disembodied voice advised; the tone of which also implying a set of solid thighs. "It needs to be left a good few months before you use it otherwise it tends to burn your brassicas. The best thing to do is to put it in a pile somewhere and forget about it until the spring."

The 'aaahh' that then slid from Sacramenta's lips went some way towards reflecting Mabel's own horror at the prospect of a dung heap festering away in her garden, and was swiftly followed by, "Oh my lord, I can't have that. We've got the Smittington-Smythes coming up from Chelsea for dinner on Saturday. Whatever would they think?"

Mabel pursed her lips. *'Well you don't have to feed them shit unless they've got their heads stuck as firmly up their arses as you do, Luv',* did hover briefly in her mind; but she let it swiftly disappear. The woman obviously required a certain amount of latitude, for it was clear that she was not one of the seen-it-all-before Bunting Hill brigade. With a name like Sacrementa, she was unlikely to even have set foot on that side of the village, let alone live there, and if that wasn't proof enough, anyone who actually lived on Bunting Hill would already be trying to sell the stuff on eBay by now. The Shittington-Shites and the Sacrementas of this world wouldn't be getting a look in, however mysteriously sacred and well connected they were. So overall, with the limited life experience that these people had, Mabel knew it wasn't fair to judge them by their own standards; they'd never make the grade. It was time to move on.

She picked her way carefully along a mottled path to the front door and rang the bell. As it buzzed, Mrs McFreece looked up angrily to see who had the audacity to set foot on the premises before the school day had ended, and squinted to get a better view. Mabel tried a wave. The scrunched up face tightened momentarily, and then softened in an un-moisturised, set-in-concrete kind of way. She was allowed to head inside.

"Mrs Milner is here, Mr Fitztumbleton," The Fridge announced, almost pleasantly, as Mabel reached the inner sanctum. "I have Ashley's paperwork here for you to go through with her."

Derek grunted back asking to be given half a jiff, and the secretary smirked

"He won't be long."

Mabel looked at her watch and brooded. She'd probably have been prepared to give the man a whole jiff if he'd asked nicely, not knowing exactly what a jiff was, but thinking it sounded like something that involved tissues.

She shrugged.

"Perhaps I should have a look at the paperwork whilst I wait then?"

She put her hand out to encourage the secretary to pass the envelope across but The Fridge bit her lip.

"You might be thinking that the dates aren't quite right when you look at it, Mrs Milner. But we need to backdate the document, you see for, err… technical reasons," she explained. "Ashley will be given the catch up time, of course," she added, still on a back-footing, "but…"

"You need it to look as though it's been going on for a while, is that it?" Mabel interrupted, the ingratiating approach suddenly slotting into place. "But the thing is, Mrs McFreece," she then continued, feeling more at ease now that she knew that this was just a matter of false personas, "Ashley has only been here three weeks, so how much difference does it really make?"

The pleading eyes staring back flared, but otherwise the face remained impassive.

"More than you'll ever know," The Fridge replied matter-of-factly, and then followed it up with a controlled sniff.

Mabel paused before replying, wary. "Well that's enough of a difference, I suppose," she sighed, and the begrudging nod that dipped back as she said it confirmed it to be so. Out of nowhere, an unexpected idea began to grow. "Still, it does rather conveniently bring me to the main reason for why *I've* come to see *you*..." she tried, and then having boldly set her thoughts in motion, she paused again, now uncertain of what she wanted to say. Was this the right thing to do? It was a strategy with risks. Maybe even unintended consequences. It was possibly against the law, but then again... Oh bugger it, she decided finally throwing caution to the winds; in for a penny, in for a jiff. "How about we scratch each other's backs, Mrs McFreece?" she proposed, and watched the beseeching eyes gazing back narrow. Mabel continued.

"I've heard that you need helpers at the moment, to listen to the kids read." The narrowed slits thinned further. "Well, believe it or not, Mrs McFreece, I can read." If Mabel hadn't known better, she'd have sworn the eyelids then completely closed but she carried on.

"I have a very intelligent daughter, Mrs McFreece, and that has to have come from somewhere, doesn't it?"

The dubious face didn't budge. "Well I'd like to help out here for a while, but I'd need us to agree that it, too, has been backdated."

"But that isn't something we…"

"It would make more of a difference to both of us than you will ever know."

The Fridge's right eyebrow lifted and she leant forward to survey Mabel more closely.

"You need a personal reference, don't you?" she muttered.

Mabel smirked, "Let's say for technical reasons it would be useful. But I do agree that backdating things may imply that which is not strictly true, and I also agree that if it ever got out, that sort of thing could have significant ramifications for a small school like this."

The Fridge's nostrils flared and she flicked her head in fury. Mabel had her and she knew it. They both knew it.

"I'll sort it," the secretary huffed, and then thrust the paperwork into Mabel's hand and pushed her towards Derek's office.

* * *

The answerphone's flashing light caught Mabel's attention as soon as she and Ashley walked through the door of number sixty nine.

"Err... Mrs Milner, Stan here," the electronic re-workings of Stanley K. Snouterton's voice announced. *"Thank you so much for your time yesterday. Troilus,*

Ricky and I were most impressed with what you have to offer." He cleared his throat awkwardly and Mabel raised her eyes to the ceiling. She knew what a de-frogging like that usually meant, but it was worth letting the man have his say. She could always ram a frog back in there if she needed to. *"We just need to check one thin."* Another throat clearing session took place, but this one had less leer attached to it, so she let it off the hook. *"You seem to have forgotten to furnish us with a referee's details. If you could just give us,"* cough, cough, *"... me,"* splutter, splutter, *"a quick bell, before Thursday, I'd greatly appreciate it."*

A final ensuring that not a single molecule of amphibious life was left in his throat then ensued, interspersed with a collection of numbers that she assumed was his personal mobile, and the call ended.

On balance, Mabel thought, as she wrote his number down, and not without a certain sense of satisfaction, she was ahead of the game for once; which was better than being on it.

Ashley looked at her, surprised. "So what's this new job then, Mum?"

Mabel smirked. She hadn't wanted her daughter to know she was going for an interview quite yet. So she tried a diversionary tactic. "Take your shoes off, Ashley. They've got mud on them."

"It will wash off easy enough, Mum, don't fret. Now come on, what's this new job?"

Mabel stared regretfully at the grime on her daughter's shoes. Her discomfort grew.

Sordid, not-something-to-be-proud-of, sneaky, lascivious dirt; that sort of dirt she could handle any day. But the good, old fashioned, salt of the earth, rural type stuff that made everything brown; that she'd not yet learned to come to terms with. It wasn't lost on her that the latter grime would wash off far more easily than the squalid stains littering the conscience of her career to-date.

She managed a shrug.

"I'm not going to count my chickens before they hatch, Ash."

"I didn't realise you could count," Ashley replied curtly, and gave her mother a sarcastic smile. "And I didn't realise that you knew what an egg was..."

"What on earth have eggs got to do with it?" Mabel snapped back, and then felt her face blush as her daughter's expression screamed '*Got you!*' Mabel grunted. "Oh, ha ha, Ashley. Not only do you mock me for my intellectual capacity but you scorn me for my cooking too. If you're not careful, I'll pass that responsibility across to Dwayne and see what you get in your lunchbox then!"

Seeing as Dwayne could barely manage toast on a good day, and even that was only if the bread was pre-sliced and the toaster already plugged in, it should have counted as a threat; but Ashley was unperturbed.

"Yeah, whatever," she sneered, and lifted her fingers to shape the letter 'W'. "So what is it going to be, Mother? McDonalds or KFC?"

Mabel's forehead creased.

"How about we get Dominos to deliver later?"

Ashley tutted loudly. "No, no. I meant what's this wonderful new job? I'm assuming that you can at least get a position at one of *those* places."

A little gasp slipped out before Mabel could stop it. They were stinging words. Dunked in vinegar and covered with salt, they were words that could have given the best chip shop in town a run for its money. And not because of the powdering of disdain that coated each one - oh goodness me no - if only it were that simple, but because at the tender age of eleven, no child could possibly appreciate how desperate a twenty-six year old would have to be to consider working for either of those employers. Even Mabel would have drawn the line at that point. A *milf*-shake versus a *milk* shake was a no brainer. She raised an eyebrow and shook her head. The child seemed to get the message, although not quite enough to apologise.

"The school do need a new dinner lady," Ashley suggested instead, and Mabel checked her face for signs of mockery; there were none, but that didn't mean they weren't there. She waited to see what else her daughter had to say before passing judgement. "Why don't you apply to the school and get a little work experience before you try for something else?"

Vaguely mollified, Mabel took in a deep, patient breath.

"Well now you come to mention it, I am going to help out at the school. I'm going to listen to the younger ones read, because, believe it or not, Ashley, I can."

"Read the name of a lipstick maybe." the cheeky child cut in, her eyes now sparkling with evil glee, but just as she was about to follow it up with a second cutting quip, her expression then suddenly lost its zeal.

Mabel held her breath. Perhaps the girl had spotted the blotch of a flush as it had begun to seep across her mother's cheeks, or maybe she'd noticed the tiny glisten of tears as they'd started to prickle their way to the surface. One thing was for certain though, if neither of those had held sway, she would definitely have seen the clench of teeth as anger was held at bay.

They looked at each other and both knew that that had been a jibe too far.

"As if you'd know what a lipstick was," Mabel replied, and regarded the strangely genderlcss features of her cruel child with composure.

"Oh, I do know what a lipstick is," Ashley whispered back, leaning her head to one side as she said it. "I just don't want to turn out like you!" she spat finally, and darted up the stairs to her room.

Mabel watched her grubby feet disappear and heard the bedroom door slam. She winced, that last bit had been very tart. Steeped in acidic punch. She felt the pang of pain and tried to put it in its place.

Normally, a mother was meant to be insulted when her daughter declared that she didn't want to follow in her footsteps. However, in this instance, if she put her pragmatic hat on and as things currently stood, and weighing up the pros and the cons, it was quite possibly, an appropriate sentiment for Ashley to have. However, if it hadn't been for Dwayne cursing his way into the house just at that moment, Mabel realised that with convincing arguments aside, she would have struggled to maintain her poise. Bloody hell! She silently screamed. What a tricky mix to balance it was; sense and sensibility.

"Oh, Mabe, those bastard busses are buggered today, AND I've got to work again tonight. When are we going to be able to afford a bloody car? I'm sick of this," Dwayne announced, and drew a droopy hand through his mop of dishevelled hair.

"But you can't drive," Mabel replied, suppressing her frustration at having to state the bleedin' obvious, whilst she was battling with inner turmoil. "And I'm not sure I'd be prepared to sit in a car with you even if you could," she then added, putting her hand up to stop Dwayne before he interrupted. "Oh please! You would not endear yourself to me if you expected *me* to be your chauffeur, as well as everything else."

Dwayne raised a coiffured eyebrow.

"Ooooh, listen to you with your new posh voice. Look, Mrs Know-It-All, I could learn to drive," he replied petulantly, but Mabel just shrugged and then smiled her '*think-what-you-like-but-now-that-you're-here-I-want-a-word-with-you*' smile. She also made sure that the smirk was edged with, '*cos-I-want-to-know-more-about-this-Thursday-business*', and the edge wasn't lost on Dwayne.

"You're just sore with me, aren't you? About tomorrow?"

Mabel's forehead buckled.

"The thing is, Dwayne," she sighed, "you keep mentioning Thursday, but you haven't yet told me why." He winced at the formal use of his former name, but she ignored him and continued. "So, now's your opportunity. What have you gone and done? Come on, spit the whole sordid little story out whilst I'm giving you the chance," she added, plopping her hands onto her hips. "Tell me what you've bloody well cooked up this time!"

Mabel thought back wryly to the conversation she'd just had with her daughter and the irony wasn't lost on her. Dwayne was no Delia Smith, but he was a Michelin starred chef when it came to cooking up a storm.

"Well," he shrugged, "I'd be lying if I said I hadn't had a casual stab at getting a date." Mabel bristled. "But it was more to put your farmer through his paces than anything else," he then explained quickly. "You know. Test him out and see if he'd succumb. It wouldn't be the first time I'd caught someone's eye ahead of you." Mabel lifted a sarcastic eyebrow, but Dwayne ignored her. "I just thought we should check his motives first rather than find out that he is a bastard later on."

"We?"

Dwayne shrugged again. "Of course, 'We'. I'm your best pal, Mabe, and despite what you think I do have your best interests at heart. But anyway, you'll be glad to know that the man is so hopeless at communicating that I don't think he's even realised that we've organised a date."

Mabel wrinkled her nose. After their little conversation in the Co-Op just now she wasn't convinced that was the case.

Dwayne carried on. "The poor bloke is torn. You're giving him the brush off and, as always, I'm sitting reliably in the wings. Well, this time I thought it was my turn, and you can't blame me, can you?" he then asked, as if fate had brutally ripped the decision right out of his dainty little hands. "He's *already* told me that his favourite colour is pink!"

Well, what more could she say? It was the ultimate form of persuasion.

* * *

"Mr Snouterton?"

"Yes." the nasal tones filtering down the phone would have confirmed it was him, even if the affirmative hadn't done so already.

"It's Mabel Milner."

"Ah!" The glint in his eyes almost shimmered into her ears. "Maaaaabel, how lovely to hear from you."

"Well, you did ask me to call."

"Yes, of course I did."

"You wanted my referee's details."

"Yes, of course I did."

"You gave me your mobile number."

"Yes, of course I did."

"Because you wanted to talk to me alone."

"Err... Yes of course."

"Because you're hoping I'm free on Thursday."

"Err... Yes..."

* * *

An insurance broker or a farmer? It wasn't actually a choice was it? Six months ago that would have been like asking her if she preferred one sugar or two: the answer was neither; she didn't like her tea sweet, and she wasn't convinced it was a choice now. Whereas one was grey, the other was, well he was strangely rosy, actually, not that she'd want to admit it to anyone. But now she'd gone and blown it and she needed to think things through.

To look on the bright side, one could say that grey was a bit like silver on a dull day. It was a colour that could be pepped up with bright lights and zing when necessary, and if she followed the reasoning through further, she could see that grey was a bit like being cold, one could always put on a jumper to warm up; whereas being hot was so much harder to solve.

But no, it was no good really. Although these thoughts made perfect, logical sense, they still didn't convince. Despite her best efforts, there remained something about the handsome burly farmer that had caught her eye and wouldn't disappear. There existed something about his rosy roughness that let her relax and be herself; there was something about his love of country pursuits that removed all sleaze.

If only he hadn't asked her best mate out on a date.

For a second, a picture of Ashley's face appeared in her mind's eye with Stan Snouterton's greying hand resting on her daughter's shoulder. Oh my god, she thought, what price to pay for security, eh?

Chapter Twelve

"Hello, Miranda? It's Derek. I was hoping I would catch you."

For a brief moment, there was silence down the phone, and then Miranda sniffed. Derek knew that sniff, it was one that had made him doubt himself many a time, yet today, more than anything, it made him miss her with every ethereal molecule of his bared soul. A plethora of different words sprang to mind, and all were focussed on telling her how much he loved her; but none found the light of day. They all seemed so inadequate, so insufficient; now that he realised what he'd lost.

Miranda capitalised on the pause.

"That was rather sneaky, Derek," she rebuked, barely suppressing her annoyance. "How did you manage to disguise your number? I mean, looking at the time, I assume that you're calling from the school."

Derek felt his cheeks blush.

"Well, quite," was the best he could do, and he cringed. He'd not thought about how obvious he'd been until that moment. It wasn't good, was it?

Miranda now tutted.

"Look, what do you want?" she asked. "I'm short of time. Marcus and I are going to the ballet later and I need to collect my dress from the dry cleaners before it closes."

The name thudded into his ears.

So the man was a 'Marcus', was he? Definitely of a different standing to a 'Derek', that was for sure. Yes, a name like Marcus implied another background altogether, and as the thought processes rattled through their binary style logic, Derek felt a burst of anger surge through his veins. Marcus was a name that characterised everything Derek had aspired to attain, and the bugger had probably just been presented with the whole bang shoot at birth. Bollocks to the bastard and bollocks to the ballet as well, he thought bitterly; their pas de deux needed dousing.

"Well." he cleared his throat and then continued. "I thought you might like to know that I found your scarf in the car. You know, the one with the horseshoes, your favourite, and I'd wondered if you'd like me to drop it off to you some time later this week?" He winced as he heard the words coming out of his mouth. They sounded pathetic even to his ears. Wouldn't fool an inhabitant of Bunting Hill let alone an expert in accessories who'd already utilised the garment's blessings to their full advantage, so who was he trying to kid?

Miranda sighed.

"No don't worry, Derek, that won't be necessary, but thank you all the same. I'll come over to collect my remaining things some time soon. Now was that all you called about? Because, as I said, I really am very short of time."

Derek's heart sank. This wasn't going according to plan at all, not that he'd had a plan, and it had only dawned on him once he'd started to dial that this may be his one and only chance, but all the same, he hadn't anticipated quite such slighting brevity. He decided he had no choice but to dig deep. Whether she was trying to fob him off or not, pride should have no call over his attention. If he could somehow tap into her charitable side, he might be able to buy himself some time at least. At this juncture, he suddenly realised, that was the best he could hope for.

"No, actually it wasn't all that I called about," he found himself saying, and once committed he had to go on. "There was one other thing I wanted to ask you, Miranda, and it's a bit of a favour, I suppose."

"I don't owe you any favours, Derek," came the chilled reply.

"Well, no!" he countered quickly, realising that that had perhaps been a mistake. "I'm not saying that you are beholden to me in any way, Miranda, I'm just appealing to you to help me out of a hole. It's not really for me, you see, it's actually for the school."

This time Miranda huffed.

Derek also knew that huff, and imagined her weight shifting from one well-rounded hip to the other as her lips gave birth to the sound. He rather envied the pair of reinforced knickers making the move with her buttocks; his enjoyment was short lived.

"Well, what is it?" she snapped, and the vision of two nicely rounded rear end balloons popped out of his mind.

"I'm not going to do the raffle prizes at the nativity play, if that's what you're thinking. My time of doing that stuff is over. It's not just you I've had enough of, you know, it's your bloody school as well."

"No, no, it's nothing to do with the nativity play next month," he assured, stolidly ignoring the callousness of her remark. "Priscilla Stoutman is dealing with that and I'll let her know that you're not interested."

He'd said it purely to pacify, but before Derek knew what was happening, Miranda exploded.

"I think I've gone beyond the call of duty many a time for your poxy little establishment, Derek!" she yelped. "So don't you speak to me with that condescending tone. I've sat through tuneless versions of *Twinkle, Twinkle, Little Star*; I've smiled at brats with snotty noses; I've clapped when one of your pitiable stragglers has finally learned to spell their name. I think I've done my bit for your crusade over the years, Derek Fitztumbleton, and now it's time for me to put some energy into myself!"

Derek pulled the handset away from his ear and looked at it in astonishment. He couldn't believe what he was hearing. Did she really not know? Did this adorable woman actually believe that he had slaved away all these days, weeks, months and years purely for *his own* satisfaction? That wasn't possible, surely. Not when he had only ever spent every second in this godforsaken village purely to benefit her.

"It wasn't like that," he whispered, placing the receiver back to his ear. "I only ever did it all for you."

A snort rattled down the line.

"Look, Derek, I haven't got time for this. Tell me what it is you need me to do, and if I can, I will. Because," she then added haughtily, "as you know, I'm good like that. Marcus always says I shouldn't put others first in the way that I do, but it's just the way I'm made."

They were noble words, at least to his ears, and they also gave him a jot of hope, although admittedly not very much. Still, a drowning man wouldn't turn down a punctured life jacket if that was all that was on offer. He rallied himself with a deep breath.

"Ofsted are arriving tomorrow," he stated and then paused, expecting her to make some sort of sound commensurate with the momentous nature of the announcement. But there was silence. Derek cleared his throat and carried on. "John Bentwick has suggested that we take the man out for dinner in the evening."

"Well you wouldn't take him out for dinner in the morning, would you?" she scoffed.

Derek stoically ignored her.

"And it would really make a difference to me if you could join us. It would give the inspector the right idea about the people who work at the school, and you really are very good at charming people, Miranda. It would mean such a lot to me if you could."

The sigh that he then heard suggested, to his relief, that she'd got the message. Derek relaxed. At last, he thought, I have something to confirm that all is not lost.

"No sorry," she then stated matter-of-factly. "I can't do tomorrow night. Marcus wants me to go with him to choose a new vacuum cleaner and I can't let him down, can I? He's planning on getting the latest Dyson!"

* * *

Derek set the burglar alarm and locked the school front door. Who was the greatest sucker here? he asked himself, as he dropped the keys back into his pocket; the head of a miserable little primary school, or a hoover? At this moment, he reckoned he could give a Henry a good run for its money, not that that would help the state of his playground, mind you, for despite the best efforts of the PTA, it still looked like god had eaten a curry the night before and not quite made it to the loo.

Was this really what he deserved? Ever since the inspector had announced his plans to visit, karma had been playing a funny game. First there had been the sewage, and after that it had been Bob. Thinking about the awful day that had passed yesterday, Derek began to wonder if he should have spotted that his career was just a flash in the pan, but now, with the aftermath of a herd of cows, and no prospect of his wife returning any time soon, was it actually a bigger message from the cosmos he was missing?

There had been other clues...

"Mr Fitztumbleton," Ashley Milner had said to him only that morning. "Do you mind if I ask you a question?" Derek had shaken his head patiently, and waited for *it* to tell him what was on *its* mind. "Can you explain to me what makes a person great?" *it* had asked, and then stared back at him expectantly.

"A good education," Derek had glibly replied, never one to miss an opportunity to emphasise what was closest to his heart. Only now, though, did he realise that that wasn't what the child had meant at all. *It* hadn't asked him that poignant question because *it* had wanted to know what tools enabled a person to do great things. *It* had asked him that question because *it* had wanted to know what defined a person as 'great' overall, and despite the wondrous education that Derek had received, he still didn't know whether *it* was a girl or a boy. That didn't spell greatness, did it? And it didn't exactly give him the right to suppose he could possibly describe what greatness was either, and just to rub his nose in it, he'd then found out that the Milner kid had been one step ahead of him all along.

"It's just that Miss Lovelock says that King Henry the Eighth was a great man," *it* had then added. "But I don't get why being a fat man, with a big name, and lots of power and dosh would make him great at all. You see, I think that would just make him a fat man, with a big name, and lots of power and dosh. What do you think, Mr Fitztumbleton? What do you think actually *made* him *great*?"

He'd not known how to answer the question at the time, and to his intense relief Sandra had come along at just the right moment and ushered all the children into class. Now though, with the memory of the conversation springing back into his mind, he suddenly realised that he still had no idea how to reply. It would seem that, not for the first time that day, greatness, as a concept, was totally beyond his grasp.

* * *

Derek wasn't surprised that Sandra lived in Cockerby rather than Lower Bushey, it had just never dawned on him to realise it until now. In fact, she didn't actually live that far from where he lived, and as it had been such a rotten day, he decided to walk the fifteen minute distance rather than drive, for the smell of Miranda's perfume was still getting to him.

Within five minutes of setting off, however, he regretted the decision. The plastic bag with the file of procedures and a dusty bottle of wine was beginning to weigh heavy in his hand. The chill of the night was also eating into his fingers, but he swiftly rationalised that even if he turned back now, by the time he'd made it to his car, he'd then still arrive at the same time. It wouldn't make much difference promptness wise, but with regard to the rest of the evening he'd have to stop at one glass of plonk if he drove. The original decision was thus reinforced as correct, and he mentally prepared himself to deal with the pain of the carrier bag digging into his palm.

Sandra looked at his alcoholic gift as she opened the door, and beamed.

"Oh, Derek. What a lovely idea! I never normally drink during the week, but the odd exception isn't a problem, is it? Why don't we make a night of it?"

Really, those last few words should have been a bit of a warning. But as Derek wasn't aware that he needed to be on alert, he didn't pick up their meaning and so instead stepped inside, innocent and unprepared. Even once he'd spotted that her attire was something which would have looked more at home on the set of *Ben Hur*, he just naively accepted it as one of those things.

Sandra stared at him with glowing anticipation, as she straightened out the bust of her toga-like dress, and then swished the flimsy material playfully and led him through to the sitting room. Derek's eyes took in the sparsely furnished room and landed on the acoustic guitar in the corner.

"I didn't know you played?" he drawled, glad to have something to focus on other than the insubstantial halter neck tied just below her hairline. "You are a woman of many hidden talents, Miss Lovelock."

"Oh, call me Sandra, please!" Sandra corrected, with surprising warmth bearing in mind her voice had been known to freeze mercury. "I'm not one to stand on ceremony once I'm out of the classroom, Derek. I really am not the person you think you know."

Up until today, Derek would have doubted the veracity of that remark, but since he'd received a muted description from Mrs McFreece of Sandra's performance that morning, he'd begun to see Miss Lovelock in a different light. Not only had she managed to deal with a very challenging situation, but she had done it utilising something he had never had; imagination. True enough, it was an imagination that reached into the dim and distant dimensions of the universe that should possibly have remain unreached, but imagination it was all the same. Miranda had chastised him for his lack of it on many an occasion; perhaps Sandra could teach him a thing or two.

"Well, quite," he attempted, still gripping steadfastly to the plastic bag as it dug into his hand.

Sandra managed a smile.

"But perhaps more of that later," she offered before he could condemn himself any further, and took the bag from him and pointed across the room. "Have a seat, Derek, make yourself comfortable." And as he wandered over, then added, "You're obviously into music; do you play the guitar?"

Without thinking, Derek shook his head and simultaneously had a stab at perching on the edge of the proffered sofa. It was an imprudent thing for a man to try to do, two things at the same time, for as soon as his rump had hit the leather, his dignity disappeared and the shiny surface took matters into its own hands. As his torso slid backwards into the vast depths of the seat, his mind wondered whether looking like a sack of potatoes was worse than confessing to what really made his heart sing, and his feet lifted to dangle absurdly over the edge. Sandra's face twitched with disappointment at his disinterested reply, and he reluctantly felt honour bound to put his tuberous concerns aside.

"I'm a bit of a brass lover, actually," he puffed, and tried to straighten himself out again, whilst his feet sought to reconnect with the floor.

There had been a time when he'd considered joining the Salvation Army, but Miranda had wanted him to drive her to her WI meetings on the same night, and all his plans had gone by the wayside. It wasn't, he decided, something to blow his trumpet about.

To his distracted relief, Sandra's eyes sparkled.

"Oh, there's nothing like a good bit of brass for blasting out the crotchets," she said softly. "I can see you playing the horn."

"French horn," he clarified and, as she nodded knowingly, made one final humongous effort to slide forward again and felt his knees give. "But tell me, Sandra," he muttered, relieved to be able to hold a reasonable conversation again now that his legs had returned to a more traditional ninety degree angle. "What about you?"

Sandra put his bag down on the floor, placed herself on the other end of the sofa, and coyly crossed one thigh over the other.

"Well," she sighed, and her granite like features softened to the solidity of soap stone. "As you have probably guessed, I'm more of a string plucker myself, but I prefer the cello to the guitar. There's nothing like having a good instrument between your legs, is there, Derek?"

Derek shook his head politely – he couldn't actually say, for he'd never had one – but bearing in mind that music was a subject closer to his heart than some that Miss Lovelock could have raised, he stalwartly ploughed on.

"No, Sandra, I'm sure there isn't. However my tastes lean more towards a bit of organ playing," he offered. "Although my wife..." and then his heart sank, "has always preferred the gentler side to wind, so we've tended just to listen to James Galway's greatest hits."

And that, he then realised, was about as much as he was prepared to divulge on the music front at this stage. Miranda's recent and sudden interest in percussion had caught him off guard, and no amount of sympathy was going to get him over that experience. He'd caught her gyrating to a DVD by Evelyn Glennie one evening when he'd got home rather late. Nothing wrong with that per se, for Evelyn G is a truly amazing individual, but when Miranda had suggested he tickle her triangle whilst she waggled her castanets, he'd spotted the empty bottle of wine and put her to bed in the spare room. Looking back on it, it should have been a sign really, shouldn't it?

Sandra wrinkled her nose.

"Oh, the flute has always seemed a little wishy washy to me," she said. "I tend to prefer something with a little more *aural* penetration. "Derek frowned as she said it but she ignored him. "Anyway," she added finally, "shall we get cracking? How about I pop your cork?"

For a second, Derek's eyes widened with surprise, but then he realised that she was pointing at the bottle still in his hand and passed it over, relieved. Picking the plastic bag up, he then followed her through to her

215

kitchen and Sandra rummaged around in a drawer for a corkscrew.

Derek watched her fumble inexpertly with the metallic wrapping on the bottle, and took the opportunity to move the subject back to more familiar territory.

"I expect you're all ready for tomorrow's impending visit, Sandra, so I do appreciate you taking some extra time to go through these policies with me. I don't think there's anyone in the school who knows the set up quite as well as you."

He smiled as he said it, and dropped the heavy folder onto the kitchen table with a thump. A startled meow issued from underneath.

"Oh, please just ignore Mr Perkins. Push him off the seat, Derek, and make yourself comfortable. He'll soon get the message."

Derek did as he was told, much to Sandra's obvious satisfaction, and he spread the contents pages out for them both to see as she poured them each a glass.

"So where would you like to start?" she asked, and they both sat down.

Derek ran his eyes over the long list of procedures with a sinking heart. It was an arduous task for someone with other things on his mind, and to make matters worse, as he tried to make sense of what he was reading Mr Perkins began to rub up against his calf. Feeling the warmth seep through his trouser leg, Derek's mind wandered. It wasn't an unpleasant sensation, seeing as nobody had rubbed themselves up against him for a good long time, but it was a distraction all the same, and as

Sandra helped him to prioritise the policies in descending order, running from statutory must-haves down to local authority job-fillers, Mr Perkins persisted in gaining Derek's attention. Finally, he gave in and allowed the cat to jump up onto his lap.

Sandra frowned.

"If he's bothering you, Derek, please just shove him off."

"Oh, not at all, Sandra," he reassured, secretly enjoying the opportunity for an interruption. "I'm more than happy to give your pussy a stroke."

* * *

It was only later, as Sandra was heating up some lasagne, that Derek remembered how her eyes had suddenly started to glow the moment he'd shown an interest in her cat. It was also only later, much later in fact, that he realised how lucky it was that Mr Perkins chose that exact moment to then cough up a fur ball.

The sausage shaped lump of soggy hair had, after much huffing and choking, eventually landed with a squelchy plop on the floor between them, and Mr Perkins had then jumped down from his vantage point clearly satisfied that the whole manoeuvre had gone according to plan.

Sandra's face had flushed with fury and then rosied-up into an embarrassed look of mortification as she'd scurried around with reams of kitchen roll and antibacterial spray. Derek had distracted himself with

217

writing out a list of the key policies they needed to check, and by the end of the odd little episode his moment of awkwardness had passed.

Blissfully unaware of what was to come, and with most of the bottle inside both their stomachs, he now sat back in his chair and watched her serve them each a tasty looking portion.

"Miranda would never cook lasagne," he sighed, his mouth watering at the sight of the hot vapour rising up into the air. "She said it was too fattening, but I tell you what; it's just what I'm in the mood for now."

As soon as the words slipped out, a smug glow began to ooze across Sandra's face. Silently, Derek gave himself a pat on the back. That was exactly what he had intended. He may not have been much of a husband as far as some were concerned, but he did at least know how to be a manager. People deserved recognition sometimes and Sandra Lovelock certainly deserved more recognition than he'd given her to-date, and as he thought that thought, it suddenly struck him how lucky he'd been that she'd stuck at Lower Bushey for so long.

"How come you've never looked for a post in a larger school, Sandra? I mean," he chuckled, "of course I'm thrilled that you've never wanted to leave us, but your talents are almost wasted here."

Sandra put a steaming plate down in front of him and perched herself on the edge of the chair to his left.

"Do you really not know?" she asked, and a strange watery look suddenly began to glisten in her eyes.

Perplexed, Derek shook his head, wondering if she'd inadvertently got some onion stuck in a lash, and then reached across, plucked a sheet of kitchen paper off the roll, and passed it to her smiling. Sandra looked at it surprised, but took it and dabbed gingerly at the corner of her eyes.

"I could say the same about you," she sniffed, and wiped at them again. "Your abilities are way beyond what is required here. I've never understood what has kept you at Lower Bushey for so long."

Derek took a slow, deliberate, deep breath.

"Well, hopefully tomorrow will be a step towards a new future for both of us," he sighed, and dug his fork into his food. "If that *Outstanding* comes in, Sandra, we'll all be looking to move on. And I don't think we'll be needing our infamous Chair of Governors to be taking the man out for dinner to achieve that either, do you?"

Sandra's face perked up.

"So you and Mr Bentwick are taking the inspector out tomorrow, are you?"

Derek nodded, naively unaware of the implications.

"Well that's what Mr Bentwick wants to do. I'm not convinced, but you never know. I actually think he has some new woman on the go and is looking to impress her."

"And who are you going to take with you, Derek?"

Derek didn't notice the note of urgency that had now entered her tone, and so simply managed a shrug.

"To be honest, I hadn't planned to take anyone. But I don't think the inspector will mind. Let's face it, he won't have his partner with him, will he?"

"But there are two of them coming, aren't there? I thought one of them was a woman... Perhaps?" she then added but paused.

Derek misunderstood.

"No chance," he interrupted. "Miranda has already told me she has something more important on tomorrow. *If* that was what you were going to say."

"No it wasn't, actually," Sandra replied, and this time Derek did catch a harsh edge to her voice, but she carried on with a more softened tone before he could dwell any further. "No, what I was going to say, Derek, was how about you and I impress that inspector together instead? There's no doubt that we will impress him during the day, but why don't we impress him during the evening too. What do you say?"

And with that, Sandra then stood up and offered Derek her hand. At the sight of her beckoning fingers, Derek raised his head and took in the bareness of her shoulders as they shone in the stark kitchen light, and still he didn't suss...

"Come on, my love," she whispered, "let's forget about the food and talk about this somewhere a little more comfortable."

* * *

Derek ran.

He tried to make it look as though he was just walking very *very* fast, but really, for him, he was running. There was no doubt that Sandra Lovelock could have had the edge on him if she'd really wanted to, but he was just hoping that his ill-thought out excuse about needing to sort out his pencil case, admittedly a very poor excuse, even for the spur of the moment, had been convincing enough.

"Don't get me wrong," he now muttered, readying himself for a conversation in case she did decide to pursue. "I think you're a lovely lady, Miss Lovelock, but my pencil case really does need sorting."

And as he prepared his mouth to reiterate his defence, an extra spurt of energy entered his stride, fuelled by the memory of the short toga-like dress tumbling to the floor.

Of course, the thought that she might actually have undone it on purpose had crossed his mind at the time, but it had swiftly been sent packing to a place where thoughts like that were kept in solitary confinement.

"Oh, Miss Lovelock," he had exclaimed instead, as she'd walked towards him seemingly unaware of the travesty that had just occurred. "You appear to have become unknotted."

She had frowned, whispering something about it being preferable to being told to get knotted, and he'd then mumbled back that actually, as far as he was concerned, knots were a very good idea. Well that was how he remembered it anyway.

"They are an absolutely wonderful invention," he had gasped, whilst trying to 'help' her pull the material back up to shoulder height again. "My father taught me all sorts of knots," he'd added, but had then admitted to himself that none of them had been specifically recommended for dresses with disobedient ties. An imagination would have been useful at that point.

He had fumbled with the two loose ends as she'd stared longingly into his eyes, but had finally managed to link them together utilising an attractive double reef of which any sailor would have been proud, before stepping away.

"Sorry about that," she'd sighed, oddly unaffected at having just displayed her bee sting breasts and bap-like buttocks to her boss. "It really is all a bit too much, isn't it? Sometimes these Romanesque fashions just don't quite cut it in today's world," and he'd nodded his head fervently in agreement.

"Yes, all a bit too much," he'd repeated for good measure, and had then looked at his watch. "Well, you'll have to excuse me, Sandra, but I've just realised the time. There is so much still be done, you see, and I've remembered that I need to sort out m-m-my pencil case before the morning."

Her forehead had creased as he'd said it, but it had been enough of a diversion for him to make a quick dash to the front door before she'd had a chance to stop him.

And now, as he continued to jog, his ears vaguely caught the sound of some comment about not needing extra lead with a woman like her, and then all was silent once more; but for the noise of his feet trotting along.

Good Lord! He suddenly thought, as his pace slowed down to a stilted skip, now he knew what the Romans had ever done for us; and they bloody well had some explaining to do.

Chapter Thirteen

Mabel hated Thursday mornings at the best of times, but as soon as she woke up to this one, her heart sank.

Throughout the previous evening, she had swung from one unlikely prospect to the other like a pendulum worried about losing its job, which, of course, was part of the problem. And now that she'd spoken to Stan-Stan-the-Insurance-Man, rashly intimating that she might be free tonight, she'd got the distinct impression that the job was hers for the taking just as long as she came up with the goods. Well, no surprises there really, and naturally, if pushed, she could perform perfectly well as the letter 'Y'. But this was not what she wanted the position to depend upon; an employed position, that is, and nothing was worth being coerced in such a way either. Mabel had never been one to let a man have her over a barrel, and unless he had kind eyes and a good sense of humour, that wasn't going to change. Stan Snouterton possessed neither. So in the cold light of a new day and with her daughter's moralistic wisdom hanging like a cloud, it was clear he needed 'dealing' with.

Mabel sighed and took a sip of her tea. *Well*, she thought, *that's that decision made then*. She could now feel a little better about herself, although what she was going to do about the handsome burly farmer, she didn't know. The bugger was as ineffective as his ram, yet she just couldn't get him out of her mind.

"I've taken some bread out of the freezer for you," Dwayne announced, interrupting her thoughts as his dressing gown flounced up the stairs. Mabel looked at her watch and frowned. It was seven-fifteen in the morning and he'd just done an all-nighter. By rights he should have been as grumpy as hell. In this instance, however, her dearest pal had been inordinately thoughtful.

Something was amiss.

"Do you want me to make you some toast?" she called up after him. "Me and Ash will be having some when she makes it out of the bathroom."

A dramatic sigh slid along the banisters and down to the ground floor.

"Oh, darling, that's very sweet of you, but no thanks. With the time that Sasha and I had last night, I need a few hours' kip before my date this evening."

Mabel flinched. As soon as he'd said it, a horrid spiky knot of jealousy had twisted in her stomach. You sneaky little chimp, she thought. No wonder you're being so nice to me; you feel guilty!

"Oh, by the way," Dwayne's more normal voice then filtered down, he obviously felt that bread exhumation amounted to penance paid. "I bought a local paper whilst I was waiting for the bus. You'll never guess who is on the front page."

* * *

So, Mabel mused, still staring at the headline as Ashley began to put on her coat, it would seem that Sandra Lovelock was also the infamous Lady Lovelick; Mistress and Minister to the Minions at Hand. Not that the paper actually said that, and Lady Lovelick had never been known to take her mask off, but Dwayne had apparently seen that whip in action enough times to have been able to read between the lines. And Mabel believed him. When it came to S&M, Dawn was your man.

She looked at the photo of Sandra's sour face glaring back and shivered. Thank god she'd put all that *Dominantics* stuff behind her a couple of years ago; if it meant one ended up becoming a teacher, it wasn't good, was it?

"Come on, Ashley, get your arse in gear," she muttered, still distracted and her daughter shot her a filthy look. Mabel ignored her. It was true that she drew the line at hopping into bed to get a job these days, but it was her house and she could use the word *arse* if she wanted to. "I need to get you to school mega early today, 'cos I want to catch old Titzfumble before the Ofsted people arrive."

She paused, expecting disapproval of her casual disregard for a key community figure, and was appropriately rewarded for her instincts.

"His name is Mr Fitztumbleton, Mum, and he deserves more respect. If you want people to respect you, you have to be prepared to respect them too. What goes around."

"Yeah, yeah, yeah," Mabel interrupted, and raised her eyes to the ceiling. "What goes around; comes around. You have to put in to take out. What goes up, must come down. And children should be seen and not heard! All these things are very true, my girl, but I still need you to get your arse in gear so I can sort out this reference before the iceberg arrives."

"Mrs McFreece is a..."

"Is a person who bites the hand that feeds her, Ashley, and you'd do well to take note of what she has yet to learn. Mind you," Mabel then added, more as an aside to herself, "I should imagine that old Titzfumble knows that there's no point in having a dog and barking yourself, so she probably fulfils a very important role for him. I am just hoping that she's a creature of habit and doesn't ever turn up to work before eight forty-five."

"Actually, I was going to say that she is a bitch." Ashley muttered and did her last button up, "To continue on your canine theme, of course."

Inside, Mabel cringed. "I think 'cow' would be more appropriate at your age."

Ashley shrugged. "They're all just animals to me. But I save *that* one especially for you."

Now Mabel winced. With cutting wit perfected before her teenage years, Ashley was without doubt her mother's daughter, of that parental lineage she was at least sure. But enough was enough. As she had already illustrated, good parenting was all about knowing where to draw the line.

"Well I suspect that you could keep this hurtful banter up all day, but I'd like to remind you to keep the noise down," she stated instead, and ushered her pitiless daughter towards the front door. "Dwayne's just gone to bed," she added, "and if nothing else, Ashley Milner, please learn that you should always let sleeping dogs lie."

* * *

The two of them arrived at the school at the unprecedented time of just after eight; and that was as accurate as Mabel's time keeping ever got. It dawned on her that she'd never seen the silhouette of the building etched into the horizon in the half-light before and checked her watch. Perhaps she just wasn't used to early mornings. And to add to her chagrin, The Fridge had broken the habit of a union led lifetime and was already sitting at her desk as they rang the bell.

"It would appear," Mabel whispered, and glanced at her daughter as the secretary buzzed them in, "that it takes Ofsted to teach that old dog new tricks." Ashley's face reflected a similar sentiment, even if she would never have admitted it in a million years, and a fragile connection formed between mother and daughter. Mabel saw it, grabbed it, and clung onto it for dear life.

"I'm going to go to the library, Mum. I'll catch you later," Ashley muttered and trotted off before she'd finished speaking.

Mabel watched her disappear, feeling the tenuous link between them stretch and stretch until it was thinner than a stripper's G-string; but still it didn't snap. She drew in a deep breath. There was hope yet.

"I suppose you've come for your reference," the mocking tone of The Fridge chafed from an invisible position within the school office.

Mabel exhaled slowly and held her response at bay until she was able to tackle the Arctic Husky face on.

"You suppose correctly," she said, and stretched her mouth into what she hoped was at least a smile with meaning, if perhaps one entirely lacking in sincerity.

The pose held for a split second longer than was necessary, but then a flash of red caught her eye. Thrown, Mabel blinked, and found to her surprise that it was still there. She leaned in to get a closer look.

Is that lipstick? She asked herself, looking more carefully at the crimson cracks bleeding around the woman's mouth. Perhaps it was cochineal. The Fridge's face creased into a scowl, and as the vein like effect distorted downwards the answer was confirmed. Yes, that made more sense; beetle juice. It could be nothing else.

"Well your reference isn't ready yet," the woman growled with irritation, clearly regretting the attention. "If it hasn't escaped your notice, we've got other things to deal with. Mr Fitztumbleton will write one when he has time, but he is currently transferring the scarecrows in the playing field to a more appropriate location in next door's skip."

Mabel cursed herself for having already signed Ashley's gifted and talented paperwork. She'd not been looking out for a McFreece shaped barrel at the time, but the woman had had her over it before the ink had dried. This wasn't how taking the right path was meant to be. But, as she contemplated giving the woman a piece of her mind, a waft of musky perfume suddenly hit her nose.

Mabel took a sniff.

"Is that *Impulse* or cleaning fluid I can smell?"

The Fridge's nostrils flared.

"I'll have you know that that it is *Poison* by *Christian Dior*. My husband gave it to me as an anniversary present."

"Figures," Mabel snapped. "But I think he meant for you to drink it."

* * *

They arrived early; as was their want. Grey suited with sensible shoes. Sour faced with clipboards in hand; organised, proceduralised and possibly even pasteurised and by the look of their pale skins. Yes, at 08:23 hours, Mr Barnaby de Ravel and Ms Diana Bonniface – a title that would have prompted litigation under the trade descriptions act, were it to have applied to civil servants – rang the bell and waited patiently to be admitted via the strict protocols required under the Local Authority approved Child Safeguarding Policy.

Mabel watched from the corner of the office and listened as the male of the inspectorate species introduced himself. Something he said caught her attention. She heard him utter his name for a second time 'de Ravel' and wondered what it was that was triggering a memory that she just couldn't quite yet grasp. The most likely explanation was that she had overheard him at the Post Office or something, for he looked far too much of an upstanding member of the community to have crossed her path in a professional capacity; and she was sure she could remember every upstanding member anyway. But unable to place the name as yet, she realised that she'd have to wait for inspiration to hit another time.

It took a good ten minutes to sign them in, but Mrs McFreece wasn't taking any chances. She checked the newcomers' identity badges. She called their overseeing body to confirm their identities were real. She called their overseeing body again to check that they had been DBS checked, and she then called their overseeing body a third time in order to thank them for their help; it was important to provide evidence of manners.

She made them sign in the visitors' book and ensured that they provided all manner of obscure details. She gave them a comprehensive run down of the fire exits, fire exit procedure, use of oxygen masks, until she remembered she wasn't on a plane, and, of course, the meeting points. She gave them visitor badges, visitor badge plastic holders, and child-safe safety pins to attach the said name plates to their lapels. She noted the numbers of the badges in the visitors' book, and then and only then, did she make them stand where she could still see them whilst she walked through to Derek's office.

Lower Bushey Primary's earnest headmaster appeared a few seconds later, white as a sheet, dark circles under his eyes, and a pencil case clutched determinedly in his right palm.

As he introduced himself to the guests, he leant across to shake their hands and only then noticed what he was holding. A regretful look flitted across his face but he put the item down on Mrs McFreece's desk, giving it one last longing glance, before finally pulling himself together.

Mabel's heart sank. There was no way now that she was going to get her mitts on that reference today, but as she prepared to leave, Derek stopped her before she had a chance.

"And this is Mrs Milner, one of my parents. Well not one of *my* parents," he corrected unnecessarily, "obviously. My two are dead and she is much younger than me, although not too young to be considered a teenage mother." he then stuttered. "Good Lord no."

A very brief, pithy, moment of camaraderie bound Mabel and McFreece together as they squirmed in the wake of his wittering. Having swapped resigned but knowing looks, The Fridge broke first.

"Mrs Milner is in the process of becoming a voluntary reader," she clarified for him, and enabled Derek to swallow the remaining waffle before it could escape. "As the whole school has PE this afternoon, she's in this morning to do some work with class three now."

Mr de Ravel smiled a chilly smile at Mabel and raised an eyebrow. Diana Bonniface went to speak first, but he DBS check please?" The acerbity of the question compounded the starkness of his ashen suit and stripped his voice of warmth. Mabel held her breath.

But The Fridge was one step ahead...

"We've applied for it but it hasn't come through yet. Mrs Milner, whilst being a very well respected member of the community, is..." Mabel imagined how hard it was for Mrs McFreece to form those words and noted the wobble in her tone, "not allowed to spend time with the children alone yet. She is never left unaccompanied or unsupervised; we expect it to come through any day. If you would like to see our safeguarding policies and procedures, they are all in that folder over there."

The Fridge pointed to a bulging lever arch file leaning precariously at the end of a shelf in the corner, and all heads turned. For a split second, Derek frowned, and then his eyes widened with astonishment. Mabel watched him take a closer look, shudder, and then peer fearfully out into the corridor. She followed the direction of his stare but saw nothing of particular note.

"Miss Lovelock in, is she?" he asked nervously.

"Of course she is," Mrs McFreece exclaimed, and cocked her head to the side. "Why?"

Derek cleared a non-existent lump in his throat.

"Err... no reason," he replied, and flicked another disbelieving look across at the folder. A second tiny tremor shivered down his spine and Mabel waited for him to continue, wondering just how much of Miss Lovelock's private life he now knew. "I was checking everyone is in on time," he mumbled. "Not that we have a problem with teacher absence," he then added more fervently, seemingly beginning to find his feet again. He then smiled what he probably hoped was a gracious smile, although it looked more like a frog with a ruler stuck in its mouth, and began to usher them through to the staff room.

"How about a cup of coffee or tea?" he offered, guiding them into the corridor. "Mr de Ravel, Miss Bonniface, does that suit you? Ladies, would you like me to get you one too?"

Mabel turned and spotted Mrs McFreece nodding. Well, she thought to herself, if he can refer to *that* woman as a 'lady' then anything is possible. She managed a grin.

"Let me give you a hand, Mr Fitztumbleton," she offered.

Derek nodded and gave the overburdened folder on the shelf a final questioning look, before guiding the three of them out into the hall and along the corridor to the staff room. As they reached the sanctuary of its walls, the doorbell rang, and the sound of a frostily dismissive groan emanated from The Fridge just before John Bentwick made his entrance.

"I've left my wellies out the front as I don't want to be treading muck into the school. Sorry about the smell." he offered. "That bloody useless ram of mine 'as been a right pain in the arse this morning and I stink." And as he took in the two inspectors, he stopped in his heel-and-toe-reinforced-socked tracks and scowled. "Oh, excuse me, Mr Fitztumbleton, I didn't realise you 'ad parents 'ere."

It was an inauspicious start, but despite herself Mabel felt a strange sense of kinship with a man who clearly only managed to get through life through luck.

"Mr de Ravel," Derek stepped in, "I'd like to introduce you to our Chair of Governors, John Bentwick. Mr Bentwick, perhaps I can introduce you to our visitors from Ofsted; Mr de Ravel and Miss Bonniface."

John did exactly what Mabel expected and took one look at Diana Bonniface and frowned.

"Is that really yer name?" he asked, and Mabel winced. "I 'ad a great aunt who we used to call bonny face," he added with a flourish, but then seemed to lose momentum. The female inspector sniffed and raised an eyebrow.

"Really?" she asked, seemingly unsure if it was a good thing to have an ancestral link with a man who smelt like an overripe stilton. "It's a very old name but there aren't many of us left. I believe its origin is linked to Saint Boniface of …"

"Oh no," John interrupted, his eyes suddenly lighting up as he remembered what he'd been about to say, "that wasn't why we called 'er that. It were more like a joke 'cos she 'ad a mouth like an..."

"Well, quite," Derek cut in, and cleared his throat. "Thank you, Mr Bentwick. But much as I'm sure our

Ofsted Inspectors," he tried to stress the two words in a bid to make some sort of impression on the hapless governor, but Mabel couldn't be sure it was sinking in. Derek continued. "… Would like to be able to spend time discussing the derivation of surnames, we unfortunately have a lot to fit in to a short space of time. So what's it going to be then? Coffee or tea?"

As Derek asked the question, he walked over to the drinks machine and gave it an optimistic pat. Barnaby de Ravel peered at the beast and frowned.

"That's a rather grand affair for a small school," he said suspiciously, and whispered to his colleague who then wrote something down on her clipboard. "Must have cost a fortune."

Derek coughed. "A thoughtful bequest, that's all, and far less grand than you would suppose. Two days ago, I was sure I'd ordered coffee, but what I ended up with looked like chicken soup, and I didn't think we even bought those refills anymore," he explained laughing awkwardly, and Diana Bonniface noted something else down on her very important piece of paper.

The Fridge appeared at the door.

"No, he's telling the truth," she muttered. "We don't buy those refills any more, so what the green bits were that were floating around, only the good Lord knows. My recommendation would be to go for a black tea; it gives the machine the least to do."

As she said it, Diana Bonniface's face lost what little lustre it had had, and she flicked a pleading look across at her boss.

"Well I'll 'ave a chicken soup, if yer don't mind," John Bentwick chipped in, the mention of sustenance obviously having triggered some sort of Pavlovian response. "I've been up since the crack of sparrow's fart this morning," he began, but to Mabel's relief the two inspectors were already walking out of the door, mumbling something about wanting to meet parents before the day began.

* * *

"I'm afraid my wife won't be able to join us this evening," Derek announced, embarrassed, as soon as the inspectors disappeared. "Unfortunately she's..."

"Oh, don't worry, I know all about 'err..." John interrupted, and Derek looked at him, surprised. "Now about that chicken soup?"

"What do you know?" Derek asked.

John flicked a longing look at the drinks machine and sighed.

"I know that she's gone, Mr Fitztumbleton. Bob told me on Tuesday. But it's no worry, we don't 'ave to take 'em out. It 'ad only been an idea."

"Well you'll have some explaining to do to my friend," Mabel stepped in crossly. "She's expecting you to take her with you, you know."

The farmer flushed.

"Oh no, I never."

"Oh yes you did!" she countered, relieved to be able to let off some angry steam. "And never mind what I think," she added. "If you let her down, neither of us will ever hear the end of it."

"Well partners aren't mandatory, are they?" Derek chipped in uncertainly, and then seemed to regret the rash statement as both Mabel and John turned to look at him as though he had two heads. He gave his nose a scratch. "I mean, Mr Bentwick, you and I could take the inspectors out on our own, couldn't we?" he then tried, clearly becoming less convinced by his own idea as Mabel raised an eyebrow. "Well, quite," he finished off and left the rest unsaid.

Mabel shook her head. "No way!" she said, and then turned to glare back at the Chair of Governors. "You are not going to let Dawn down. You've made your bed, John Bentwick, and you can damn well get used to having to lie in it."

He winced as she said it and Derek did too, although, it transpired, for a very different reason.

"But I don't have anyone to take except Sandra Lovelock," he gasped with dismay. "And. Well..." And then even his usual catchphrase failed him. He was a spent man.

John shuffled from one foot to the other and made what appeared to be an attempt to speak, but Mabel put up her hand to stop him.

"Oh, go and get yourself a soup, will you? I think we're all dying to see what you make of the floating green bits, and whilst you're sorting yourself out, I'll deal with Mr Fitztumbleton here." Derek, who continued to stare into space as she'd issued her

238

instructions, suddenly jerked up his head at the mention of his name.

"I'd never meant for it to come untied," he mumbled. "They looked like fried eggs."

"Oh yes, that's it!" John cried, his face lighting up with excitement. "What I wouldn't give for a fried egg now."

"Soup!" Mabel barked, and pointed to the other side of the room before turning back to Derek. "Mr Fitztumbleton, listen to me," Derek's eyelids fluttered, "I'm not sure what you're talking about at the moment, but please don't mention food again until we've got this sorted out."

"Fried eggs on top and baps down below," he whispered. "I've never seen anything like it."

"Oh yes! Even better! An egg butty!" John exclaimed, and Mabel realised she had no choice.

Without stopping to think, she lifted her hand and walloped the side of Derek's face with all her might. As the clap of the slap rang out, bouncing off the blu-tacked timetables and milk rotas, it reverberated through the air and Derek came to with a shake.

"Don't say any more!" she warned, and he looked back at her in surprise as a crimson, palm-shaped flush began to seep across his right cheek. "Just don't say another word. Ok?" He nodded. "Good. Now. If I go as your partner tonight, does that solve your problem?"

From her viewpoint, the suggestion had merit in more ways than one; the main one being Dawn's 'misunderstood' gender, and the problem that was going to cause, and of course, had nothing to do with the little heart flutters she was experiencing every time she looked at John. Now, however, both men stared at her with consternation.

"Well there's nothing wrong with me going, is there?" she countered, their perplexed expressions beginning to test her patience. "I am a voluntary reader, after all. It wouldn't be inappropriate for me to come along. Or perhaps, Mr Fitztumbleton," she then added, plucking at a better strategy, "you really would prefer Miss Lovelock?"

The phrase hit the spot.

As she said it, the colour that would normally have populated the blood cells in his cheeks swiftly emigrated to his ears. His eyes opened wide, more with fear than with surprise, and his jaw dropped into a fetching pose that suggested an IQ of twenty three.

John's face, on the other hand, did the polar opposite. His cheeks glowed red, his eyes narrowed, and his teeth clenched until the sinews in his jaw nearly snapped.

Mabel averted her look to his filthy socks briefly and then turned to stare determinedly into Derek Fitztumbleton's forlorn features.

"Do I take it that is a good idea then, Mr Fitztumbleton? To have a parent in your entourage would certainly give a good impression, wouldn't it? Perhaps you'd like to pick me up at seven?"

Just at that moment, footsteps sounded in the hall. It would have been nice to have been able to see who it was, but Mabel didn't want to break the contact until she'd got his agreement. Too much was resting on this moment not to see it through to the end: the protection, with careful management, of a headmaster's career; the saving, with careful handling, of a farmer's face; the rekindling, with a good dose of luck, of a mother's self-respect. All these things, every one of them, hinged on a solitary nod.

Derek dipped his head up and down.

Mabel sighed with relief.

"Excellent! Well if you would excuse me for a minute," she said, "I have to make a call. I had made other plans for this evening, but they now need to be changed. In the mean time, Mr Fitztumbleton, if you would be able to do that paperwork for me quickly, I won't have to bother you again."

The furrows on Derek's forehead deepened.

"I'm talking about my reference," Mabel added in clarification. "Backdating it is not that big a deal is it?"

But it was only then that she realised he wasn't staring at her any longer but at the person standing at the door.

Chapter Fourteen

"No, Mr Perkins," Sandra admonished, as the cat meowed for attention underneath the kitchen table. "I'm not talking to you today. Your behaviour last night was unacceptable."

The moggy looked back at her with an expression suggesting 'fur ball, smur ball', although there was definitely a hint of 'I told you so' in there too.

She took a sip of her tea and weighed things up.

Yes, perhaps the tumbling toga bit had been a step too far. She hadn't meant for it to fall all the way to the floor, more drape suggestively across one breast. But such was life when one chose to use ancient Roman technology originally designed for the more buxom woman, and besides, putting Derek's rapid disappearing act to one side for a moment, had the evening really gone that badly?

She took a larger gulp and weighed things further.

It was true that there had been more encouraging reactions in the past from other less interesting victims, but she and Derek did at least now have plans to go out together later. Plus, to have established that they had a common interest in the occasional quivering quaver was going to be useful in the future. On balance, therefore, it was probably safe to assume that he'd get over the premature nudity in time, just as all obedient little minions did when they finally realised what was good for them, and things would work themselves out.

All was sorted then. Excellent!

With that straightened out in her mind, she was free to face the rest of the day with an optimistic heart.

* * *

"I see you are enjoying your fifteen minutes of fame," Mrs McFreece stated with curt contempt as Sandra arrived, pointing to the local paper on her desk. "Mr Fitztumbleton will have fun trying to explain that lot to the inspectors if they see it."

Sandra glanced at the headline and, and as always, retained her composure with ease. The journalist had been true to his word, *Flasher's Trashers' Fifty Lashes*; nothing to get uptight about.

"Has Derek seen it yet?" she asked, and tried to intonate that she was hoping that he had, so that they could all brush it under the carpet and move on. But The Fridge wasn't having any of it.

"Well *Mr Fitztumbleton* was mumbling something about a pencil case earlier, so you may be off the hook for the time being. But," she added, waggling an infuriated finger for good measure, "don't think that I won't ensure that he has taken note of all the sordid details before our visitors arrive. Forewarned, as they say, Miss Lovelock, is forearmed."

Sandra rather wished the woman would forego the lecturing tone, or she could foresee her telling the frosty cow to fornicate off, it was just a fore-thought. However, for the sake of forthright speech, she chose a different approach.

"Forget it. I'll speak to him."

Mrs McFreece's nostrils flared with humdrum predictability, and Sandra was just about to write the reaction off as ignorable when she suddenly spotted a new frequency to the quiver of the splaying gristle. The remainder of her sentence went unsaid.

Hmmm, this was interesting. Was this indignation tinged with something new that she could see? A rebel sentiment perhaps; all be it one that McFreece wasn't yet prepared to admit to herself. Intrigued, Sandra waited for the woman to respond.

"I will forget nothing," the secretary fumed theatrically, whilst this disconcerting intruder now also began to shine in her eyes. Sandra noted how it complimented the gaudily crimson lips and waited to see what was coming next. The Fridge did not disappoint. "You can't just turn up one morning, crack the whip and expect it to go unnoticed," she continued. "People are going to ask questions, Miss Lovelock. People are going to want to know how you learned to do such a thing. When you get your practise in. And where..." And then suddenly her mouth froze mid-sentence and not another word passed her lips.

Sandra took in the wide-eyed look of dismay, and it struck her that these may well have been the words of someone who actually wanted answers to other non-questions they weren't asking. It was certainly an odd 'striking' to have, but so it struck all the same. She frowned.

"So let me get this right, Mrs McFreece. What you are saying is that people are going to want to know where best to purchase such well crafted works of art," she replied, her mind racing to make sense of it all. "Where to get these obedient instruments of control. Is that what you were going to say?"

The ruby lips facing her puckered pre-response. The cheeks flushed with the clashing pink of shame, and were swiftly accompanied by a reddened set of ears, nose and throat. Sandra held firm and let the silence hang. Mrs McFreece broke the deadlock first.

"I w-w-wouldn't know w-w-what you're talking about, Miss L-l-lovelock," she stammered, clearly despising herself more and more with every syllable. "N-n-now if you don't mind, I have some p-pencils to sharpen," she added a little more evenly, and held a handful of HBs up for Sandra to see.

Sandra surveyed them critically. They looked brand new and distinctly in need of leaving alone rather than sharpening. She scowled.

"Did Derek ask you to sharpen them?"

"Oh good gracious me, no," Mrs McFreece exclaimed, clearly back on home territory once again. "It is simply the least I can do for a man whose nib has been blunted by such cruel turns of fate. He was bemoaning his stationary career to me only this morning."

245

* * *

Sandra caught sight of Derek's expression as she appeared at the doorway to the staff room, and quickly rattled through her inventory of memories to gauge when she'd last seen that particular look. The night before was a clear contender, but having thought things through earlier she was prepared to show tolerance. At the end of the day, he had still asked to stroke her pussy so it couldn't all have been a waste of time.

Mabel Milner brushed past, mumbling something about needing to make a phone call, and then hers and Derek's stares locked.

For Sandra, the moment was electric. Pounding shockwaves of possibility pulsated between them as unspoken love merged with a suggestion of submissive respect. A million hopes and dreams suddenly tumbled within reach. And he seemed to feel it too.

"Fried eggs on top, and baps down below," Derek whispered, and she felt a rush of exultation; everyone knew that the way to man's heart was through his stomach.

An expletive from the far side of the room shattered the golden moment.

"Oh bloody 'ell, I can't find bloody chicken soup on 'ere," John Bentwick growled, and kicked the drinks machine with frustration. As boot met metal, it rumbled and then gurgled its displeasure, before falling silent once more. The farmer grunted. "I can only see minestrone and I can't be doing with that foreign rubbish."

Sandra breathed in a long deep breath and took stock of the situation. She and Derek needed to have time alone together before tonight. She needed to put his mind at ease and explain that whips and pencils weren't everything when two people had love and obedience on their side. But first things first; the bull had to go. She cleared her throat in preparation for what needed to be said.

"We no longer buy the refills for chicken soup, Mr Bentwick. We found that the croutons were gumming up the inside."

"Croutons?" he asked, aghast. "What, in chicken soup?"

Sandra resisted the temptation to raise her eyes to the ceiling and nodded instead.

"Yes croutons, Mr Bentwick, so probably not to your liking either if you don't have a stomach for foreign sounding words. I suggest you head over to the shop if you're looking for anything more substantial than a cup of tea."

The Chair of Governors weighed up the wisdom of her words and huffed.

"Well I'll take myself off to the Co-Op then," he muttered, disgruntled. "And I'll come back once I've 'ad something to eat," he added, as though it was meant to be of significance to his audience. But Sandra just shrugged, relieved.

Thirty seconds, she calculated, and then they'd be alone. That was all the time that remained before their mutual declaration of love could be enshrined by a magical kiss.

She tapped her foot to pass the time. Tap-tap-tap it went. Get-the-hint. Bug-ger-off. But John Bentwick's fingers began to drum the same beat on the glass of the drinks machine, and he gave his stomach a rub.

"Oh, I don't know," he murmured, clearly changing his mind. "It's a bit early for a proper meal. What do yer think?"

Desperate, Sandra went to remind him of his quest, but to her dismay Ashley Milner suddenly appeared at the door and her heart sank.

"Miss Lovelock? Can I please ask you a question about Henry the Eighth?"

Frustration bubbling, Sandra managed a curt nod and channelled all her annoyance into a short, sharp stamp instead. It helped, things swam back into perspective. She reminded herself that Derek's eyes had sparked at the mention of the name of the epic historical figure, so perhaps this could at least be another common interest.

"Ah yes, that great man," she crooned, and pulled herself together. "What would you like to know, Ashley?"

The child smiled appreciatively, but then bit her lip.

"Well, it's just that I've been reading up on him," she quickly explained, "and I don't see what made him so great. I mean, sure he turned the religious world upside down, married lots of birds, and even managed to have more than a brace of kids, just. But he also lopped the head off anyone who disagreed with him, spent all his dad's dosh, and ended up as fat as a pig."

"I think you'll find he was more like a hippopotamus when he died," Derek chipped in, and although it was a disconcerting contribution, Sandra took it as an encouraging sign that he was slowly returning to normal. "They're amongst the most dangerous animals on this planet, you know, which probably suits this analogy too."

At this point, however, she felt it was time to step in.

"But he was a very accomplished musician, Mr Fitztumbleton. I am sure that you are one to appreciate that." She hoped that the strand of musical togetherness they had enjoyed the night before would bind them yet closer now. But, unfortunately, Derek seemed to be gathering his wherewithal via a more serious inclination.

"I think The Reformation was of far greater significance, Miss Lovelock," he corrected. "Henry the Eighth was a man who wanted to rule with absolute power. And overall," Derek continued, "it has to be said that he found it utterly intolerable that all major decisions in England were in the hands of the Italians."

"Well if they're the ones that started all this Latin lark then I don't disagree with 'im," John Bentwick announced, and shot a final offended look at the drinks machine in the corner. "And none of this minestrone rubbish for me neither. I'm off to get meself a pasty." And with that major announcement, he walked out of the room.

Even Ashley's face showed an element of surprise at the odd outburst, but she clearly didn't want to waste the opportunity she'd been given and so focussed back on her chosen subject as soon as he'd disappeared from sight.

"Yes, I know all that," she said quietly, and then paused to check that Sandra was listening to her again. "But what I want to know is this; what did Henry the Eighth actually do that made a positive difference to the lives of those around him, and not just to himself? As far as I can see, that's the most important question to ask."

Sandra was stunned. Not so much at the astounding knowledge this eleven year old had, but more at the purpose of the question at all. Surely if one ruled with absolute power, it simply didn't matter.

"You see, I think," Ashley added, before Sandra had a chance to cogitate further, "that a great person is one who makes sacrifices so that others may gain; someone who puts others first. What could possibly be greater than that?" she asked, and then appeared to be about to articulate another philosophical belter, when the tinkle of the outside bell sounded in their ears. "Oh, it's roll call," she finished off. "I'd better go."

And with that poignant question left hanging in the air, the child disappeared off.

* * *

The morning assembly came and went.

Why assemblies were so important, Sandra didn't know. Crowd control was all about 'divide and conquer', not 'let's have a communal hug and pray'. But on the up side though, she did note that Derek had at least moved on from worrying about his pencil case.

After that, other than an odd two minute diversion where she had to explain the vagaries of whip choice to a coy but insistent Mrs McFreece, the rest of the morning was spent waiting for the assessors to visit her class. "A whip chooses you, Mrs McFreece," she had had to divulge in the end, just to shut the woman up. "Not the other way round." The secretary had rather liked the mysterious aura to it all and had returned to her record keeping making a strange noise that was peculiarly akin to a hum.

The droll exchange helped Sandra get through the tedium of the morning, and her moment of glory with Ofsted finally arrived during the last session before lunch.

"I'm sorry to interrupt your class, Miss Lovelock," Derek said quietly, as he entered the room. "As you will have been expecting, Mr de Ravel and I shall be sitting in on this one. Good morning, children," he then announced, and as one they all replied;

"Good morning, Mr Fitztumbleton. Good morning, Mr... Drivel."

Sandra frowned. She'd been determined to take no notice of the visitors when they arrived, as it wasn't de rigueur to do so, but this mention of a 'de Ravel' suddenly caught her attention.

Or perhaps it was more its derivative; *Drivel*.

Her frown deepened. This was not the first time she had made the acquaintance of a Drivel, however the previous individual had been introduced to her as a doctor wearing a mask and a dog collar, canine, of course, so it couldn't possibly be the same man... or could it?

"Well, please continue, Miss Lovelock, just as if we're not here," Derek said, and guided de Ravel across to a pair of seats especially set aside for the occasion. Sandra watched the inspector's confident strut, irked.

"So, where were we?" she asked, keen to focus back on the moment. Ashley Milner's hand shot up.

"You were introducing us to the use of zero in numeracy," she advised, and Sandra felt a flush of gratitude.

It was, however, short-lived, for Peter Drayton then went and cleared his young throat.

"So let me get this right," he said cautiously, the determination on his face suggesting he was onto something significant now that he'd had a couple of minutes to think things through. He struggled on. "If you *times* somefink by nuffink, then you always get a nuffink, yes?" Sandra nodded and he carried on. "But if you *divide* somefink by nuffink, what you get is f-f-f-finitony, is that right?"

Sandra winced and did her best to ignore the newcomers as they settled into their seats.

"Well, sort of, Peter, well done. But if you divide something by zero, what you actually get is *infinity*," she corrected, and then to her astonishment and for the first time in his life, Peter Drayton's face lit up with comprehension.

"Oh, fantastic!" he exclaimed, and it was true that Sandra felt like celebrating with him. But her joy proved to be fleeting, for his next question then rekindled old concerns. "But does it *only ever* give you finitony?"

"Yes."

And at this, his face fell. "Oh, that's a shame, 'cos I don't much like that Italian cake."

"What Italian cake?" Sandra asked, before she could stop the question leaving her lips, and to her regret, Peter found an answer for once.

"Finitony," he repeated, grimacing. "It's like a sponge with bits in."

"Are you sure you don't mean Panettone?" she tried, despairing at her desperation to sound reasonable in front of her judges.

Peter scrunched up his face. "Oh, yeah, that's it," he replied, disappointed. "But that's a right bugger 'cos I thought I'd had it all sorted when you said that if you divide somefink by nuffink you get finitony. Sorry," he then corrected, "I mean panettone." Sandra went to interrupt him, but unfortunately Peter was now in full swing. "I'd already planned to tell my mum to divide our Sunday treat by nuffink instead of in half, 'cos then me and my bruvver could eat cake all day. But," and as he said the word, his face fell further, "as I've already said,

253

I don't like that Italian stuff so there's not much point now, is there?"

Sandra licked her lips slowly. It wasn't the first time that day she'd been presented with a reticence for cultural specialities, but if there hadn't been a panel of judges waiting to score her out of ten she'd have actually felt a strange sense of elation. It was true that Peter was missing the point on more levels than one could count crumbs on a plate, but in a strangely flaky way, his answer told her that he had actually grasped what infinity was, sort of, when discussed in baking terms with a zealous helping of self-raising flour.

"Well, Peter," she settled for eventually, "I accept that Panettone isn't everyone's cup of tea, but I'm delighted to learn that you have such an excellent understanding of the foods of our European partners." Peter's forehead creased, but she ignored him. "However this morning I am simply introducing you to the use of zero in your numeracy. Divide by zero, you get infinity. Multiply by zero and you get nuffink. I mean nothing; I mean zero," she double corrected quickly.

Peter made one last ditch attempt to see some hope in the lesson.

"And never Bakewell Tart?" he asked forlornly, but Sandra shook her head.

"No. Never Bakewell Tart."

"Bakewell Tart, makes you fart," burst from Billy Barber, before she had a chance to shut him up. "And custard powder makes it louder," he then added for good measure, but to her relief she spotted Derek mouthing the word *Tourette's*, which seemed to put the inspector's mind at rest.

"Now, I think that's enough talk about cake, don't you, Peter?" she suggested and waited for him to nod his head.

"Yes, Miss Love*lick,*" he mumbled, and then his jaw dropped with dismay.

As the silly mistake sounded out, the class erupted into guffaws of laughter.

Sandra froze. She'd been paranoid that they'd shout *Titzfumbleton* earlier, and she'd cringed when *Drivel* had sounded out instead, but this one she really hadn't been prepared for.

Mr de Ravel's head jerked up and he gave her a perplexed look.

Damn, damn, damn! She cursed in her mind. Billy's Tourette's was one thing, but to look as though she didn't have proper control over her class was inconceivable. Her back stiffened.

"Perhaps you would like to rephrase that, Peter."

Already as red as a cherry, Peter's cheeks took on a new shiny, glacé appearance as the sweat began to form.

"S-sorry, Miss L-l-love-l-lock," he corrected.

But it was too late. For already, an odd look of recognition was seeping across what was, now without doubt, *Doctor Drivel's* face.

* * *

Some might think that to inadvertently bump into one's minions away from one's club would be an awkward thing to happen, but to a dominatrix such as Sandra it was a mere walk in the park, although admittedly she had left her dog lead at home.

Of course, it may well have been a different matter if a rival dominant had turned up to weigh, measure and find her wanting. But the rivals she knew tended to work as traffic wardens or airline check-in staff, so there was little chance of them meeting in a professional capacity. And, fortunately, today was no different.

As soon as he had sussed who she was, she had given him the secret signal, and a mutual vow of silence on the subject had been agreed. And that was as much lowering down to his level as she was prepared to go. If word got out that Lady Lovelick had ever bowed to Dr Drivel's will, then her mastery as mistress over the minions would be a thing of the past. He knew that. She knew that, and she also knew that this would be an experience he would harbour as a gratifying memory for many years to come; probably literally. Nice for him, but a bit of an intrusion for her, as far as she was concerned.

"Go to the staff room, now, Mr de Ravel," Sandra ordered once the class had emptied out for lunch, expertly guided by their headmaster. She was conscious that someone might overhear her and so kept the commanding note in her voice low key. "I will join you when I am ready. Mr Fitztumbleton will look after you until I arrive."

She looked at her watch to show her disinterest and waved him away with her hand. It would be alright, it was lunch time. There was no reason why a lone Ofsted inspector shouldn't be wandering around the classrooms during break, but he'd be following her around like a bad smell if she didn't nip it in the bud now. And besides, Mrs McFreece would no doubt begin to think something was going on and start taking notes.

"Of course, Lady..." Drivel simpered, but Sandra widened her eyes in fury.

"Miss!" she barked, and then huffed a decisive sigh in order to channel her irritation. "And as punishment for that insubordination, you will ensure your colleague is on message for giving this school the excellent inspection rating it deserves," she then added, not sure when she would get another opportunity.

Dr Drivel bowed.

"Of course, Miss Lovelock. Whatever you command," he said and then sidled out of the room.

Sandra watched him leave, and only once he'd disappeared did she then let her shoulders slump. Oh my, this was too much. She'd never have believed it unless she'd experienced it for herself, but to be performing constantly in character, in what was otherwise her 'normal' everyday setting, was harder than she'd have thought. It was draining.

Giving herself a few minutes of rest, she laid a text book on each desk in preparation for the next lesson, and only then went to join the rest of the team for sandwiches and cocktail sausages on sticks in the staff room.

As she wandered along the corridor, jovial voices filtered through from the little gathering.

"Oh no, I've already 'ad a pasty this morning thanks," John Bentwick's booming voice announced to whomever was offering him a sandwich. "Didn't know that you would be going all posh today, and I need to save my appetite for this evening."

Sandra heard Derek cough his funny little awkward cough and slowed her pace.

"Well, quite," her hero said, and then added, "Actually, Mr de Ravel that reminds me..."

Now Sandra stopped. She could only hope that Derek was going to say what she was expecting him to say, but for some reason it didn't seem right to appear at the door until it had all been agreed. The poor man had been so twitchy recently that the invitation to dinner might never make it out of his mouth if she interrupted the proceedings at the wrong time. Instead, she held her breath.

"Would you and Miss Bonniface care to join us for a spot of dinner this evening?" he asked to her relief. Sandra took a silent step forward to hear more. "Mr Bentwick and I had wondered if, seeing as you're not in this area much, you might like to experience a bit of rural hospitality whilst you're here."

Sandra could imagine the sour faced puckering of the female inspector's mouth and thanked St Sebastian, the unofficial patron saint of masochists, for working with her on this one. Drivel would not be able to resist.

"What a splendid idea!" he exclaimed, and she clenched her fists for joy. "I can't think of anything better."

A sharp, feminine cough sounded an irritating note of caution.

"But Mr de Ravel," Diana Bonniface said softly, and Sandra felt herself tense. "We are not supposed to accept offers like that. At Inspector Training last week, I am quite sure they said that if an offer could be construed as currying favour then it is our duty to resist."

"Oh, I don't know that we need to worry about curry, Miss Bonniface," he countered, far more commandingly than Sandra would normally have allowed from a minion. "I'm not sure that chicken tikka has even reached this part of the world yet."

Diana Bonniface went to speak, but John Bentwick's brash pointlessness overrode her.

"Well, The Three Sided Thicket 'as been known to do a chicken take-out," he now offered enthusiastically. "And I believe they can also put on a nice steak and chips, if that's any good to yer."

"I think that sounds a splendid idea," de Ravel said genially, expertly ignoring his colleague's well-meaning but over-zealous contribution. "Miss Bonniface and I would love to join you, and would I be right in assuming that Miss Lovelock will be joining us too?" Sandra held her breath even more. "Plus any other members of staff, of course," he then added, clearly remembering the need for political correctness at the last minute.

"Well, we were thinking it would be more like partners, so to speak," John answered, before Derek could get a word in edgeways.

Sandra crossed her fingers. If Derek could just grasp the nettle now, confirm to the world that this farmer person had actually got it right for once and that Sandra was going as Derek's partner, and not as a member of staff, then everything that she had endured for the last seven years would have been worth it.

Unfortunately, it was John Bentwick who spoke first.

"Well, I'm bringing a friend," John continued, and then paused as though he was struggling to find the next word. "Well, she's more a friend of a friend, really, called Dawn," he managed eventually. "And Mr Fitztumbleton is bringing 'er friend, who is my friend too actually, and 'er name is Mabel."

* * *

It was the mother of all bombshells. And being a person who was used to calling the shots, Sandra found it almost impossible to deal with the Mabel-Milner shaped grenade as it hit its target with wanton disregard. Even controlled deep breathing in a hidden corner of the playground wasn't doing anything to help.

Percy had done his bit to buy her some time, dropping a shell on an unsuspecting member of the PTA as they wandered a little too close with their wheelbarrow. It had been enough of a distraction to send the woman trotting away in search of a wet wipe, and had given Sandra a few extra moments to quell the rising tension. But she wasn't sure it would do the trick.

Seven years of boredom, rural inanity, and childish chatter about chickens she had borne, and borne with relatively good grace too, all in the hope that he would finally see the light. Seven sodding years!

For seven tedious years, she'd quashed her desire for daily sating through the fawnings of a minion.

For seven dreary years, she'd funnelled her efforts into one condensed weekly savouring of masterly control on a Monday night; as Dr Drivel knew well.

For seven bloody years, she'd successfully channelled her unfulfilled cravings into an alter ego that had, only recently, started to test the boundaries she had set.

And all these actions had taken their toll. The pressure had begun to mount. The hunger for acknowledgement, any acknowledgement, of her pathetic meaningless existence had started to grow too strong. Well, now this extraordinary other-self she had so carefully crafted had begun to build a life of *its* own.

Only *it,* suddenly, could offer the promise of release. Only *it* could give respite where otherwise there was none. Only *it* didn't care.

The public-facing Sandra Lovelock may have worried in the past about the outcome of *its* actions, but with *its* growing sense of identity, *it* now believed fervently that there was nothing left to lose...

Chapter Fifteen

"Don't worry, Mr Fitztumbleton, I'll have that whipped it into shape for you in no time."

Mrs McFreece spoke with surprising relish. Not that Derek was one to look a gift horse in the mouth but he'd only asked her to tidy the stationery cupboard; there were pencil shavings all over the floor.

He wondered briefly if there was a catch, and then let the idea go. If he asked himself any more introspective questions today, he suspected it would be like flogging a dead mare; unrewarding, uncompromising and probably rather messy.

"Thank you, Mrs McFreece," he said instead, and the smile that came fluttering back added to his naive false sense of security. Unaware of impending doom, Derek carried on. "Now I'm going to accompany the inspectors outside whilst the pupils are doing PE," he advised. "So do you think you can hold the fort?"

It had only been a throw-away line, one of those friendly, disposable parting gestures, but the disgruntled look that shot back immediately informed him that a longer lasting type of quip would have been a wiser choice. Her face crumpled into its usual position and the moment of helpful camaraderie was gone.

Derek sighed. It was a shame, but at least things were back on an even keel; and boy, oh boy, was he in desperate need of some stability. The last twenty four hours had, if he was being honest with himself, left him rather numb.

Or was that strictly true? No, perhaps not. The 'honest with himself' bit demanded clarification.

Derek replayed the thought in his mind.

It was perhaps more accurate to say that the last twenty four hours had, in fact, seen him play second fiddle to a vacuum cleaner; endure a cat's fur-ball warming his; and suffer the embarrassment of not being an upstanding Roman citizen. So, if he was actually being properly honest with himself, it was more appropriate to say that he had been broken hearted, disgusted, horrified and then left numb. He didn't dare think about the last seventy-two hours; that would require a book to set it all down.

But there had, at least, been one very small blessing. Miss Lovelock had made a hasty exit during lunch, and he and The Fridge had managed to explain her disappearance away as an unplanned trip to the dentist. The mood of the place had lifted once she'd gone, despite Mr de Ravel seeming disappointed, and at the time of the announcement, Derek had ruefully accepted it as a mark of poor planning against his name and had revelled in the boost in atmosphere anyway. Even if it had led Miss Bonniface to attack her clipboard with renewed vigour such that she had now run out of ink.

Hence his discovery of the stationery room floor, and hence why they were now running slightly behind schedule.

Concerned about time, Derek led de Ravel and his acerbic sidekick along the corridor and through to the changing rooms. It wasn't the most scenic route to take to the back playground, but it was the quickest, and as the musty smell of yesterday's socks and sweaty pants hit their nostrils, Miss Bonniface wrinkled her nose. Derek spotted a half-eaten pepperami on the floor and kicked it to the side with his foot. Well that was one thing at least, he thought, there was nothing quite like touching base with reality to keep one's sensibly shoed feet on the ground.

He opened the rear door and stood back to let them through. To his relief, the inspectors emerged outside to the delightful sound of happy high pitched voices.

Wow! Did Derek love that sound. Every time he heard it, it elicited a joy in his heart that nothing else could touch. It was so positive; so of-the-moment; so full of innocence of what their futures held. Yes, it was a sound that always brought a smile to his face and, turning to his left, he noted with pleasure that de Ravel's features had softened too. This was what being a small, rural, primary school was all about. This was what these examiners needed to see; children learning to be together regardless of gender, age, or parental disposition.

Inspired, Derek turned to his right and found Diana Bonniface looking as glum as ever. Suddenly, her miserable demeanour slotted into place. She's not a country girl, he caught himself thinking somewhat critically, and she wouldn't know the arse end of a bullock from a heifer. It was an oddly gratifying thought for one who had previously considered himself so urban, and it gave him a little boost.

The three of them began their walk along the edge of the playground and the November breeze twiddled with the trees and stung their bureaucratic faces. Derek watched Miss Bonniface pull her thin jacket in tighter and wondered if he should offer her his. No, he decided. Inspector Training wouldn't approve; a chilly inspector was undoubtedly better than a curried one.

A football suddenly whistled passed his nose and the three of them paused on their journey. De Ravel slapped his hands onto his hips and took a good look around.

"You really do have a first-rate team here, Fitztumbleton," he proclaimed, puffs of hot breath blowing out into the air. Pleasantly surprised, Derek pulled himself from his contemplations. "Small but perfectly formed, I'd say," de Ravel added indulgently, and nodded with satisfaction. "Absolutely top notch."

"Thank you," Derek replied, and was about to add something suitably inane to the unexpected compliment when the inspector carried on speaking.

"That Miss Lovelock of yours, what a cracker, eh? Outstanding teacher, excellent second in command when you're not here…" Derek thought of the newspaper article and wondered if it had been spotted yet. "And nice bit of eye candy to boot, wouldn't you say?"

The man gave Derek a knowing wink as he said it, and Diana Bonniface choked.

"When I was at Inspector Training last week," she stuttered, but de Ravel interrupted her.

"Yes, yes, yes," he snapped, and raised his eyes to the heavens in irritation. "When you were at Inspector Training last week, I expect they told you that calling an attractive woman *eye candy* could be construed as sexist. I however, Miss Bonniface," he then declared in no uncertain terms, "with my many years of inspecting experience, like to think that recognition should be given to talent where recognition is due. And I am sure that Mr Fitztumbleton would agree with me. Is that not so, Mr Fitztumbleton?" Derek nodded before he could stop his head from moving. But it seemed to do the trick, as the inspector already had his next comment lined up. "I like to call a spade a spade," he asserted, and having spotted the tremor of Miss Bonniface's lips decided to cut in before she could make a sound. "And no," he stated finally, "before you mention Inspector Training again, that isn't some sort of racist remark."

The woman's face shrank into a scowl. Inspector Training had clearly not prepared her for rebellion on her own side of the fence.

Even Derek was unsure as to what was going on, but he'd never been a person to pass up a good opportunity when it arose. There was only one thing he could say to that.

"Well, quite," he managed, and felt it was more than appropriate for the occasion. De Ravel was unperturbed.

"So tell me, Fitztumbleton," he continued, returning to the purpose of his visit and clearly enjoying his underling's discomfort. "What sort of health and safety assessments do you carry out with regard to the outside playing areas?"

Derek relaxed. For the first time in this conversation he believed he was on safe ground. He and Mrs McFreece had anticipated this question and the completed forms were all in the office: Regular health and safety checks; frequent risk assessments; annual nil-returns on foot and mouth, an unfortunate requirement due to the fact that the playing field was actually listed as farmed, greenbelt land.

"I have the paperwork in a folder," Derek replied confidently. "Mrs McFreece likes to keep it all filed together."

To his joy, his response seemed to do the trick. De Ravel nodded and Derek's hopes began to rise. It was hard to put his finger on what had happened since lunch time, but the chief inspector had suddenly become his best friend. The same, however, could not have been said for the man's over-eager accomplice. Her mouth had barely morphed out of the downward crescent in which it had been set, even when she'd eaten her fig roll. The woman was impenetrable and, though clearly thinking better of referring to Inspector Training now, she turned to a different approach in an effort to thwart his success.

"I. Err…" she muttered, and dug the clipboard out from under her jacket. "I. Err… took the liberty of reviewing the risk assessments first thing this morning, Mr de Ravel. The secretary did a copy of the latest report for me." She handed him the stapled sheets. "The last one was carried out two and a half weeks ago."

De Ravel looked at them.

"Well, they all seem in order, Miss Bonniface, don't you think?"

Having at last been formally invited to give her opinion, her eyes now took on an evil glint. She licked her lips and smirked.

"Well, I did think that, Mr de Ravel, until we came outside. This netball court seems fine, but take a look down there," and as she spoke, she pointed across to the expanse of grass that served as the school's football pitch. "It's not as green as one would expect," she added cryptically, and Derek cringed inside.

He had hoped that they would be able to get away with simply reviewing the PE lesson from the protection of the school building, but this over-efficient excuse for a recent inspectorate qualification was one step ahead of him.

"I think we should investigate, Mr de Ravel," she continued smugly. "From what I can see, there are some very unhealthy looking brown patches dotted around which are giving me cause for concern."

As the damning words slipped out, the expression on her face twisted into the happiest it had been all day. Like a caterpillar stretching out in the sun, her lips straightened into a taut line and her municipal mind concluded that there was no getting out of this one. She'd got the school well and truly cornered.

De Ravel followed the direction of her finger and then leaned forward to get a better look. He scrunched up his eyes.

"You know, Miss Bonniface," he deliberated, and Derek's heart skipped a beat, "I think you'll find that they are cow-pats. Which makes me wonder..." he then added, and straightened up again, rubbing a finger thoughtfully along his chin. "Whether you have only attended the *Urban* Inspector Training course. There is a rural version as well, you know, where they teach you to expect such things. Would I be right, Mr Fitztumbleton?"

"Err..." Derek scratched his ear awkwardly and shrugged. "Well I don't know what training courses are on offer actually, Mr de Ravel."

The inspector laughed and shook his head.

"No, no, no. I meant would I be right in saying that those are cow-pats?"

Derek winced but nodded. "Yes, you are correct."

De Ravel shifted his weight from one foot to the other.

"Well," he sighed, and managed a little smirk as he said it. "I expect that Lower Bushcy Primary is working towards its 'Greener Schools Award'. And being the first rate institution that it is, I also expect that it has chosen to fertilise its land organically rather than wasting money on expensive agricultural products. Would I be right there too, Mr Fitztumbleton?"

269

Derek nodded again, only this time more fervently. "Greener Schools Award," he repeated for good measure, just to add weight to the explanation even though he'd never heard that such a thing existed.

Miss Bonniface's face fell. Once again she'd been thwarted by her own kind, and with friends like that who needed enemies? But, just as Derek thought they'd got this little matter of a few meadow muffins cleared up, her features then lifted again.

"Well," she said, sporting a new victorious tone, "it doesn't matter how green the school is, if the children are escaping in front of our noses, does it?"

And as she asked the question, she pointed across to a conspicuously thin but surprisingly tall and athletic looking football figure escaping through the hedge.

* * *

It was hard to say which was more gratifying for Derek; the look of dismay on the female inspector's face when she found out it was a scarecrow, or the look of delight on de Ravel's when he did too.

Derek had pulled the Peter Crouch look alike out of the gap in the hedge, explaining the reason for its existence in multi-syllabled health and safety terms, and de Ravel had simply muttered, "Ingenious," all the way back to the staff room.

At this point, Diana Bonniface had begun to walk meekly five steps behind the two men, and Derek had got the impression that her faith in Inspector Training had been severely dented. Even when she discovered that a child had done a 'number two' in the boys' urinals, she never batted an eyelid. She simply recommended that the Reception teacher refocus on the teaching of the numbers one to ten, and that was all there was to it.

"It would seem," de Ravel muttered conspiratorially to Derek, as they headed off the premises at the close of day, "we have our eager beaver beat. Miss Lovelock will be pleased when we tell her later, yes?"

Derek scratched his nose. A 'well, quite' was probably pushing things, so he chose a simple nod as his response and ushered them towards the front gate.

"Oh, you'd better watch where you're walking," he whispered wryly to de Ravel, as they marched across the playground. "There are still a few deposits towards our 'Greener Schools' initiative to contend with this side too."

Expecting the man to chuckle, he felt his mouth go dry as de Ravel stopped and looked around with a frown.

"But there's no grass here," the man stated matter-of-factly, and Derek's stomach leapt into the back of his throat.

Oh what a fool! Derek cursed his stupidity. He'd let himself be lulled into a false sense of security and now the bugger had gone and caught him out. This was no time to think that an inspector was on his side, and it was certainly no time to start being blasé. Yet now he'd gone and alerted the man to a seriously unsanitary situation.

"Well, quite," was his immediate reaction, of course, but then to his surprise, a stroke of genius struck. "And that is exactly what we are trying to illustrate by laying out dollops of the stuff down here too. As you quite correctly state," he added, growing in confidence with every word, "not a blade of grass has sprouted despite the application of fertiliser. The children are going to write up this part of the experiment some time next week."

De Ravel cocked his head to the side.

"Miss Lovelock's idea?" he asked, and Derek took his cue.

"Oh yes, absolutely."

"I thought as much," the inspector replied gratified, and turned to speak to his colleague, who was still staring around in dismay. "Sheer brilliance, don't you think, Miss Bonniface? Nothing like a bit of practical investigation to show these children how nature works, eh?"

Bonniface weighed up the situation and swallowed hard.

"Yes, it's a very novel approach, Mr de Ravel, but clearly extremely effective," she agreed. "We should highlight it in our report as an example of the innovative teaching methods used here."

De Ravel liked the sound of that and nodded his assent.

"Well, we'll see you later, Fitztumbleton. Both you and Mr Bentwick have my mobile number if you need to contact me in the mean time. What was the place called?"

"The Three Sided Thicket in Nether Bunting," Derek replied and bravely waved them off.

Only once the two of them had driven away, did the ballooning panic finally begin to grow. He'd been lucky today, no doubt about that, but how long could that luck hold? His senior teacher had disappeared without an explanation; his caretaker was on suspension for unproven acts of obscenity; and his Chair of Governors struggled to spell PTA. How the hell was he going to get through another twenty four hours and still retain their respect?

* * *

Ambling along at five miles an hour, Derek drove past the house with the abandoned cooker twice before he realised it was hers. He gave his inside jacket pocket a nervous squeeze, and accepted the bitter-sweet reassurance that Miranda's discarded scarf offered. He was going to need all the luck he could get.

To his relief, Mabel had been looking out for him, and as he parked up she was already closing the front door behind her. Derek watched her totter along the garden path, demurely clad in a little black shift dress and high heels, and found to his surprise that he felt proud.

"I've had to pay for a proper babysitter," she explained, as she clambered into the passenger seat and straightened out her coat. Derek regretted the disappearance of the shapely calves and put the car into gear. "So I hope we're not going to be too late. I never realised how much they charged per hour," she added disconsolately. "I think I'm in the wrong business."

Derek suspected that this was very true, although not for the reason suggested, and agreed.

"Has John Bentwick been and gone then?"

"He has," Mabel said stiffly, and followed it up with a sniff. "They left about ten minutes ago."

Surprised that that was all she had to say on the matter, he peered left and right, waiting for a gap in the traffic, and then pulled out onto the main road.

"I don't think I've met your friend, have I?" he asked, once the engine was chuntering up to economy performance once again. "Dawn, isn't it?"

Mabel cleared her throat.

"Yes, her name is Dawn," she replied, and then hesitated before continuing. "Look, she and I have known each other for a few years," she now said cautiously, "and I might as well warn you that she's a little," she paused and scratched her head. "Well, she's a little unusual, that's probably the best way to describe her. She's not like many other people you'll meet, Mr Fitztumbleton, but she's got a heart of gold. I'd just ask you to remember that when I introduce you."

Derek laughed despite himself; John Bentwick wasn't exactly your run-of-the-mill type either.

"Well, good for John then," he smirked. "Who knows, perhaps they'll hit it off."

It had just been a jovial retort but Mabel sniffed a little louder this time, adding a snorty tinge to the sound as she did. Derek wondered if this was some new-fangled mode of communication, after all, he'd only just got the hang of texting, but then remembered that the noise still needed a reply.

"You don't think he's right for her, eh?" he asked. "Too brash and farmerish, perhaps? You think she can do better?" He paused, expecting a sniff, snort, or snuffle in response, of which there was none, and took the ensuing silence as a sign to carry on. "Well, I'll admit that our Mr Bentwick is about as rustic as they come but, like your friend, I believe he too has a heart of gold. He means well."

This, however, elicited a huff, which in turn, then put him firmly back in the dark again.

"And he's as honest as the day is long," Derek added, grabbing at a cliché for comfort. "He's a lucky man all things considered," he sighed finally. "One of the few people who can spend their time doing what they really love."

A 'humph' now met his ears.

"Well, I expect you're right," she muttered, "if rams are your thing." And despite his diplomatic comment, Derek backtracked and found himself silently agreeing. She carried on. "I mean it's all very good and well being able to do what you really love, if you've been born into it, inherited it, and aren't actually capable of doing anything else, isn't it?"

There too, Derek conceded, she had a point. But there was more.

"And it's all very good and well wasting all your time doing it, if you haven't got the wherewithal to spend your time doing other stuff with the person who is right for you," she then added, and not without a small dose of bitterness.

As the words tumbled out, Derek caught the mournful note in her voice and felt it tug on a string in his heart too. It twanged, and then resonated so wretchedly with his own maudlin state of mind, that he waited to see if there was more before he could respond. There was.

"You know, Derek?" she added finally. "Life would be much easier if it happened like that for all of us, but it doesn't, does it? Most of us have to grab at straws to make ends meet. We have to take any tiny stalks that Lady Luck allows to fall from her bale and make the most of them. I'm not proud of my past, Derek, and I'm not particularly proud of the things I've had to do to make ends meet either in, err, more ways than one," she added, and something told Derek not to ask. "But I've only ever done those things for one reason, and that reason is Ashley."

At the mention of the child's non-gender specific name, Derek's stomach lurched. In his desperate bid earlier to remove Sandra Lovelock from the evening's proceedings, he had totally forgotten his dilemma.

"Well, quite," he managed, just, and then pretended to do a double take at the dashboard just to stall for time.

If he let her continue, her words might give him more of a clue.

"I could have been a dancer," she mumbled wistfully to his relief. "You know, a proper one. Not the sordid nasty stuff that I do now. I had a teacher once who said that she'd take me to the top, and I tell you what, she meant it. But then, well, life got in the way, didn't it? Ashley came along. Me and my sister had to sort ourselves out and I'm probably telling you far too much, but there you have it. And now I'm trying to change things for Ash. I'm trying to get myself out of this hole and into an office job. And only god knows how that fills me with dread. The thought of it makes me feel dead, Derek, like I'll turn grey inside, but I'll do it for Ashley. I'd do anything for Ashley." And then her voice tailed off.

Derek checked his rear view mirror. The line of traffic behind them looked like an articulated snake, but now was not the time worry about inconsequentialities like that. He flicked the indicator left, put his foot gently on the brake, and brought the car to a stop halfway up the grassy verge.

Mabel looked back at him, worried.

"Oh gawd," she exclaimed. "I've gone and said something out of turn, 'aven't I?"

Pressing the button to activate his hazard warning lights, Derek pulled the handbrake and then turned to look properly at the woman who had just opened her heart to him with a frankness he'd do well to take on board. A horn sounded somewhere behind them as cars began to file past, angry voices shouting rude words, but he ignored them.

"Tell me, Mrs Milner," he said, but she wasn't listening. Instead, she was just staring forlornly into the distance.

He tried again.

"Tell me, Mrs Milner," he repeated, and this time she turned her head.

"Mabel," she offered and grinned weakly back.

"Mabel," he agreed, nodding. "Tell me, Mabel; what do you think makes a person great?" She frowned as he asked the question and Derek realised he had better explain himself. "I only ask because Ashley made an astute observation this morning, when we were talking about Henry the Eighth."

Mabel pursed her lips, swallowed, and then pulled a stray hair from her eyes.

"Henry the Eighth?" she asked. Derek nodded again. "Well I don't know about him, I'm afraid," she admitted, clearly embarrassed. "I'm not big on keeping up with the news, and I tend to leave the soaps alone. But if you really pushed me for an answer to your original question, then I'd say that a great person is someone who always puts others first."

Derek laughed to himself and Mabel flashed him a peeved look.

"I may be ignorant, Mr Fitztumbleton," she started angrily, but he overrode her quickly.

"No. No! Please. Mabel, I was laughing because that is exactly what Ashley said too. You know, your..."

Derek suddenly struggled to find the next word, felt sick, swallowed and then plucked at the first appropriate noun that came into his head. "Your child is wise beyond their years."

"Who, Ashley? What that precocious little turnip?"

"Yes, Ashley. You see you have already made a significant impression on *herrrrim*," he mumbled this time, inspiration utterly spent. "And you need to recognise that. He..." Mabel frowned, so he corrected himself. "She..." the frown didn't change, so he realised that she was simply waiting to hear what was coming next. "Ashley," he reverted to finally, "may well understand you better than you think."

* * *

Derek was none the wiser as to the gender of Ashley Milner by the time they reached their destination, but as soon as he drew up in the car park and saw John Bentwick had parked up already, he realised that that was the least of his worries.

As far as he was aware, The Three Sided Thicket was meant to be a public house. However, in its present state, it looked as though the public hadn't been for quite some time. In fact, it was more accurate to say that it looked as though it had been so unfrequented, that it was now boarded up with aluminium slats with a padlock on the door. In the background, the rumble of the odd car engine sounded on the road, an occasional sheep baaed, but otherwise silence rang out from what could only have been ghostly inhabitants now left behind.

Derek waved to his Chair of Governors and tried to peer through the window to get a look at this mysterious 'friend of a friend'. Unfortunately, the interior of the vehicle was too dark to get a good view, and he realised that his curiosity would have to wait to be assuaged. He got out of his car and met the man half way.

John Bentwick swiftly, and succinctly, explained what had happened.

"It's a right bugger," he said. "I was only 'ere a couple of days ago and the buggers didn't say a word about buggering off."

Derek looked around.

"Well, quite," he said, more for something to say than anything else. "Where's Mr de Ravel and Miss Bonniface?"

To his surprise, Bentwick smiled back.

"Already ahead of yer there," he said with satisfaction. "Dawn in there," he pointed to the inside of his vehicle with his thumb, "'as already given 'em a ring and told 'em to meet us in Cockerby at a venue she knows. She says it's nice and discrete, so we should 'ave some privacy to chat."

"Which venue is that?"

Bentwick shrugged. "I can't remember the name, but if yer follow me, we'll find somewhere to park in town and make our way there on foot."

Derek couldn't see any reason to object, so whilst John clambered into his vehicle, Derek did the same and switched the engine back on.

"What's up?" Mabel asked, peering apprehensively through the windscreen as John and Dawn drove off.

"Pub seems closed," Derek replied, stating the obvious. "But your friend has suggested a place in Cockerby, and we're going to follow them and meet the inspectors there."

"What's its name?" she asked suspiciously, but Derek just shrugged.

"No idea."

"The No Eyed Deer?" she asked, and frowned. "I don't know what one."

For a split second, Derek entertained correcting her. But she was already distracted, gesturing to her friend as if to say 'what are you up to?', and he realised that it wouldn't be necessary.

They followed the Land Rover all the way into Cockerby and found a space in the multi-storey car park. Derek looked at his watch; quarter to eight. It was later than he'd planned, but it appeared that Mr Bentwick and this Dawn had it all under control.

He searched them out in the gloom and spotted that they had found a space just two rows up. The thud of the man's brown brogues soon sounded in tandem with the click of his companion's heels, and the pair headed across.

Derek scrunched up his eyes. The light was dim, but even in the artificial murkiness, the silhouette walking at the side of the farmer didn't seem quite right. He couldn't put his finger on what it was, but there was definitely something odd about the woman's gait. Perhaps her feet were too far apart, or maybe they were just too large. Either way, though, her legs looked thin but muscular; her skirt was sitting particularly squarely on her hips; and the Edwardian arm-length gloves were definitely a little OTT. Individually, none of these aspects would have elicited comment; it was just that when they were presented altogether, questions started to arise.

He felt Mabel watching him and drew his stare away.

John and Dawn reached them and introductions were made.

"Well, where are we going, Mr Bentwick?" Derek asked, relieved to have a distraction. "I hope we don't have too far to walk. It is rather chilly tonight."

Dawn answered for him.

"We're going to *Bobby's Bar*," she said. "I've already called ahead and reserved a table."

Mabel's eyes widened in surprise.

"*Bobby's Bar*?" she gasped. "But that's owned by Bob the Bastard, and he owns *Domin...*" and then she shut up.

Dawn looked demurely at her gloves and straightened them out slowly.

"Yes, I know, Mabe darling," she cooed softly. "But it wasn't my idea... It was Drivel's, and after what I told you this afternoon, you and I both know what he's like, so who was I to argue?" She looked up and shrugged when she saw Derek's perplexed face. "Well, don't look at me like that. I thought you guys wanted to keep the little sod sweet!"

Chapter Sixteen

John could feel the misgivings rumbling in his stomach as he looked around *Bob's Bar*. True enough, he'd normally have eaten his supper by now, so hunger could have had something to do with it, but overall the rumbles still had a dubious nature to them.

He tried a sniff and then did something that he, as a farmer, wouldn't normally do; he smelt what he sniffed as well. The place had the aroma of a recently vacated barn; suspiciously damp and heading towards mouldy. Noises from the room next door implied that whatever herd of animals had been in this room just before had now moved on to olfactionally infect another area instead. There were cheers, jeers, and what sounded like wolf whistles bellowing through a set of double doors, and they were leaving little to the imagination. If he'd not known for sure that he was in the middle of Cockerby Town, he'd have hazarded a guess that it was a cattle market.

A group of lads on a stag night erupted into laughter on the other side of the bar. John looked across at them and spotted a blow up sheep standing forlornly on a stool. Poor thing, it was clearly missing the rest of its flock, the doleful glint in its eye belying the cheeky grin on its face. He felt his misgivings grow.

De Ravel took a sip of his Bacardi and coke and sighed with satisfaction.

"So will Miss Lovelock be joining us later?" he asked, and put his glass gently back down on the table.

From the edge of his vision, John saw Derek shift awkwardly in his seat and risked a glance to his left; Miss Bonniface too seemed uncomfortable, although that was perhaps the natural state of affairs for her, so maybe it was only Derek who was bothered by the question?

Or maybe not…

Suddenly, he realised that Dawn and Mabel had also swapped knowing looks. It hadn't been an equal trade, of course, for Dawn's face was coated in such a thick layer of makeup that movement of her facial muscles was mostly deadened. But there had still been an exchange of sorts, and it was at least the third such exchange that had taken place since de Ravel had arrived. Whatever it was that the man's arrival had proclaimed, it had proclaimed it good and proper.

The rumbles in John's stomach grew louder.

"Excuse me," he murmured, and gave his belly a rub. "The pickled onions I 'ad for my break are playing 'avoc."

Derek cleared his throat.

"I'm sorry, Mr de Ravel," he replied, "but I don't believe that Miss Lovelock will be joining us later," and then he paused before continuing. "My understanding is that she had a pre-arranged commitment she couldn't break."

He spoke as though he were the bearer of bad tidings but, to John's surprise, de Ravel's eyes lit up.

"Ah!" the inspector mused, the corners of his mouth turning upwards just slightly. "I'd hoped as much," and lifted his glass in a toast.

Confused, John looked back down at his pint of bitter. Warm beer was all very good and well normally, but it wasn't slipping down nicely at all this evening. There were too many things that didn't fit together when they should, and perhaps too many things that did fit together when they shouldn't; like Mabel and Derek. Yes, it was all turning out to be very disturbing, and he really didn't like the way Derek kept tapping Mabel on the shoulder to get her attention. For a start, it wasn't Derek's shoulder to tap, and yet the man seemed to think he had exclusive rights over the 'tappability' of said lovely piece of anatomy. And secondly, well, secondly, it still wasn't his shoulder to tap.

John huffed.

He looked across at Mabel in the hope of catching her eye, but she was watching the headmaster like a hawk and his glance unfortunately snagged with her friend's instead. Dawn raised her cocktail glass to her lips and winked; a shiver squirmed down his spine.

Oh Lord, how had he got himself into this situation? He was a simple man, with simple needs and tastes. It had been said long before this moment that he had more money than sense, and despite his good nature being taken advantage of again and again, he had never taken exception to the remark, for he really did have an awful lot of money. However, he was now wondering if he'd bitten off more than he could chew. What with inspections and beautiful women, this week had turned into one he'd never known the likes of before. It had started badly and gone downhill from there. From the moment Roger had entered the tupping paddock, in fact.

A thought struck him and John cocked his head to the side.

Perhaps that was what this was all about. It was a sign; an omen. As his 'relationship' with the woman of his dreams had floundered at the first hurdle, so too had Roger's with his flock. Although come to think of it, he wasn't convinced Roger had even reached the first hurdle. There certainly hadn't been any indications that he'd tried, but whichever way John looked at it, the prognosis still wasn't good.

The notion made the grumbling in his stomach worsen, and a volcanic gurgle erupted just as Frank the barman arrived with a huge platter of steaming plates.

Frank looked at him askance and lowered the tray.

"Oooh, it sounds like I've arrived just in time," he joked, and John shifted in his seat, stolidly ignoring the overly-friendly wink that followed. "The next show is on at eleven," Frank then advised, and handed a plate of ravioli to Miss Bonniface. "Let me know if you'd like to reserve some seats next door; although standing room is always available," he added as an aside. "We find patrons often like a little extra *standing* room."

De Ravel's eyes glistened with appreciation. "What's on?" he asked, and accepted the surf 'n turf as Frank passed it across.

The waiter smirked and ran his eyes over the motley audience. As his glance bounced across Diana Bonniface, an eyebrow lifted and he bit his bottom lip.

"I think the next performance tonight is *Puss in Boots*," he replied. "Err... The musical." And left the rest unexplained, whilst he concentrated on doling out the remaining meals.

Derek was the first to speak.

"Oh gosh," he muttered, as he spread his paper napkin across his lap. "The panto season must have started early. I never realised these little theatres existed in Cockerby, did you?" he asked Mabel, in a not unfamiliar way. John felt his hackles rise. Oblivious to this, Derek smiled as Mabel shook her head and turned back to the inspector. "Well, it's not what I'd originally had in mind, Mr de Ravel, but if it sounds like something you'd like to go and see, I'm sure we'd all be delighted to join you."

Out of the corner of his eye, John watched Mabel's face turn pale.

"To be honest, Derek," she whispered, "I'm not sure it's the sort of show you'd want to see."

"Nonsense!" de Ravel interrupted and flicked her a knowing look. "From what I can gather, Mr Fitztumbleton and I are men of one mind when it comes to these things. Any man who has the inspired instincts to employ a teacher like Miss Lovelock must occasionally rally to the cause. Come, come, Mrs Milner," he said jokingly, winking as he spoke, "we're all consenting adults here tonight. Even Miss Bonniface."

Mabel and Diana Bonniface both flushed at the same moment, although John had the impression it was for entirely different reasons. He looked at the young female inspector and scowled.

"I wonder what the performance is that we've just missed." de Ravel pondered as he picked up his fork, and dragged the farmer from his thoughts.

Frank forced a cough. "Dick Whippington," he replied, and then turned to Dawn with the final plateful in his hand. "And I expect the coq au vin is for you."

* * *

John allowed himself a sly glance around the table as their plates were cleared away. Other than Miss Bonniface, who was determinedly not living up to her name, the rest of them seemed reasonably at ease; even Derek. But then why wouldn't he be? Not only had the man skilfully stepped in and pinched his bird, but he was now in the process of rubbing his nose in it too. John listened to the tickle of Mabel's heart-warmingly delightful laugh as the headmaster recounted the story of his last visit to a Christmas show, and hated him. What on earth was so amusing about Peter Pan? he thought. Captain Hook could fook off, for all he cared, and he'd bloody well be tinkering with Derek's bell soon if the man wasn't careful.

Eventually, he'd had enough.

"I'm not a panto man, me," he boomed suddenly, and surprised even himself. "And besides," he added, "all this watching of Christmas shows is going to make it rather a late night, isn't it? I've got a ram to sort out early in the morning, yer know."

Miss Bonniface raised her hand to try to get someone's attention but nobody took any notice. To his irritation, it was only Derek who got the hint.

"Oh yes, Mrs Milner, don't you need to get back early for your babysitter? I'm so sorry, I've only just remembered. Perhaps staying for the late show isn't such a good idea; I can take you home after we've eaten if that suits you."

Miss Bonniface lifted her hand a little further, but still to no avail.

John felt his stomach lurch.

"She's not going to turn into a bloody pumpkin, yer know." he bawled, and Mabel shot him a furious look.

De Ravel laughed.

"Nobody mentioned Cinderella, Mr Bentwick," the inspector guffawed. "And I'm sure that a bit of Puss in Boots will finish the evening off nicely. Mrs Milner and her friend aren't immune to the idea of a little theatrical stimulation, are you ladies?"

Mabel now shot de Ravel a furious look. It was true to say that she looked distinctly uncomfortable at the thought of staying for the show after the meal, and it was also true to say that John felt distinctly uncomfortable at the thought of Derek taking her back. Quite how he was going to resolve the conundrum, however, he didn't know.

At this point, Diana Bonniface now stood up and raised her arm as high as it would go. De Ravel stared at her, and Derek put her out of her misery.

"Miss Bonniface," he said softly, "please, go ahead."

With the spotlight now shining in her direction, she lowered her arm to her side and took a deep breath.

"Well," she started, and then dislodged a frog from her throat before continuing. "When I was at Inspector Training last week, we were specifically told to look out for examples of pupils being given the opportunity to go on excursions. I expect that Mr Fitztumbleton could put this down as a pre-visit risk assessment. Is that not right, Mr de Ravel?"

Despite the woman's good intentions, de Ravel raised his eyes to the ceiling and then turned to John with an irritated look on his face.

"Perhaps, Mr Bentwick," he chimed tersely, "you would be so kind as to give Miss Bonniface a lift too when you head home in a minute. Mr Fitztumbleton, Mrs Milner and I can stay to enjoy the proceedings."

"No I bloody well will not!" John exploded. "I'm not bloody going anywhere without 'err..." he added, and pointed directly across at Mabel. "I'll give yer all a lift if I 'ave to, but she's got to come too."

To his dismay, Dawn now threw a spanner in the works.

"No! I refuse to go home so early."

Mabel's eyes widened in surprise. "I think you mean ... yes."

Dawn gave her a sarcastic look. "No, I definitely mean no."

"Yes."

"No!"

"Yes! And maybe you'd like to accompany me to the bathroom to freshen up as well," Mabel added, gritting her teeth as she said it.

Dawn's mouth pursed but she said no more. John rubbed his chin.

"Well, perhaps I'll get us some coffees. Whilst we sort this all out," he suggested and stood up. It was the only thing he could think of to bring this matter to a close. "Ladies, would you be up for a coffee at least?"

"No," Mabel now replied.

"Yes," Dawn countered, and grabbed Mabel by the arm. "Come on, sweetie, let's freshen up first. You said you want the toilets, and they are just over there." She pointed across to the other side of the room and stepped aside for Mabel to lead the way. Mabel glared at her, but stood up and grabbed her bag.

John followed them towards the bar. He watched Dawn's strange waddle and Mabel's beautiful sweep of the hips, and plodded, mesmerised, as the two of them continued their argument, oblivious of his existence behind them.

"We have to stop them going to the show," Mabel whispered urgently. "Derek will be mortified."

He felt a tinge of jealousy at the familiar way she said the man's name and, for the first time that evening, felt himself warming to her friend; Dawn wasn't having any of it.

"But Drivel is up for it, Mabe. You know that as well as I do," she explained.

And although John didn't know who this Drivel was, it sounded as though it was heading in the right direction.

Mabel sighed.

"But Derek doesn't know who Drivel is..."

"But Drivel thinks he does."

"Well, why on earth does Drivel think that?" Mabel asked, exasperated, and suddenly stopped in her tracks.

Not concentrating, John nearly bumped pelvis long into her back and only just swung to the side in time. Dawn glowered at him, and then put her hands on her hips.

"Well I don't suppose you understand a thing we're talking about, do you?" she snapped, acknowledging him at last. Despite himself, John obediently shook his head. It seemed to be an acceptable response, for she then 'tutted' and turned back to face her friend as if he wasn't there again. "Look, Mabe Babe," she huffed. "Drivel thinks Derek knows who he is because Lady Lovelick works for him. He's put the wrong two and two together and thinks that not only do Derek and Lovelick do this all the time, but that Lady Lovelick will be performing later on. I mean, did you see his face when he realised he'd missed Dick Whippington? At the end of the day, if

293

your darling Derek wants to get his outstanding grading he'd better stay and pretend he is Drivel's kindred spirit, or else."

John jolted in surprise. He didn't like the words *Derek* and *darling* sitting so closely together in a sentence. And who the hell was Lady Lovelick?

His ignorance was irrelevant. The three of them started walking again.

"I see your point." Mabel conceded, and John suddenly realised with regret that he'd reached the bar. The two women continued to walk away, deep in conversation, leaving him behind.

The last thing that reached him before he was out of earshot was Dawn's mordant tones saying, "But for god's sakes, Mabe, we've got to ditch Bonnie Langford first."

* * *

"Right!" de Ravel exclaimed, and rubbed his hands together. "Are we off to see this performance then?" His eyes sparkled with expectation.

Begrudgingly, John stood up. Quite what was so exciting about going to see a pantomime, he didn't know. Besides the women being dressed as men, and the men being dressed as women - which was something he couldn't comprehend, full stop - wasn't the audience meant to be mostly made up of children?

And whilst he was still trying to get his head around this odd contradiction, a deflating plastic blow up sheep wandered past and removed what little sense of reality he had left. At that moment, John gave up trying to understand why the music was so loud, and simply followed the rest of them into the other room.

As they walked through the dividing double doors, he breathed in and immediately regretted it. This time, far from being damp and mouldy, the malodorous perfume that hit his nostrils just stank like a barn full of randy steers. There was nothing stale or fading about this smell. Oh no, the aromatic stench of testosterone and recently soiled underwear was unique.

Briefly, he wondered if it was the kind of thing that might help Roger sort himself out, but then the beat of a new song began and the thought slipped from of his mind.

He turned his back to the empty stage and peered to his right. De Ravel was staring, captivated, waiting for the show to begin. To his left, Mabel's face was impassive, and next to her, Dawn's foot was tapping away. Further on, Diana Bonniface had turned whiter than a toothpaste technician's teeth. It was, however, the switch in Derek's expression as the performer appeared on the podium, however, that then made his blood run cold.

John turned around to see what had forced the headmaster's features to freeze, and his stare locked on.

Suddenly everything slotted into place. No red blooded male could have overcome the magnetism that was drawing all eyes to the front. As the thump of the rhythm began, the performance tapped into a primal instinct like a groin high Mexican wave, and left him in no doubt as to what was bothering old Fitztumbleton.

Derek was a punctilious man; he didn't like inaccuracy, and when John thought about it, it didn't make sense to him either. For how on earth could this be called Puss in Boots? As far as he was aware, cats had fur, and in this instance there wasn't a hair in sight. There were lots of tassels dangling around, and a few could even have been said to be providing whisker-like protection, but as it was, most were simply pivoting in a circular fashion from two vantage points far above the apex of the boots. So there wasn't a feline element to be seen.

All in all, it was both very perplexing and imprecise. And embarrassingly disturbing in the trouser department to boot, bearing in mind the woman of his dreams was standing nearby.

The song changed. A pelvic thrust marked the start of a new key, and the room was treated to the shine of a perfect full moon.

At this point, John managed to drag his eyes away and sought out Derek's face.

It hadn't altered.

He edged across to Mabel.

"I'm not sure this is quite what Mr Fitztumbleton had in mind," he whispered, but she couldn't hear a word. He tried again, only louder.

This time Mabel turned to him; her eyes narrowed.

"Well, tell that to your date," she spat, and pointed angrily across at Dawn, who had now progressed to perfecting her own groin grinding gyrations to the rhythm of the beat. John took in the tightly moulded top, short skirt and super sized earrings, and spotted what he'd not spotted before; the sight brought a lump to his throat.

He turned back to Mabel, dismayed.

"I never meant for 'er to be my date, yer know," he said as loudly as he could, and Mabel raised a sceptical eyebrow. "No, really," he reassured. "It was all an 'orrible mistake. She'd said that yer weren't going to be free tonight, 'cos yer were working, and then it just sort of 'appened."

"What did?"

John shrugged. "Well, I don't really know, but you seemed to know all about it on Wednesday when I saw yer in the shop, and then by this morning it was all too late. And I don't even remember mentioning Thursday to 'err at all. All I'd wanted to do was ask yer out again, but I never 'ad the balls."

His voice began to tail off as he realised that Mabel was struggling to hear again, and what was the point anyway? He'd already been usurped. This was like closing the stable door now that the horse had bolted. "Would yer like another drink?" he asked instead, imagining the clop of hooves as they headed off into the distance.

Mabel shrugged.

"I'll have a G&T if you are buying," she replied, and handed him her glass.

John looked at it. G&T, he repeated. And then repeated it again...

G&T.

G&T?

Wasn't that what Sandra Lovelock had prattled on about only earlier that week? *If I were to drink gin and tonic at school, I'd want ice and a slice to go with it, wouldn't I?* She had said, and she'd been particularly adamant too.

It gave him an idea.

"Would yer like ice and a slice?" he asked, and then added jokingly, "Yer can't possibly 'ave a G&T without ice and a slice, can yer?"

To his relief, Mabel smiled and nodded, giving her glass a little tap.

"Ice and a slice sounds good," she mouthed, and as she said it, her grin broadened and his grateful heart flipped.

This was the sign he'd been looking for, wasn't it? The connection. There was now a sparkle in her eyes which was giving him permission to hope; a chance to see opportunities, where others would normally see none; to take risks, when many would choose to keep their gobs shut.

But John Bentwick wasn't like the many.

As far as he was concerned, what he was being given here wasn't just hope; it was another chance. With all the machismo of his strength, and the sharpness of his mind, he had to show this woman that he was worthy. Prove that he was both a man of action and of words, which from the homework he'd done over the last few days he now felt that he could do. Fitztumbleton, Mabel, McFreece, the lot of them, they'd all told him to *Seize the Day*.

And now, he decided suddenly, he was going to seize it in style.

John Bentwick's little brain raced.

Seize the Day, it said, again, and again, and again. A good place to start, what with its Latin alter ego also beginning with '*C*'.

In farming, words beginning with '*C*' had value, there was Crop, Combine, Cow , so he was prepared to take this as a sign. And even if Google's long list of Latin expressions had now all but left his mind, '*C*' and *seize* had at least still forged their bond.

Finally, his mouth engaged, and his lips parted to shape the words that were going to set him on a new path.

"I really want you to know..." he began, but Mabel creased up her face as if she couldn't hear him. John tried again.

"I really want you to know..." he said, louder this time, whilst the music continued to pump away.

But still it was no good, and as they looked at each other, the blonde beauty removed her final tassel, and yet all John knew was that he had yet to seize the day.

This time he took a deep breath.

"I really want you to know..." he cried, and as the remaining grind of the hips ground, he repeated it one more time in a bid to outdo the last lingering chord, and finally managed to move on. "That I've decided to adopt your motto!"

Mabel raised her eyebrows expectantly and John felt a burst of pride.

"*Caveat emptor!*" he yelled, just as the music died and the room fell to a deathly silence.

The words rang out, bouncing off the stripper's wobbling breasts and then swiftly seeking sanctuary in the crease of her feminine buttocks; as all self-respecting words would when a man was talking out of his arse.

Mabel's hopeful features fell. Tears glistened in her eyes, and the look of hurt that bevelled every furrow in her forehead pierced his confused soul.

"What do you mean?" she rasped breathlessly. "What do you mean *buyer beware*? I'm not for bloody sale you know!"

And with that, she ran out of the room.

* * *

At that moment, one could have heard a flea fart.

Miss Bonniface appeared to be rattling through a mental image of the Inspector Training manual before she could frame a response, but otherwise even de Ravel seemed to wince. Derek scratched his ear awkwardly and muttered, "Well, quite." And the swish of the double doors swinging behind Mabel's disappearing form sounded in John's ears.

Dawn managed a 'tut'.

"Probably not a good idea to use that particular phrase, John Boy," she sighed, looking carefully at a nail. "Mabe's never been one for a pimp."

Mortified, he backed out of the room to a slow chanting applause.

John could feel his heart pounding. As the sound of jeering hushed behind the closing doors, it felt like it was going to burst. He could still picture the look on her face as she'd run out of the room, and it burned his sorry soul. Branded it. If she'd not reached the point of hating him before, she sure as hell had now.

He looked around; the bar was empty except for Frank, who was standing drying glasses with a 'you'll-not-sort-this-one-out' look on his face. John cleared his throat.

"'As a young lady run through 'ere just now?" he asked, quite pointlessly as Mabel couldn't have gone anywhere else. It seemed a good enough ice breaker though.

Frank put his cloth down and leant against the bar.

"Well, I've not seen a lady run through here," he mused, and then his face lit up. "But if you're looking for Mabel, she's just gone through to the front."

John faltered. Something told him that his loved one had just been insulted, but the full rationale had yet to sink in. On a bright sunny day, when he'd have had time to chew the cud with a young bullock such as Frank, he'd have stopped to mull this over and chat it through with the lad. But as things were, with the time nearing midnight, he opted instead for the bellow-like-a-bull option; snorted, and lumbered off.

Outside, with the moon hidden behind a thick layer of cloud and a broken street lamp flickering across the other side of the road, his vision took a few seconds to adjust.

A small crowd had gathered on the far pavement and its bulky shadow sputtered on a wall each time the light flashed. His eyes sought out Mabel's familiar shape, softly moulded breasts and a waist he could have fitted snugly within his hands, and spotted it.

John bristled.

Next to her, Stan Snouterton's willowy form stood firm against the bustle of newcomers as they joined the throng. Even in the dimness, John could see the man's hand edging up towards her buttocks, hovering with intent, lascivious to its fingertips.

His hackles quivered harder. He wasn't having that and marched across, barging a union jack t-shirt aside.

"Get yer 'ands off of 'er," he yelled, but the jeering crowd swallowed the noise and Snouterton went untold. Desperate, he tried to reach over to touch Mabel on the arm instead, but the man's broad hanger-like shoulders moved to block his path.

Frustration began to bubble. He needed to get her attention. The easiest thing would be to simply shove the bastard aside, but just as that decision was made, another patriotic beer drinker barged up from behind and knocked him squarely up against Snouterton's backside.

Snouterton shifted forward awkwardly and then looked around in surprise.

"Ah, Mr Bentwick," he oozed, "want a better view?"

As he spoke, he drew his left shoulder back to allow John to slip in next to him, blocking his path to Mabel even more. John glared but Snouterton ignored him.

"I never realised you were a school governor," he shouted.

It was an odd statement to make at this juncture, but the man clearly wanted to make a point about something. John eyed him suspiciously.

"'Ow did yer know that?" John yelled back.

Snouterton laughed.

"Mabel told me this morning when she phoned to rearrange our date. Said that she needed to do her bit for the inspection, and that she'd been invited to go out with the headmaster. Rather a tedious evening I expect."

John went to respond but the roar of the crowd suddenly reached a crescendo. He was out of time.

As the Cockerby church bell chimed midnight, out of the corner of his eye he caught a flash of white, a streak of red, and then the tinkle of a Christmas bell peeled.

An, "Ooooooh!" quickly aaaahhhed in unison from the crowd.

And a high-pitched, "Ho, ho, ho!" swiftly followed.

Chapter Seventeen

Sandra shivered. She'd thought that with a nice thick coat and black fur-lined boots she'd be warm enough. But no, not tonight. The day's events were obviously getting to her more than she'd realised. She adjusted the floppy winter hat further over her ears and strode on.

So this was what being in love with Derek Fitztumbleton had brought her to, was it? Marching through Cockerby Town on a chilly November night; all dressed up and nowhere to go. It wasn't good, was it? In terms of scraping the barrel she'd definitely reached the mouldy bits; despite having her misery as a worthy excuse.

Well. She thought it was a worthy excuse; for it had bloody hurt to hear it at the time.

Partners, the farmer had said. Yes, he had specifically referred to *partners*, and dearest, darling Derek had said nothing to disagree.

The memory stung even now as she thought about it; and the rest had become history. Her burbled explanation that she had a need that required fulfilling, had been consigned to the annals of verbal diarrhoea.

Then McFreece's abnormally sympathetic nod, was now confined to the annals of unexplained moments of empathy.

And the note made in the attendance register that Sandra had an emergency trip to the dentist... A Testament that would be there for ever more.

Absolute proof that history was in the making.

The school would survive without her. Drivel and his miserable sidekick would understand; *he'd* been instructed. And, most poignantly of all, Derek wouldn't even care. He probably never had.

She'd got home in a desperate state, banished Mr Perkins to the downstairs toilet, and cried her eyes out on her bed. They had been tears of frustration and hurt; tears for opportunities missed, those that were always just out of reach, and now would never be. Her eyes had burned with the viciousness of the salty liquid, and they were still, even now, as red as the rosy cheeks she'd painted on just before she'd walked out the door several hours later.

At least now, however, the cool air was beginning to help. It would have been nicer if the stars had been out, but the artificial glow of the odd street lamp was enough. And at this moment, with the safety of her suburban house far behind, she was striding into the future once again, determined to dig deep, change her aspirations and find a new pathway to happiness.

And with that thought, she adjusted the strap around her waist, hoisted the big brown sack she was carrying across to the other shoulder, and put her best hobnail-booted foot forward.

* * *

Bong! The first stroke of midnight struck.

Sandra could hear the catcalls. Admittedly, they were muffled by the wig, hat and beard, but a mocking jeer was a mocking jeer whatever the amplitude, and part of her was thrilled. It was the part of her that revelled in a crowd's attention, and she certainly had them captivated now. They were like putty in her hands; malleable as a crowd should be. Soft and squidgy and drunk, or so she hoped; the thought of there being someone proudly sporting a solid staff didn't appeal, that wasn't what this was all about. Mind you, she didn't really *know* what this was all about, but a stiffy brought on by a flasher dressed up as Father Christmas definitely wasn't part of it. Putty was, by far, the preferred option.

Bong! The street lamp briefly flickered off.

But there was also a part of her that was petrified. Adrenalin spawned from the exhilaration of performing in front of an audience was fine, that made perfect sense. But the adrenalin that was pumping through her veins at this moment had a different resonance; a resonance with which she wasn't familiar and one that, when coupled with a crowd with which she wasn't familiar, was making her feel uncomfortable. To *not* be mistress in command would be tantamount to needing help.

Bong! The street light sputtered on.

A puzzled voice jostled through the melee and fell, unwelcome, into Sandra's ears.

"He's rather skinny," it said, not without disdain. "I'd thought the FC Flasher was going to be a big lad, you know, a happy fatty, but this fella looks as though he'll barely have any flesh covering his bones when he finally undoes his coat."

"Yeah!" another similarly dismissive judge chipped in before Sandra had a chance to respond. "And now you come to mention it, where is his boner? Come on, Santa," it added, much to her chagrin, "show us what you've got."

Bong!

Behind the beard, Sandra scowled. This wasn't how it was meant to be; people weren't supposed to be telling *her* what to do. They were supposed to be shocked, horrified, perhaps even strangely fascinated, but certainly not telling her what to do! There was only one thing for it...

Bong!

She braced herself with a huge deep breath, and belted the bastard out.

"Ho, ho, ho!"

The words boomed into the night and the empty present-like boxes in the brown sack shuffled irritably on her shoulder.

The crowd guffawed.

"Ha, ha, ha, more like," someone said, and another laughed. Sandra bit her lip.

It hadn't been like this at M&S the other day. The people there had stared, be it briefly, she had held them in her thrall. When she'd carried out the act of revelation, displaying with pride the professionally moulded and perfectly skin-toned prosthesis, they had gawped with disbelief.

Well, that was how she wanted to remember it. Deep down, she knew the truth was slightly different, for in reality there had only been an eighty-five year old pensioner whose carer had dropped a bag of Werthers Original just at the critical moment. But, and this is still a point of note regardless of what anyone else thought, silent they had both been when they had eventually looked up, each gumming a sweet.

Bong! Impatience hung in the air. Still six more chimes to go.

Ye gods, Sandra thought miserably, as feet started to stamp with the chill. Have these heathens no sense of *the moment*?

The mob read her mind.

"Come on!" someone shouted with irritation. "It's getting cold out here. Show us yer bits and then we can all bugger off 'ome."

"Oooh look, I don't think it's going to be long. The wait that is," a new spectator clarified. "I can see a bulge under his coat. He *has* got something down there!"

Bong!

"I bet it's a courgette."

"I bet it's a parsnip."

Several people winced.

And in a bid to get a better view, a small group broke ranks and pushed their grubby bodies forward. Sandra gasped. This wasn't in the script; she hadn't given them leave. What in Saint Nick's name was she meant to do?

Filled with panic, she stepped back and felt the wall block her way. The chilly hardness pressed resolutely against her shoulders, and even through her thick woollen coat she could feel it thwarting her escape, indomitably standing its ground. Without thinking, she put her hand coyly over her groin and leant away to the side. Her eyes searched through the crowd, trying to read their faces; trying to work out which way things were going to go, and as the next bong chimed, she cursed herself. This had not been properly planned. All previous revealing's had been orchestrated in advance, considered down to the second, timed to perfection; But this had been a rush job. She'd allowed her precarious state of mind to sully her thinking and now she'd gotten herself into a pickle with a prickle that wasn't going to fool anyone up close.

Oh Derek Fitztumbleton! she cursed, as the next Bong! sounded out. What have you done to me? What have I become?

"Come on, Santa," a voice growled and interrupted her cerebral ramblings. "We can't spend all night staring at those two sticks of celery poking out from under yer coat. I can look at skinny legs, knobbly knees and big boots any day of the week. Bloody well get on with it, mate. Show us your North Pole and we'll give you a seasonal cheer!"

Applause rippled through the crowd.

Sandra cringed. It had only been a matter of time before that one had made it out, but hearing it now, it sounded even more naff than when she'd imagined it.

In the name of Jude, she thought in exasperation, what on earth had ever induced her to pick this particular disguise?

Bong!

But there was no time for inner contemplation. She ran her gaze across the crowd, and in the flicker of the street lamp the figure of Barnaby de Ravel caught her eye on the other side of the road. Sandra's mouth went dry. If he was here then Derek would be somewhere nearby too. She should have known he'd bring them to a place like this. The man was, without doubt, the most debauched of all minions. But putting aside such flattering accolades, it wouldn't do for him to recognise her whilst being derided by a crowd of drunks. If he thought she couldn't handle it, it might give him the wrong idea; it might give him delusions of grandeur and overegged ambition. It might – even - give him cause to consider taking over!

For one extraordinary second, Sandra realised she didn't care.

Bong!

But it was too late for such thoughts now. She'd started so she'd finish. With a flourishing wave of her arms, the sack of useless boxes fell to the ground, and the crowd jointly held its breath. As she waited one second longer for the final bell to chime, Derek's hunched form scuttled across her vision and she realised she was stuck between a wall and a hard thing, but at least she knew how to use it.

Bong!

The last button slipped undone.

The crowd gasped as if as one.

And John Bentwick said, "Bloody 'ell. That's the sort of 'elp my ram needs!"

* * *

"It's a woman!" someone exclaimed, and pointed, somewhat unnecessarily Sandra thought, in the direction of her groin. "Look!" the observant one added, "that thing's not real."

The click of a dozen mobile cameras sounded in unison, and another female voice added with a countrified, authoritative air, "No, it can't possibly be real. They don't come in that size naturally."

The reaction to this statement was mixed. The women giggled, and the designated drivers of the group agreed in sober manly tones that this sentiment was correct. There was some puffing out of chests amongst the over-the-limit brigade, but on the whole a sense of solidarity bound the men firm. This was not a moment for comparisons to be made; cold night and suchlike.

One pissed renegade, however, did fight against the grain.

"Oh, I don' knoww," he countered none too clearly, and wobbled in tenor right at the end. "Mine coul' cive it a goo' run for its money on a goo' nigh'."

A caterpillar load of worried eyebrows shot up, but the dissenter's girlfriend chuckled with cruel mirth and laid his claims to waste.

"Oh, shut up, Gary, in your dreams," she scoffed. "You just don't know when you're seeing double." And the wave of relieved laughter that rippled through was palpable.

The click of more cameras sniggered in the background, and someone cursed that *Facebook* was down.

Sandra realised with dismay that she was losing her audience. She tried a little wiggle and felt the strap-on sway menacingly from side to side. It was an impressive beast, even in daylight it was built to take your breath away, but from her vantage point the shine to the mock ridges and veins gave it a look of stunning authenticity. She watched it swing left then right, and admired its beauty.

For an instant, it held both her and her audience transfixed; but the moment was only brief.

"Don't you wave that thing at me, luv," a gruff latecomer warned, "or I'll 'ave to shove it somewhere where the sun don't shine," and the moment of magic was gone.

As the words landed in her ears, the straps began to cut in; this was all starting to get uncomfortable. Mentally, she rattled through ideas for reinforcement, but Natasha was safely snuggled up in her car boot, out of reach. Frantically, she wondered where else she could turn, and suddenly the naked truth hit her squarely, where no other truth could. There was nowhere else; she was exposed. Physically, of course, but that worried her no more than usual. No, what was most bothersome was that she had found herself unexpectedly stripped and displaying her inner stuff; she was suddenly emotionally nude.

Her eyes swung across the crowd and then on further to the other side of the road in desperation. They needed something to snag on, something to give her strength. Catching on de Ravel's nonchalant form briefly, she dismissed any hope of help from him, and moved her gaze on until it landed on his doleful associate instead.

Despite her precarious position, Sandra grimaced with disgust. She'd not liked the woman from the first moment they'd met. Sometimes, people with sour faces looked bitter and twisted because they were unhappy and that, on the whole, was a state of mind one could do something about. But sometimes, people with sour faces looked bitter and twisted because they didn't know how to be anything else. They simply lacked imagination, and the one thing that Sandra Lovelock thrived on was imagination. Imagination was what gave the world colour; imagination was what gave the world hope; imagination was a band from the eighties that still got her toe tapping on occasion. People like Bonniface, with their insatiable appetite for facts; the facts and nothing else, were the capitalists of the world of education. Left to their own devices, they would strip every layer of magic and mystery from learning, and hang each enchanting quality out to dry until it fell, desiccated, into a pile of dust. They would reduce every moment of wonder to a formula on a spreadsheet. They would dampen every lateral thought until all obeyed only the laws of the bottom line. For capitalists, the bottom line was about efficiency, supply and demand. For the likes of Miss Bonniface, the bottom line was efficiency and performance tables. Get that bottom line right, and the bun fight for school admissions each year was simply a replay of supply and demand. Nothing more; nothing less; it was a dog eat dog world. You snooze you lose; both were as blinkered, prescriptive and soul destroying as the other. Both had lost touch with what truly mattered.

Suddenly, Sandra knew what her quest tonight was to be. There wasn't much time to plan it, but Bonniface had to be brought down.

Booting the sack with a derisory kick, she breathed in deeply, submerged her pride and joy beneath the folds of her coat once more, and strode across to the other side of the road.

The crowd hushed and shuffled collectively behind her.

At first, only de Ravel spotted the shift in emphasis and, true to form, his eyes lit up with excitement. Behind her beard, wig and hat, he had no idea who she was, but he was waiting for whatever was coming next with eager anticipation. Sandra smirked; he was about to be impressed.

In the intermittent light of the street lamp, she came to a halt in front of the female inspector and wrapped her fingers around the edges of her coat.

The woman froze as her jaw dropped in horror, she turned to de Ravel for support, but he was already chuckling away.

"Take this, you silly sour faced tart," Sandra spat, and yanked the two halves of her coat apart again.

Behind her, a communal intake of breath sucked itself in. As the plastic member glistened in the flashing light, Bonniface's eyes widened with terror, and Sandra added a couple of pelvic thrusts for good measure.

"Go on, have a good look," she goaded, loving every second of her nemesis' discomfort. "Imagine what you're missing," she added, twisting from side to side to ensure that the woman could see the cockle in all its splendour. "Tell me how you'll put this..." and as she said the word, she did an extra hard thrust, "into your performance tables, and tell me how you'll add this..." again, another thrust added emphasis, "to your pupil progress charts, and let this..." one more time, "sort your gifted and talented from your tripe..."

She was getting into the swing of things now. It felt good to tell this blinkered bat that she was a leech that drained the life out of every teacher's enthusiasm; a blood sucker that left nothing but the dry bones of academia scattered on the ground.

As her mind rattled through more insults and her pelvis continued as if it had a mind of its own, the screech of tyres sounded in the background, and suddenly Sandra became aware that the crowd had started to part. Her gyrations ground to a halt.

"Let me through, please. Let me through," a rather indifferent, wearied-by-the-years-but-not-quite-ready-to-be-pensioned-off voice said. "*Coming through.*"

Someone laughed and then stifled the giggle instantly. Office Groundnut shot the offender a glare. He'd been separated from his cuppa for ten minutes now and he wasn't in the mood.

"Watch out, darlin'" a voice called. "'E's got one 'ell of a truncheon!"

And with that, the glimmer of a black and white uniform hovered in Sandra's peripheral vision, and then something tapped her on her knob.

Sandra looked down. Whoever it was that had called out the warning was absolutely right. Groundnut's baton did indeed put her appendage to shame.

"Come on then, Miss," he said dryly. "I'd normally say *Let's be having yer*, but in this instance I'm not sure that it's entirely appropriate."

A pair of handcuffs swung gently in his hand.

At that moment, both the sound of a second set of tyres squeaked in the background and de Ravel's eyes glittered with recognition.

As Sandra took in the inspector's appreciative but knowing look, Cockerby Chronicle's sleaziest reporter panted his way to the front.

"Oh fantastic," he puffed with relief once he'd clapped eyes on the scene. "I can see the headline already."

* * *

The last thing Sandra could remember hearing as she was bundled into the back of the police car was Drivel's bleating words, "Bonniface will behave, Your Ladyship. I will make sure she does!"

They were brave words for a minion, too brave perhaps, but she was too damned tired to worry about that now. It was hard to say whether anyone else had recognised her, but did it matter anyway? She gave her beard a little tug to test the hypothesis; it clung on firmly in place and the knowledge provided relief. Bugger! she thought; perhaps it mattered more than she wanted it to.

Disconsolate, Sandra reached over and started to pull the seatbelt across. It snagged, looping uncomfortably over the protruding bulge in her groin. Groundnut stared at her unflinchingly through the open car window, and smirked.

"You've been over-doing the limbering up tonight, Mrs Claus, I expect. Putting the *rude* into *Rudolph,* no doubt. Hubby out on the tiles elsewhere, is he?"

Sandra smiled sarcastically and watched as Groundnut turned away again, his huge arse leaning against the door and bulging through the open window. It was inevitable really, wasn't it? Policemen weren't known for their imagination either. She raised her eyes to the ceiling and yanked the strap-on dildo to the side and clicked her seatbelt into place.

This is it then, she thought. This is the end. What's left to look forward to any more? Derek Fitztumbleton will never be mine; Dr Drivel could be - woo hoo – not; and I'm a dominatrix who's lost her stuffing.

As the last thought rallied, all her enthusiasm for masterful control slid away. Where had it got her up to now? Nowhere, and when she looked at it carefully, she'd not been particularly good at it anyway. Of course, Monday evenings at *Dominantics* had not been a problem, people had always arrived in role right from the start. But otherwise, well, her command was hardly a resounding success. The Fridge had never succumbed; not even Billy Barber had managed to get the hint; and as for Peter Drayton, well, quite.

Which summed it up.

She was no more dominating than the failing head of a forgotten primary school.

As her maudlin thoughts escalated, Groundnut tapped on the roof of the car and the officer in the driving seat turned the key in the ignition. She watched him eyeing her in the rear view mirror as the engine sparked to life.

"Fancy women with beards, do you?" she asked caustically.

The eyes held her gaze. He cleared his throat.

"Shut up," he said firmly.

Sandra went to snap his head off, and then thought better of it. She sat back against the seat.

That was odd. Very odd.

It was a strange sensation, being obedient, submitting to the will of another. Yet inexplicably, she felt that it was actually rather nice having someone else to do all the thinking.

And as the seed of that idea took root, she looked at his smart uniform, all crisp and imposing, and mused that it wasn't an unappealing sight at all.

The car began to move forward and the crowd stepped to the side as it snailed its way through. From her goldfish bowl position, she looked out at the world, and the small subset of the world that was interested, admittedly very few, looked back at her. Suddenly, she felt vulnerable.

Sandra glanced down to find the button to shut the window and pressed it. But nothing happened. She pressed it again, and then again, but still there was no response. The cool outside air began to play with her beard whilst the noise of jeering voices rang in her ears and she felt a knot form in her stomach.

"Please," she rasped, and then faltered before continuing. "Please, can you shut the window?"

The chilly, commanding eyes looked back at her from the front and blinked.

"I said, shut up," he growled, and Sandra felt the knot leap into her throat.

She was at his mercy. There was nothing she could do. He had full control and she so wanted to ask him one more time, beg him to afford her a little protection from the leering faces, but she daren't. For he had spoken.

She peered outside, full of horror at her position, and only then realised with relief that the cogs were beginning to turn. As the glass slowly slid up, the authoritative eyes at the front continued to watch on. She felt his stare burning and finally recognised what that stare meant. She was safe. He was keeping her safe. As much as it was the duty of a minion to obey, so it was the obligation of a superior to protect, she flicked her glance back to the rear view mirror and revelled in the overseeing eyes. With his great strong uniform, and his truncheon by his side, he was watching and protecting; as long as she obeyed.

Sandra took her hat off and let herself relax. It felt good and it felt right.

Suddenly, extraordinarily, this new incarnation felt it had a future; Sandra the Serf.

Chapter Eighteen

"And so what did the flasher do next, luv?" the reporter asked an eager onlooker standing next to Mabel, pad in hand.

Mabel took a step back, keen to put some distance between herself and the press; it was best to leave all that to someone who wanted to waste their fifteen minutes of fame on a night like this. They'd all watched in fascination as the police car had driven off, Father Christmas' disconsolate face disappearing as the window had closed, but now the crowd was looking elsewhere for entertainment. Like a young child, its collective consciousness was getting bored and needed some light relief.

The interviewee thought earnestly for a couple of seconds and then answered the question.

"Well, she just sort of waggled it a bit."

Riveting stuff, Mabel thought. The papers were going to have to embellish things a little if that was the best they could get.

"*Just sort of waggled it a bit.*" the journalist repeated back to himself, as he wrote the quote down. "And tell me, was it a big 'un?" he then asked, pen held poised, and Mabel realised that she'd had enough.

She spotted John Bentwick ambling in her direction and pulled her coat tighter across her chest. God, this was all she needed, hadn't the man said enough already?

"I reckon Roger could do with seeing something like that, yer know," he drawled, and offered her his jacket. "Might make 'im up his game a bit, what do yer think?"

Mabel shook her head; at the offer, not the question. She presumed the latter was a pathetic attempt at a joke, and with *caveat* bloody *emptor* still echoing through her brain she wasn't in the mood for humouring him.

"Well best you go and have a chat with your pal Roger then," she snapped, but found to her disappointment that it didn't do the trick. More venom was required. "But failing that," she then continued, "why don't you just go and shag one of the sheep yourself? Set Roger an example, and make the most of the opportunities you've got 'cos you sure as hell ain't gonna have success anywhere else!"

There! She'd got the poison out at last; it was said.

For one whole second, Mabel felt a wonderful sense of euphoria, but then it disappeared and a dollop of self-loathing settled in instead. The man was uncannily like her daughter. He seemed to bring the worst out in her and she suddenly felt ugly and gnarled inside.

John frowned and looked as though he was trying to make sense of the suggestion. But to Mabel's relief, Dwayne sidled up, and snapped the conversation in half. Ditching her unhelpful rural chum, he dragged her aside, and Mabel gave the farmer a final rueful look before letting her mind move on.

322

"You'll never believe it, but it's Lady Lovelick!" Dwayne whispered louder than he'd intended and the journalist looked their way. Mabel surreptitiously moved another step back and grimaced.

"Who is?" she asked.

Dwayne smirked.

"The FC Flasher; it's Lovelick. I know it is. I've just heard Drivel muttering to himself."

"Oh my god, does Derek know?"

Dwayne raised a flawlessly manicured eyebrow.

"I doubt it," he scoffed. "Darling Derek is not exactly the brightest bulb in the circuit when it comes to these things, is he?"

Mabel shrugged. It was a reasonable assertion to make. Derek Fitztumbleton was currently wandering around like a lost lamb, and signs that he knew his senior teacher had just been arrested weren't apparent. Poor man, so helpful in some ways and yet so useless in others. It was hard to see what Ashley saw in him. Mabel's gaze roamed as she contemplated and, as if drawn by magnetism, landed on the Chair of Governors again. She noted that he had now been cornered by the reporter, and the unmistakable words, "well in fairness, she's right. Roger's scrotum is the size of a football," filtered back to her ears. She marvelled at how men could only ever focus on one thing at a time, and then parked the thought and turned back to Dwayne.

"Best Derek doesn't find out about Lovelick until this Ofsted thing is over," she decided. "The news would break him and then the school would fail."

Dwayne weighed up her words. "But how are you going to stop Drivel from saying anything, Mabe? He probably thinks your pal has a little red suit too and likes to join in on weekends."

Mabel glumly ran her fingers through her hair. For all his failings, Dwayne was right; she needed to think objectively here. Drivel obviously believed that Derek knew about Sandra's antics on a Monday evening, and he also undoubtedly knew that Dwayne wasn't a real Dawn too; which didn't help the picture at all. Derek Fitztumbleton was probably fast approaching the status of god just now, so close were his links with the likes of Lady Lovelick *and* the pussyless posse. Thinking logically, therefore, for the inspector to believe that there were two FC Flashers wasn't beyond the realms of possibility, and he'd probably want to join in to make it three. It was a tricky one. If Derek let slip that he was ignorant to all this malarkey, then who knew what de Ravel would do. Having worn his heart on his sleeve so blatantly this evening, the man could easily turn inspectorially hostile. These imaginative sorts were unpredictable at the best of times.

Mabel sighed.

"Leave it with me," she said, although not without hesitation. Her mind had already begun to hatch a plan but it wasn't one to relish. Life had taught her that answers often lay in the least obvious places and, Inspector Training notwithstanding, Diana Bonniface was beginning to look like her only hope. As she mentally rattled through ways that The Inspectorate's manual could interpret this situation, Officer Groundnut sauntered over to them and stalled her plans.

"Evening, ladies," he said and then did a double take at Dwayne.

Momentarily, Dwayne held his pose, but then a fascination with inanimate objects suddenly took precedence and Mabel knew something was up. First he looked at his nails, then the pavement, a brick wall, broken streetlamp, and only after all that, did he eventually pick a spot six inches above Groundnut's head on which to focus his stare. Groundnut cleared his throat. "Oh, it's you," he said disdainfully, and added a contemptuous cough. "I should have known that you'd be involved."

Dwayne huffed.

"Involved, me?" he snorted with indignation. "I'll have you know, Officer Groundnut, that I am no more involved in this whole thing than he is," and as he said it, he pointed arbitrarily at the person closest to them, who just happened to be John Bentwick. Groundnut followed the direction of his finger and frowned. Details of the finer points of a ram's penis were already jumbling through the air back at them, and Mabel noted that the journalist had stopped writing.

Groundnut heaved a deprecating "*hmmmmm*".

"That man made me spill my tea," he muttered, more to himself than anyone else, but it was clear that he was now distracted.

Dwayne flicked a questioning look across at Mabel, who shrugged and shook her head. Tea spilling hadn't ever been specifically listed as something to avoid. Of course it made perfect sense not to spill tea, just as it made sense not to fall down a flight of stairs, or serve up smoked mackerel with chocolate gateau. It was just one of those things one shouldn't do, but if one had to list all the things that one shouldn't do, one wouldn't have time for anything else.

Groundnut muttered something to himself, seemingly lost in replaying the great spillage in his mind, and Dwayne tried to wheedle his way out of the mistake whilst the man wasn't concentrating.

"Ah," he said, "well perhaps he's not a good example then. I was going to tell you that if you knew that man well enough, you'd know that he didn't have the imagination to be 'involved' in anything like this. And," he took a deep breath and then carried on, "with him being my date for tonight."

"He's your *date*, is he?" Groundnut interrupted, as a look of comprehension swiftly settled across his features. Dwayne shut up and nodded; Groundnut puffed. "Well that figures," he muttered. "No point in trying to get any sense out of you then," he added, and began to walk away, still mumbling something about PG Tips.

Mabel watched him wander off, thrown. The moment John Bentwick's name had been mentioned in the same sentence as the word 'date', a sharp pain had shot across her chest. She could feel its horrid little green tentacles already starting to dig in and taint her sorry soul. Oh for god's sakes, she screamed in her head, this is ridiculous!

It's only Dwayne, it's not even a proper date. Yet still she found the thought of anyone even *believing* that John was out with someone else a distinctly unpleasant concept. Nobody, not even Ashley's father, had caused this sort of ache, and that was the last time she'd felt anything this bad. It irked, really irked, and worse still it was an irksomeness that was tinged with a horrible sense of loss.

Dwayne grabbed her arm.

"Look, Mabe," he said urgently, and Mabel pulled herself together. "That reporter is heading towards Bonnie Langford. We need to stop him."

But just as he said it, Diana Bonniface looked up, spotted the journalist too, and disappeared inside Bob's Bar as quickly as she could.

* * *

Dwayne dashed in after her and Mabel tried to follow, but John caught her arm.

"I need to talk to yer," he said in a loud whisper.

"I think you've said more than enough," she spat back, pulling against his grip whilst her mouth responded before her brain could stop it. She'd meant the words, of course, if not quite the sentiment carried by her tone, but they were hardly going to help move the needle on their stalemate; which had grown very stale indeed. She went to put it in a different way, but a slimy condescending accent suddenly joined the proceedings, and Mabel watched John flinch.

"Well I think we have to say, Mr Bentwick, that we should both admit that the best man has won, hasn't he?"

It had seemed, only half an hour ago, that Snouterton had done a runner as soon as the police had arrived. But it was now apparent that he was no more able to miss out on the fun than de Ravel. John looked up, surprised. Mabel stood and shivered.

"Best man won what?" he asked, and Mabel despondently pictured him searching around for a rosette pinned to someone's lapel. She thrust the vision from her mind as Snouterton's smile widened.

"Why, the lady, of course," the insurance broker explained, still eyeing Mabel with his lustful gaze. She shivered for a second time, realising it was an odd sensation to have someone mentally undressing her and not want to follow it up with the real McCoy. Misinterpreting her shake, John went to take off his coat, but then changed his mind and Mabel cursed herself for being so short with him earlier.

"Lady? Who?" he asked instead, and Mabel bristled.

"I think he means me," she said coldly, and Stan K. nodded.

"That headmaster is a lucky man," the snout explained, and this time it was Mabel's turn to frown. John Bentwick's face darkened.

"And why is 'e a lucky man?" he asked, and Mabel sighed.

"I think he means me," she repeated, and again Stan K. nodded.

John's face darkened further. "Bloody 'ell 'e's a fast worker," he grumbled. "'is wife only left 'im a few days ago. I wish my..."

"Yes we know," Mabel interrupted and shot him a frosty look. "I expect you wish Roger would take a leaf out of his book. Well, I think I need to break something to you, John Bentwick. Roger can't read, and if his cock isn't working quite how you want it to, it probably has something to do with the pair of football size knackers stealing the show. You shouldn't judge a book by its cover!"

There, she thought, that'll throw him; and it did. John went to reply, opened his mouth but nothing made its way out. He tried again, opening it a little wider, but still remained mute. Even Stan Snouterton was stunned into brief silence, although that probably had more to do with the fact that he didn't have a clue who Roger was. Mabel looked at him and decided she wasn't in the mood for providing enlightenment, which was lucky, for at that moment, Dwayne reappeared, with a very worried expression.

"Oh my god, what's wrong?"

Dwayne dipped his head towards the inside of Bob's Bar, and was about to reply when his eye caught sight of Stan. To Mabel's frustration, all that was waiting to be said then instantly flitted out of Dwayne's brain as he switched into seduction mode. A hand straightened out the hair, a tongue ran across the lips, and a twinkle suddenly sparkled behind two sets of batting lashes. Mabel had seen it all before; nothing could be done.

"Well, hello, big boy," Dwayne purred, and pressed his lips together in a smooch. "Look what Santa left behind," and true to form, Snouterton's eyes lit up.

Mabel raised hers to the dark, cloud-ridden sky, and took a deep breath. When distracted, Dwayne was impossible. It was likely that even Snouterton had met his match.

"Well, hello to you too," he slimed back. "Didn't your friend and I meet the other day, Mrs Milner?" Mabel nodded, the new formality not lost on her, and Stan raised an appreciative eyebrow before turning back to the farmer. "Well, it looks as though you and the headmaster have both been enjoying a lucky night, Mr Bentwick. I didn't know you had it in you to pull a little corker like this."

As he said it, he winked at Dwayne again, who tittered predictably back, and John Bentwick's jaw fell.

"Oh, n-n-no," he stammered, "she's not with me."

Dwayne sniffed dismissively.

"Oh yes she is," Mabel snapped, and forced a terse smile at him for good measure.

"Well only temporarily," John insisted. "If Mr Snouterton 'ere wants 'er, 'e can 'ave 'er. I won't stand in 'is way."

John looked imploringly into Mabel's eyes as he said it. She could see that he meant every word and, of course, it was exactly what she wanted to hear. Except. Mabel wavered. Her loyalty to her friend demanded a degree of indignation, and her loyalty to herself, well, come to think of it she'd not got that bit sussed in life yet. There was only one thing for it; to speak in terms he'd understand.

"Now listen to me, John Bentwick," she said slowly but meaningfully. "Dawn's not one of your sheep that you can just pass around, you know. My friend is a human being." Dwayne nodded as she said it. "With feelings and self-respect," Mabel faltered slightly at that, but carried on "and you can't just shout *caveat emptor* at every woman you see."

His forehead creased with concern.

"Oh I never said she were for sale," he replied defensively, but that only inflamed Mabel even more.

"But I am, I suppose!" she cried.

"I'd buy you," Stan chipped in, and John and Mabel turned to look at him.

"No!" they both shouted in unison, but then Mabel remembered she was talking to her prospective new boss and decided that the adamant nature of that statement needed tempering. "I mean, I'm not for sale either," she added quietly, and then felt all her energy dissipate away. "Look, I'm sorry, gentlemen," she muttered finally, "but I'm cold and I need to go and speak to somebody inside. So if you'll excuse me," and with that, she smiled a pathetic smile and left the three of them to it.

The last thing that Mabel heard as she walked back into Bob's Bar was Stan K. Snouterton saying, "So where does this Roger chap come into all this, you gorgeous little thing? And will it be fisticuffs if I take my turn first?"

* * *

The bar was empty but for one dazed female inspector, a disoriented headmaster, and a punctured plastic sheep. Mabel looked at the blow-up beast, wondering if the horns were in the wrong place, and then kicked herself. Stop it, she thought; forget the farmer and just enjoy the warmth.

"I don't think any of this was covered at Inspector Training," Diana Bonniface lamented, as Derek disappeared off to find the gents' loo. Mabel passed her a tissue and took a seat. "And I really don't remember Puss in Boots being quite like that. I always thought the lead part was a girl dressed as a boy, or perhaps," her eyes suddenly lit up as she said it. "Perhaps that was what outside was all about. Gosh," she then added, "I hadn't thought of that, do you think that's what it was? A new theatrical device to have half the show inside, and half the show out?"

It had to be said that Mabel had overlooked this option when she'd rattled through the possibilities earlier, but the twinkle of temporary madness glittering in Bonniface's eyes did offer some sort of explanation; and a gift horse was still a gift horse however it was presented; an oral inspection was not required.

"Yes I'm sure I saw something on a flyer somewhere," she replied vaguely, hoping it would suffice. "It's the latest fad; gives people a little exercise," and then she realised she was losing it too; probably best just to leave it there.

Bonniface nodded, reassured. "Not really material for children though, is it?" she said, appearing to have recovered a modicum of school-mistressly sense. Mabel shook her head. The female inspector reflected further, "Lucky Mr Fitztumbleton decided to do a full pre-visit inspection then. I mean, trying to keep tabs on all the pupils whilst moving from one location to the other in the dark, it wouldn't have been easy, would it?" Again Mabel shook her head, but decided that the insanity had, if anything, gone up a notch. "I'll have to check he writes up his report properly tomorrow," the woman added finally, and then seemed to run out of steam.

Mabel spotted her chance.

Without thinking, she sniffed. It was something she often did when she was about to say something bordering on dodgy, one could call it her 'tell', but she didn't reckon the woman would notice and the current conversation had undoubtedly had its day. It was worth taking the risk.

"So," she started, and then cleared her throat awkwardly before continuing, another sign to those who knew her well, "You'll be, er, giving the school a good grade then, will you?"

It was a mistake. Whether it was the deep-seated passion that the woman had for the subject, or just that her moment of lunacy had passed, Mabel didn't know. But as the words slipped out, Diana Bonniface instantly held Mabel in the iron grip of a steady rational gaze, and 'tutted'.

"Mrs Milner!" she exclaimed. "You aren't trying to get me to admit to a predetermined opinion before we have finished our inspection, are you? At Inspector Training, they told us again and again that we must keep our eyes and our minds open right up to the end of a visit. We have to stick to the six 'Ps'; never allow prejudices, preconceptions, pupils, parents, paperwork, or piña coladas to prevent us from seeing the truth." Mabel's forehead creased. "Yes, the last one is a bit odd, I'll grant you," Bonniface conceded, wrinkling her nose too, "but an inspector was caught over indulging during a visit recently, and the powers that be felt they needed to be more precise from now on. They couldn't sack him, you see, because the union proved that his training had been inadequate as it hadn't specifically warned him against the dangers of drinking piña coladas whilst on duty, but suffice to say, Mrs Milner, the six 'Ps' is a creed I have sworn to uphold, and uphold it I will!"

Mabel nodded automatically; integrity was no reason to dislike the woman. Obsessive rule following without question was an issue, to be sure, but one had to let integrity have its head. Besides, it now struck her that once Diana Bonniface had given her word on something, she stuck to it; the quest, therefore, was to get her to give her word. Mabel knew of only one way for that to be achieved. She suggested a vodka and tonic and the woman went to start another lecture but Mabel overrode her.

"Don't worry, Miss Bonniface," she assured with compelling firmness, "there won't be a piña colada in sight," admittedly, the words did slip out accompanied by a wince, for the phrase was particularly pertinent to what had gone on just that very evening, but fortunately it appeared that Inspector Training had not covered such double entendres in its manual. The woman was oblivious and Mabel was free to continue without further worry. "It's just to enable us to wind down after all the excitement this evening," she finished off, and then flashed a surreptitious wink at Frank before sitting back in her chair.

Bonniface looked dubious, but already the chink of ice could be heard in the background. As the glug, glug, glug of multiple measures sounded, followed by the momentary ssshhhh of tonic topping up, Bonniface relented and Mabel felt herself relax.

"Here's to Lower Bushey Primary," she said once their drinks had arrived, and then raised her glass, keeping her eye steadfastly on the woman's face, as she dropped her next bombshell. "And here's also to hoping the papers are kind to you and Mr de Ravel in the morning."

It exploded with deadly accuracy; Bonniface's head jerked up.

"Papers? What papers?" she gasped, horrified. Mentally, Mabel patted herself on the back.

"Oh," she replied, and waved her hand dismissively, "hopefully just the Cockerby Chronicle. Well, unless the nationals are a little short on content in the morning.

335

When we go outside, the journalist will be able to tell us."

"Journalist? What journalist?"

"The one outside, following the policeman around like a lost sheep."

"Policeman? What policeman?"

Mabel sighed. The conversation, although now a little predictable, hadn't yet got her to her goal. Stating the bleeding obvious was obviously required.

"The one taking statements outside?"

"Statements? What..."

"The statement that you will no doubt be asked to give as an upstanding member of the community keen to support our law enforcement officers in every way she can."

Bonniface went white. "But Mr de Ravel and I. We can't... I mean... it wouldn't... How can we...?" And then her words petered out.

"Oh, you don't need to worry," Mabel soothed. "I'm sure your superiors will understand. I mean, they couldn't possibly judge you without hearing the whole story first, could they? Wouldn't that be basing an opinion on a preconception? Isn't that what you call predetermination?"

For a brief moment, Mabel wondered if she'd overdone the convincing argument, for Bonniface actually seemed to consider what she was saying as though it had merit. But then the anticipated doubts began to set in and the woman's face turned paler by the second.

"I think they only apply the six 'Ps' to inspector visits. I'm not sure it works that way internally amongst the staff. But putting that aside, Mrs Milner, couldn't we just disappear out the back? We'd avoid having to make a statement altogether and then we'd also be able to keep out of the way of the journalist."

Mabel sucked in her breath. She'd guessed right; the unfailing hidden shallow entitled *If all else fails, protect the good name of The Inspectorate* had been ingrained by Inspector Training. Inwardly she celebrated; outwardly, her forehead creased.

"But wouldn't you be faltering in your duty as a public servant if you did that?" she asked. "I mean, an influential person like you, Miss Bonniface, would bring credibility to the proceedings. That poor policeman out there is having to work with nothing but drunks at the moment. Your words of wisdom could make such a difference to his task."

"But is there not a way out the back?" the woman asked again, ignoring the suggestion, an increased note of desperation now creeping into her tone.

Mabel shrugged. Hurrah for Inspector Training! Time for stage two.

"We'll have to ask Frank," she replied, and turned to get Frank's attention.

The barman looked up on cue. She knew Frank. She and Frank went back a long way. She knew that he would have been listening to every word of their conversation whilst pretending that glass wiping was what he lived for. He'd help her out. "Frank, this young lady is hoping to avoid the police. Is there a way out the back?"

It was Frank's turn to suck in his breath.

"Oh, I don't know," he grimaced apologetically. "The management are keen to keep on the right side of the fuzz." Unfortunate turn of phrase, bearing in mind the nature of the establishment, but Mabel wasn't going to split hairs at this juncture; Frank was doing ok.

"Oh, please!" Bonniface implored. "I really can't be seen out the front again, it would be the end of my career. Oh, Mrs Milner, is there anything you can say to convince him?"

Mabel paused. She could push her luck and go another circuit on the argument just to make the charade look wholly convincing, but if she took that risk Bonniface might crack and all would be lost, and besides, she needed to keep Derek away from de Ravel and she'd already worked out a plan for that which required accurate timing. So in the end, she nodded.

"There might be, although you'll probably need to offer him something in return."

Bonniface's eyes widened in horror. "Oh good Lord," she gasped.

Mabel saw her chance to go in for the kill.

"Well," she huffed, "if you're not prepared to have a little how's-your-father with him, then I don't know what to suggest."

The woman wriggled in pain. "I'll do just about anything but that," she promised. "Please, just let me know what," and Mabel thanked Frank's lucky stars for him, and prepared to thrust home the final blow.

Leaning forward, she wiggled her forefinger for the female inspector to come nearer, and then looked over her shoulder as if to check that no one else was listening.

"Well," she said softly, and Bonniface moved in even closer, "Frank's daughter is at Lower Bushey Primary," she lied. "And a fantastic inspection grading would definitely make Frank both a very happy, and a very amenable, man. If you could give him your assurance that you'll look particularly favourably on the school, then I'm sure he'll be happy to look more than favourably on your situation. But," Mabel then sighed, and sat back in her chair, "I guess the six 'Ps' get in the way, don't they? What a shame. What a perfectly, petty but pissing, pain in the proverbial posterior, eh?"

The woman shook her head.

"Consider it already arranged," she assured without a second thought, and also sat back in her chair relieved. "The only thing now is to work out how I'm going to persuade Mr de Ravel."

Mabel was about to say that she doubted that that would be a problem, but Derek returned from the bowels of Bob's bogs just as she was about to speak.

"Persuade Mr de Ravel to do what?" he asked, and lowered himself into his seat.

Bonniface looked at Mabel in panic, but Mabel had it covered.

"Persuade Mr de Ravel to take her home," she answered, and winked at Bonniface as she said it. "And that reminds me, Mr Fitztumbleton, I need to get home as soon as possible too. Do you think you could give me a lift now? I think it might be best if we all sneak out the back."

Chapter Nineteen

John looked through the windscreen and rubbed his eyes. God they were tired. They felt as crusty as a cow's arse, which was making judging distance almost impossible, and as he thought the flaky thought, he realised that he'd pulled up onto the verge a bit short and wondered if it was worth reversing and trying again. It wasn't a busy road, but the last thing he needed at this moment was for someone to ram themselves up his backside. Which reminded him, where was Roger?

He scanned the tupping paddock for signs of life, but the flock were obviously just over the brow of the hill; out of sight, playing hard to get.

Bugger! This wasn't going to be a two minute check then. John gave his chin a thoughtful scratch and concluded, having not got things quite right most of the time recently, that the extra effort to straighten up the car was probably required.

The chassis creaked its objection, as the tyres slipped on the dewy grass, but once the handbrake had declared definitively who was boss, John let the engine die and the place fell silent again.

He sighed.

He'd always liked coming here, away from the hurly burly activity of Lower Bushey and the thronging crowds in the Co-Op. It was a place of solitude, somewhere where he could think without too many things making demands upon his mental capacities; which in this case, was very much needed today. Four hours sleep wasn't enough for an active man to live on. He could get away with it once in a while, but that was his lot. His mother had always warned him about burning the candle at both ends, and he'd not understood the cryptic message until this moment. She'd waxed lyrical about the benefits of a simple lifestyle, early to bed, early to rise; that type of thing, and only now did it make sense; she had married *into* the Bentwick family, but John was a Bentwick by blood. The thought of him adding a new facet to the name had always been a concern.

A great tit suddenly chirped from the protection of the hedge, warbling for the world to take heart and take stock, and John closed his eyes. Such a revitalising call it was, so invigorating. It was a noise that could nourish the weariest of souls and fuel the weariest of minds, and boy did he need that. There was a lot that required sorting in his head; not the least being that of women.

Take Mabel for starters; bloody hell hadn't he gone and blown that one good and proper? After all the ridiculous stuff that had come out of his gob, unintended as it had been, it was no wonder that she had wanted Derek to take her home. He had tried to offer, really he had, but she had insisted on Derek driving her back and it had made him feel sick to the core. Not even stinking

Stan Snouterton had got a look in. Although to be fair, he had been attending to 'other things' by then.

A horse whinnied in a paddock nearby.

Which brought him to his next point.

This Dawn woman. How on earth had he ended up taking her as his partner?

How?

No really. HOW?!

Even as he asked the question of himself now his shoulders lifted in despair. Not a word had passed his lips to prompt such an event, and yet so it still had been. He'd not have believed such things possible if he'd heard his pathetic little story recounted in the pub. Could arrangements really be agreed when no sound had been made? Apparently so, although, to her credit, she had at least tried to repay him with some advice.

"Ditch the ram," she'd counselled, as he'd driven her home. "If he's not rogering like a rabbit by now he never will be. And," she'd then added, eyeing him up and down as though the very fact that he could speak English was a surprise, "leave the use of foreign languages to foreigners, for god's sakes. Stick to what you know. And really," she had eventually finished off, "if you want to win Mabel over, all you have to do is make her feel special."

And that had been the suggestion that had flummoxed him most. The honour he had bestowed upon the woman only earlier that week had hitherto been unknown. What more could a person have wished for than to be the first to be introduced to Roger? She'd even been ahead of Bob; that was how special she was to him.

He'd pleaded his case as he'd driven, and Dawn had listened politely.

"Well it must just be a man thing," she had offered finally, and that had then been the end of constructive conversation for the subject had moved on to her own concerns. Saturday was the day of the big date, and boy-oh-boy, apparently, did she have a surprise for Stanley K.

John had cringed when she'd said it, and thinking about it now made him squirm even more. Was that how Mabel thought about Derek? Was she cooing over his heroic status? Was she replaying his every word in her mind? John shuddered. Well, quite. The thought was too 'orrible to consider.

A cow mooed in a neighbouring field.

No, he decided adamantly. All thoughts of Mrs McFreece would have to wait; it was definitely time to get moving.

Taking himself in hand, John clambered out of his car, slammed the door and stretched. Whatever else was falling apart in his life, he had to remember that glorious mornings like this made it all worthwhile. They were nature's way of putting what had happened the day before firmly in the past and starting all over again. They brought perspective, and as a more optimistic sheen nestled into place, the dew laden air slipped into his lungs and chased away the stale mouldiness from the night before. Within two more breaths, he felt like a new man and no longer quite so tarnished by the ravages of his failings.

He scanned the horizon for signs of life and caught the chirrup of what sounded like a blackbird; nature's bugle-call for action.

Listen to the little bleeder, he thought. Singing its little heart out, again and again and again. Always the same sound, never a change, just a warble and a beep, a warble and a beep, and again a warble and a beep, pause, beep, beep, beep.

Beeeeeep.

John sniffed. Perhaps he was more tired than he'd realised; Blackberry vs. blackbird wouldn't normally have been a contest, and he now had a voice message to deal with.

He listened to the crackling recorded tones of Stanley K. Snouterton and grimaced.

"Just wanting to clear the air. Believe you are a man of your word. She really is a delicious little thing." John scowled; if the man was back onto Mabel again he'd kill him. *"Totally unique"* Snouterton's drone continued. *"And you did say you wouldn't stand in my way,"* John's frown hardened. *"So I reckon I need to get in there before this Roger chap makes too much headway."* The furrows deepened. *"Plan to show her my good side and give her friend, Mabel, the job."* Relief slipped in. *"Just need that reference from your Titzfumble fellow and it will be sorted."* The seedling of a plan took sprout. *"If you can't buy 'em to try 'em, then you have to use a*

different ruse, eh?" And Snouterton's slimy laugh slid into John's ear and the message ended.

Puzzled, John threw his phone onto the passenger seat and hauled his tired body over the gate. Something Snouterton had said had given him an idea, but if he'd learnt nothing else this week, it was that ideas needed to be left to rumble before being let loose. Let an idea run too soon and all went horribly wrong; like trying to seize the day when what one was thinking about was buying a second hand tractor. Do what comes naturally first, John, a little inner voice insisted. Wait until you've checked yer flock before yer start to think.

Reassured by the strategy, he put his best foot forward. Unfortunately it was his right foot, which also happened to be the wrong foot, for the left one would have done a better job at missing the pile of sheep droppings. He imagined, rather than felt, the subtle yielding of the pellets as they gave generously under his sole, and philosophically made a mental note to take his wellies off when he got to the school.

A cow lowed again in the distance.

Yes, Mrs McFreece would give him no end of grief if she saw him marching around the place in his boots.

Accepting his fate wryly, he started to plod.

As he walked, heartening baas began to filter into his ears, bouncing over the furrows from somewhere beyond the crest of the hill, and he pondered whether they were more vocal than usual today. A happy bunch perhaps; footloose and fancy free. By Jove, he reflected wistfully, what it must be like to live the life of an unfettered ewe.

Free to roam and gain fulfilment from the simpler things in life. Who knew? Maybe Roger was even doing the fulfilling right now. After the night John had just had, it would certainly be a gratifying sight. Not perhaps enough to outweigh his despondency regarding Mabel but enough to give that rumbling plan of his a bit more of a spurt.

John's pace quickened.

He reached the top of the knoll, breathing heavily, and cast his eyes around. His glance bounced across the hillocks and hummocks, searching for a sign, but the little sods appeared to not to want to be found. Where the bloody hell are they? He wondered, hearing their regular calls but still not able pinpoint where they were. Something didn't feel right. They'd never played hide and seek quite this determinedly before and it was beginning to get on his nerves.

He forced his gaze to soldier on till eventually it found what it was looking for.

John swallowed hard.

People didn't believe in ascribing animals with emotion but, as far as John was concerned, sheep didn't appreciate bad news any more than humans did. The spinney at the bottom was making it hard to see things clearly, but the ewes were definitely steering clear of one particular part of the field, and from the sounds of things they were staying upwind too.

His eyes strayed on and finally rested on a lone muddy mound lying in the longer grass. It wasn't moving. Either Roger was taking his morning snooze more seriously than normal, or something was wrong.

Within a few steps, John realised his worst fears were the correct ones. He found Roger terminally slumped in a heap, with his humongous appendage lying pink and glistening in the grass.

Despite himself, he let out a sorrowful sigh. He'd had such high hopes for this ram, such dreams, but now it looked as though just as Roger had discovered his purpose in life he'd gone and bloody snuffed it.

John thrust his hands on his hips to think.

Shepherds weren't meant to be sentimental types, he knew that, but he was going to miss this bastard. The two of them had shared an oddly ambivalent interest towards the fairer sex until recently and, without realising it, that joint hesitancy had helped them forge a bond.

He drew his eyes away from the prostrate lump with difficulty and looked up. This was a sad day, but as that great tit had reminded him only minutes earlier, one had to take stock, didn't one? One had to grasp one's memories and tuck them neatly away. Dig deep and find the strength to go on; peer around and seek for signs of hope.

And that was what he did. Along where the sky met the earth, his eyes roamed and took in the undulating brown patches that inferred the ground was nicely manured. What he saw confirmed what he needed to have confirmed. Life went on. Always, in its own inimitable way, it never gave up.

And taking strength from that thought, he let his eyes move on to track where his flock had now moved, and where his future lay.

His heart gave a jolt.

An unexpected splash of blue was mingling amongst the natural hues. John looked closer to be sure, and took in the sight of a herd of cobalt coloured backsides parading their wanton fecundity.

He sighed in disbelief.

Not only had Roger discovered his purpose in life, but he had set his owner an example as well.

Not only had they shared a bond, but the two of them had secretly shared ideals too.

Well, John thought to himself as he jumped back into his Land Rover, I'm not one to be told twice, which wasn't strictly true, but it sounded good. He would come back and sort Roger later, allow him a bit of oneness with nature first. But for now, he had more pressing things to do. Yes, he had to seize the day, yet again, only this time do it properly, without resorting to redundant verbal gimmicks.

* * *

John wondered briefly if he should turn his wellies upside down as he slipped them off outside the school, just to thwart the local pigeons, but then changed his mind. Crushed sheep droppings and ram's semen were not what welcoming entrances were based on. It didn't cross his mind that school entrances were not renowned for their stinking man-sized wellies full stop, and so continued in blissful ignorance to de-boot before ringing the bell.

Mrs McFreece looked up.

"You're not due here until later," she said with consternation as he walked in. "The inspectors have a lot to get through this morning without you getting in the way."

John felt suitably welcomed and took another step forward.

"I know. It's Derek I've come to see."

"Well he's not in yet."

He stopped in his sweaty socked tracks. That wasn't what he'd been expecting and now he felt his stomach twist.

"Well, what time are yer expecting 'im in then?" he asked, desperately shoving aside visions of Derek and Mabel locked in early morning coital bliss.

The Fridge humphed.

"He'll be here when he gets here, Mr Bentwick," she responded dryly, and then added, "but he also has a lot to get through without you bothering him too."

Don't we all, hovered on his tongue, but John held it at bay. Unsubstantiated visualizations aside, he had a plan to pursue and he needed to keep this woman sweet. Only once he'd got what he had come for would he give the grumpy old sow two barrels, possibly literally, but not a minute before. As Roger had so well illustrated, patience was a virtue and all good things came to those who waited. So in honour of his ram's memory, he shrugged amenably instead.

"Well don't worry, Mrs McFreece, I won't be taking up much of 'is time. I just want to sort out a little outstanding matter regarding a reference for a friend of mine, and then I'll be out of 'is way."

The Fridge lifted an eyebrow. "A reference?" John nodded. "It's not for that Milner woman, is it?"

John cocked his head. "And what if it is? I'm 'ere to make sure Mabel Milner gets the reference she deserves."

Mrs McFreece's nostrils now spread into a fully-fledged flare.

"But that's just it, Mr Bentwick," she stated wryly. "What Mabel Milner deserves is not what Mabel Milner has requested, although she's got you all running round like mad march hares, hasn't she?" As she said it, her nose quivered further with indignation. "I bet," she then muttered, "if I were to ask any of you for a reference, you'd all run a mile." More like thirty, John estimated, but kept that thought to himself. "I've worked my fingers to the bone here trying to keep this place straight, and all the thanks I get is, is..." she stumbled on, and John waited for confirmation that anyone had ever thanked her for being such a stroppy mare, but it didn't come. She grabbed a tissue and dabbed the corner of her eye instead. "That woman is a tart, Mr Bentwick," she finally finished off. "And at the end of the day, one should always call a spade a spade."

At that moment, the front door buzzed. The Fridge reached across in irritation and pressed the button to admit the next poor unwelcome visitor, and then turned back to him.

John cleared his throat. He was now confused by her mixed metaphor. How could Mabel be a tart and a digging implement at the same time? Both had their merits, of course, but he still needed some clarity. Was Mrs McFreece likening Mabel to an apple, rhubarb, or even, dare he hope, blackberry tart? Or was she referring to something else far more unpleasant altogether?

"Is that a fruit one or something more akin to the Bakewell variety?" he asked, deciding to tackle the spade aspect after this had been cleared up first.

The secretary frowned.

"What on earth are you talking about?" she snorted, her face creasing up with disdain.

Two sets of footsteps sounded behind him, one pair stopping and another younger pair, trotting off to the cloakroom. John was desperate to see who it was, but now was not the time. So instead, he steadfastly held the secretary's glare with his and bent down closer for good measure. She wasn't going to get away with this.

"Well," he said in a tone so soft but firm that the woman's eyes widened with surprise, "you've just said that she is a tart, Mrs McFreece, and I want clarification as to which type of tart you're talking about. I mean, a woman as clever, kind and gifted as 'er needs to be referred to in the correct way."

The Fridge sniffed.

"But a tart is just a tart."

John smirked. Now he knew he had her.

"Oh no," he sighed meaningfully, "there's no such thing as *just* a tart. There's all sorts of wonderful combinations that yer can 'ave, and I think the right one needs to be identified if you're going to describe an extraordinary woman in such a way. Of course, my simple tastes lead me to go for something naturally flavoursome like good old bramley and raisin. But it could be argued that one should look at the more exotic types like lemon curd instead. All in all, therefore," he then sighed, "I would say..."

At that moment he was interrupted.

"I'm so sorry to cut short this fascinating culinary conversation," a sweet but embittered voice said, "but I need to let you know that Miss Lovelock won't be in today."

John swung round in surprise to see Mabel's drawn face staring back. She looked tired, dark circles and pale cheeks deadening her features. Yet still she was as beautiful as ever, with a natural loveliness that even now warmed both his heart and his underpants. To his discomfort, he felt himself rise to the occasion.

The Fridge frowned, oblivious. "What makes you think that?" she snapped, but Mabel shrugged before she'd even finished speaking.

"I've just bumped into Miss Bonniface on the way in," she explained, and her expression implied that said bumping had not been entirely by mistake. She continued, "We had a long chat, she and I, and most significant to this discussion is that she has apparently spoken to Miss Lovelock already this morning, and the upshot is that you'll need to get a supply teacher in." Having communicated her point, she then paused, holding The Fridge's stare with her own, clearly determined to ensure that the message was received. The secretary's face went as dark as a blueberry pie, but she nodded. Only then did Mabel turn to John again, and he was able to see properly in her face what he'd suspected he'd just heard in her voice. It cut him to the quick. "And that's a very lucky lady you're describing, by the way, Mr Bentwick. I'll pass the compliments on to Dawn later when I see her. I'm sure that she'll appreciate them."

John went as pink as a raspberry crumble.

"Err... no," he stuttered, "it wasn't 'er we were discussing actually. I think she would definitely be more of the pecan sort," he muttered, diplomatically avoiding the term nutty. Mabel's sad eyes searched his.

"I had been hoping you'd say gooseberry," she mumbled, and John went to correct her but Mabel shook her head.

"Don't," she whispered. "Please. Let's just leave it at that, eh?"

The Fridge looked away, smirking. "I wonder what sort of tart I would be?" she then muttered to herself, and leant across to pick up the phone. "Sweet or..."

"Very, very unsavoury," Mabel answered for her, and before anyone had a chance to say another word, she turned and walked away.

John watched her go, hips swaying, the smell of her silky hair and succulent perfume still filling his nostrils. For a minute then, he'd thought they had connected once again, just like the good old days two weeks ago when they'd crossed paths in the local shop, but now he wasn't so sure. In fact, bearing in mind that she didn't turn around to look at him as she disappeared, he reckoned his final opportunity had just gone. He felt deflated.

"Right," Mrs McFreece announced, and broke his maudlin reverie, "I'd better call the agency and get someone in to replace Miss Lovelock for the day. Oh and by the way," she then added, reaching for her phonebook, "if you're still looking for clarification, Mr Bentwick, I think you've just called a spade a spoon."

* * *

John slipped his feet back into his wellies and such was his misery that he was only vaguely aware of the moist bird dropping sitting at the bottom as he said good morning to Bob. He checked his watch. His instructions had been to arrive for a formal meeting with the Inspectors at break time, which meant he had time to do the honourable thing by his ram, and he wanted to think this through.

Normally, he'd just send a carcass for incineration, but he'd realised almost immediately that he couldn't bring himself to do that to Roger. He and Roger had been like brothers in arms, and despite dying so young, Roger still had something to offer the world. The bugger had had a uniqueness of character which was a shame to lose, and as one didn't come across an animal like Roger often, when one did, one had to do right by the world as well as right by Roger.

All in all therefore, he decided, he was going to offer him up for medical research.

It was a nice thought, but John wasn't actually sure how one went about donating an animal in such a way, and on a Friday too. He could imagine that Fridays weren't good for animal donation, as the cadaver had to be stored over the weekend.

He scratched his head. Perhaps he should put Roger in his chest freezer until Monday and sort it all out then. His mind really wasn't in the right place for making such important decisions.

He looked at his watch again. Yes, he had time.

* * *

"I think it must have been a particularly complicated extraction," Derek was explaining to the small group gathered in the staffroom as John walked in; namely an over-excited de Ravel, a surprisingly supportive Miss Bonniface, and a particularly diligent looking Mabel. "Very stoical woman, Miss Lovelock, I have to say. Never gave so much as a hint this week that she was suffering, and toothache can be so debilitating you know."

John watched Mabel twitch a sniff and then turn to peruse the photocopier instructions on the wall, avoiding Miss Bonniface's stare.

Miss Bonniface raised her hand.

De Ravel ignored her and laughed. "Yes, a good dose of oral treatment can be very..."

Mabel's head swivelled to look at him and she narrowed her eyes. "I suspect, Mr Fitztumbleton," she interrupted tersely, still glaring angrily at the lead inspector, "that Miss Lovelock has suffered a bit on the wisdom front recently."

Derek shrugged congenially.

"Yes, I had to have all my wisdom teeth out a while ago," he said. "Agony it was at the time, but it made all the difference to my bite."

"One has to get one's mastication right," de Ravel proclaimed, winking, and Mabel's eyes glared harder.

The female inspector stretched her arm higher and Derek broke first.

"Yes, Miss Bonniface. You have something to add?"

The woman nodded. "Lifestyle choices can have a significant effect," she started to say disapprovingly, but Mabel suddenly began to choke and drowned out the rest of the sentence.

"I think you'll find, Miss Bonniface," she explained finally, once her coughing fit had subsided, "that Miss Lovelock is simply dealing with a nasty dose of gingivitis."

De Ravel wrinkled his nose. "Not into redheads myself."

Mabel ignored him. "And she said to tell you, Mr Fitztumbleton, that she is off to see a specialist today because one of her canines is playing up as well. Is that not right, Miss Bonniface?"

Bonniface swallowed heavily and nodded.

"Ahhh," Derek exclaimed in a sympathetic tone. "Dear old Miss Lovelock. Her bark really is worse than her bite, eh? But I thought you said it was a wisdom tooth, Mrs Milner. One's canines are much closer to the front."

John watched Mabel shrug as if to say 'oh well, you know more about these things than I do', and was about to try to add something in support when Bob tapped him on the shoulder.

"Hey, everyone, guess what?" the caretaker joyfully announced, and winked theatrically to all those gathered in the staff room. "Not only have they gone and caught that FC Flasher, but you'll never believe who it is..."

* * *

John didn't know quite what to make of the news. He suspected it was meant to mean more to him than it did, but as the penis Sandra had sported had not been a patch on Roger's, her performance hadn't bothered him much in the end. He felt a moment of great pride at the thought, and then his underlying sadness returned. He looked dejectedly around the room and only eventually did the something register.

Despite the unexpected revelation, both Mabel and the two inspectors seemed distinctly unsurprised. In fact, he mused as he shifted his weight onto the other leg to aid the thinking process, if he opted to accept what his eyes were actually seeing, it was definitely only Derek who was shocked in any way.

John was at a loss. If the Inspector Training manual didn't cover such occasions, and Miss Bonniface clearly didn't seem to think it did, then he didn't know what to do, and so often as was his want when all other ideas failed, he said the first thing that came into his head simply to break the awkward silence.

"Well on the bright side, there was a flock of blue arses for me to see at the field this morning," he announced, and to their credit both Mabel and Bob swiftly grasped the full import. Mabel managed a thin smile.

"Roger finally bitten the bullet and got his act in gear has he?" she asked softly.

John felt a tingle of relief at her interest, but it was quickly tainted with grief. Roger had certainly bitten something; but sadly it was mostly dust.

"Well," she added, and her kind smile broadened, "I'm glad that at long last he has met with your approval."

John's gut churned.

"Actually," he admitted, only just managing to ignore the nasty twist of sorrow, "Roger 'as now met 'is maker. But only after 'e'd given 'em all a good seeing to, as yer'd say," he added, and then paused, suddenly realising that he'd run out of words.

His burly frame slumped. This whole bloody week had been a series of poorly chosen words, but now that he'd completely run out of them, all he could feel was the weight of his sadness, hopelessness and despair. "I'm s-s-orry, but I think I need some air," he stammered, and stumbled into the corridor.

Leaving their astonished faces behind, he staggered his way past the office and out through the front door. The dulcet tones of The Fridge saying, "If I had the choice of a sweet, I'd rather be a walnut whip," followed him partially outside, and were then truncated as the click of the latch sounded in his ears.

John looked around. He cast his eye across the tired playground and growled; what was it all about, eh? What was any of this living lark about? It seemed that even if he did try to 'seize the bloody day', it all went to rat shit in the end. What was the point of anything?

Just at that moment, in the midst of the most philosophical discussion he had ever had with himself, a loud clank sounded and the school gate opened and closed. He looked up and saw a woman striding towards him. Well, he guessed it was a woman, the skirt gave it away, but it could possibly have been a poodle which had learned to walk on two legs.

"I'm looking for Mr Shitzwombleton," it barked as it came near enough to speak, and then peered with surprise at a piece of paper and delved into its handbag to pull out a pair of glasses. "Sorry," it then corrected, "it's Mr Fitztumbleton that I'm looking for. I'm here to cover the Year Six class today. Can you point me in the right direction?"

John frowned. If he followed the request literally, he suspected that he'd be joining Miss Lovelock in a cell within the hour.

"Derek Fitztumbleton is inside," he said instead, and leant across to ring the bell just as Mabel opened the door.

Both women looked at each other in surprise, but Mabel swiftly pulled herself together and allowed the bubble haired supply teacher to pass by before stepping outside herself.

"Oh, thank goodness you're still here, John," she said softly. "I was worried you were off. Look," she then paused, appearing to struggle to find the right words. "I just wanted you to know that I'm sorry about Roger, really I am."

John cleared his throat.

"Oh, don't worry," he sighed. "I'm just being stupid. I 'ardly knew 'im really, and 'e was right awkward bugger if I'm being honest with myself."

"But he got there in the end, didn't he?" she offered, and followed it up with a shrug. "And that is something that I've finally done too," she added, but her comment made him frown. "Got to the right place in the end," she explained, and laid her hand gently on his arm. "I just hope I'm not too late. Although I do have one question left," John held his breath. "Do you really think I'm a tart?"

Her face creased anxiously and he watched her lick her lips. Was this what he'd been hoping for? Was this another chance? Did life really work that way; take with one hand, but give generously with the other? He'd never known it to before.

"A blackberry and apple one for sure," he croaked, "but not any other kind."

"And you're not going to make some horrid remark about adding cream?" she asked nervously.

John managed a smile.

"Oh, no," he assured her, feeling on safer territory now. "Yer should only ever 'ave custard with blackberry and apple tart."

Mabel risked the smallest of grins.

"Well, I don't know what you're doing this evening," she said quietly, but the way she said it gave him the warmest feeling he'd ever had. "But I wanted you to know that I'm free later on." She paused and looked at her feet. "Perhaps you could tell me more about the superb qualities of Roger's scrotum, as well as yours, I mean about yourself," she corrected quickly.

And John then did something he'd never done before; he took her hand.

Mabel lifted her gaze and peered into his face. "Can we get things back on track?"

As he stared into the big hopeful pools that were her eyes, John's heart swelled. For once, he thought, I should keep my mouth shut. But the thought never became a decision, for then he nodded, parted his lips and silently gave her a kiss.

Chapter Twenty

As Bob told them the news, Derek caught himself abstractly wishing he'd worn a fresh suit rather than just grabbing the first one that had come to hand. Wearing the same suit two days in a row wasn't good, was it? Not what a headmaster attempting to pursue a successful career would do when he had important people to impress.

And even when John Bentwick disappeared outside, Derek steadfastly continued to refuse to engage with what he was hearing, and moved on to think about what he should wear, if he should be lucky enough to persuade Miranda to have dinner with him later.

It was only when the caretaker passed him a copy of the latest Cockerby Chronicle that things started to sink in.

''You Say Dildo, Santa. We Say Dildon't!' it proudly announced; snappy little headline.

Derek felt his face turn white.

De Ravel gave him an unexpected wink. "Dentist, eh?" he said, and chuckled.

Derek felt his face turn red.

"Well, quite," he tried, but for once it didn't do the trick and he frowned. Something else was wrong, wasn't it? And then it struck him that the inspector's tone hadn't been as surprised as it should have been.

Derek felt his face turn grey.

"You knew where she was this morning, didn't you?" he gasped.

As he asked the question, his gaze fell upon de Ravel, who simply shrugged, and then moved on to Miss Bonniface, who'd already turned as purple as a beetroot. His eyebrows lifted in surprise.

"Don't tell me, Miss Bonniface, you knew too?" he cried in amazement. "But why didn't you say anything earlier?"

Bonniface's head swivelled in Mabel's direction, the look of pathetic appeal pulling her blush right up into her hairline. Mabel sighed and switched her weight onto her other leg.

"I'm afraid that's my fault, Mr Fitztumbleton," she confessed. "I convinced Miss Bonniface this morning that it was better for your health if you got through today without knowing. But now that the truth has been laid bare, so to speak," she added, turning to the female inspector again, "I think you'll have to explain everything to him, and as you'll not want parental witnesses, I'll just go and see if Mr Bentwick is alright."

By now, Bonniface's expression had run out of space in which to eke, so she simply managed an awkward shrug and let her mournful gaze follow Mabel out of the door.

Derek slapped his hand on his forehead.

"Not want witnesses?" he repeated, appalled. "I wonder what Inspector Training would have to say about that."

Bonniface bit her lip. "Mr de Ravel revealed the flasher's identity to me last night as we drove home," she explained apologetically. "And then when Mrs Milner caught me this morning, she, err…" the flush on her face fired back into position. "Well, she, err… persuaded me not to say anything."

"But how did Mr de Ravel know in the first place?" Derek asked, beginning to feel that he was the last person to know that his top teacher had a fetish for displaying plastic penises whilst dressed in a little red suit. To say that he felt slightly under-informed at this moment would have been an understatement.

De Ravel chuckled.

"Oh, come, come, Mr Fitztumbleton, there's no need to pretend with me. You're rubbing shoulders with a fellow fiend here. You and I both know what Sandra Lovelock gets up to on a Monday evening." And as he said it, a disquieting glint began to shine in his eyes.

Derek's brows knitted.

"She goes to cookery club," he put forward, and then added, "We discussed it only the other day." But as de Ravel's smirk broadened, his faith in this conviction slipped away. In fairness, he suddenly remembered, she hadn't said anything to that effect at all, and the knowing look on the inspector's face was now becoming very disconcerting. "She likes a nice piece of cod," he tried as a last ditch attempt, and then finally gave up. There was definitely something fishy going on, but it had nothing to do with gastronomic desires.

It was now the turn of de Ravel's features to crumple into a scowl.

"You mean you don't know about *Dominantics*?" the man asked, and as he said the word, Miss Bonniface seemed to shrink further into her jacket. Derek watched her and realised he wished he could do the same.

"No," he replied, "I don't, and I'm not sure that I want to either."

De Ravel's frown paled.

"But I'd had you down as one of her minions."

"Whose minions?" Derek exclaimed.

"Lady Lovelick's!" de Ravel cried, and then a tinge of embarrassment eked slowly across his cheeks too.

Derek was now thoroughly confused.

"But who on earth is Lady Lovelick?" he asked, just before he realised that he wasn't sure he wanted an answer to that question either. After the antics of the previous night, the very mention of a name of that ilk in the same conversation as Sandra Lovelock didn't bode well. Oh, this was all too much for his tired little brain; when was he going to wake up and find it had all been a horrid dream?

"I thought Lady Lovelick was just something the children called her by mistake," he mumbled in the end. "Just as they called you Mr Drivel yesterday, which I've been meaning to apologise to you about."

"Actually," de Ravel coughed, "it's *Doctor* Drivel, but that's mainly on Monday evenings."

"You're learning to cook too?" Derek tried, but deep down he knew it was fruitless. The man lived up to his expectations.

"Only if you call hiding the sausage and buttering the buns cooking, Mr Fitztumbleton."

Just at that regrettable moment, Mrs McFreece appeared at the door. She glanced around at the motley group and her dour features lit up at the sight of their miserable faces.

"If you're putting in a lunch order at the shop," she said, "I'll have an egg sandwich and a chocolate sundae; it is Friday after all." And then she remembered what it was that she'd originally come to say. "Oh and by the way," she said, "the supply teacher has arrived, Mr Fitztumbleton. Bit of an odd one if you ask me, so she'll fit in well here." The Fridge finished the statement off with an uncharacteristic snigger.

Derek raised his eyebrows. Odd? In Lower Bushey? Was that possible? At this moment in time, even if the woman had white curly hair and answered to the name of Shep she'd still have ranked as mundane as far as he was concerned.

"I'll be along in one minute, Mrs McFreece. I just need to finish off here."

The Fridge swung a dubious look across them all, and then nodded curtly and waddled away. Derek gave himself a couple of seconds to collect his thoughts.

He could see out of the corner of his eye that de Ravel was now not in quite such confident spirits as he had been but five minutes before. Something was bothering the man, which, Derek reflected, was probably not surprising. People like de Ravel were peculiarly volatile. They had countless procedures and methodologies to which they referred religiously, but eventually the need for impulsive behaviour always grew too strong. He'd seen it in many pupils down the years, but this was the first time he'd seen it in anyone over the age of ten.

And to his surprise, he suddenly felt within reach of an advantage he'd not spotted before; adults were different to pupils; adults had motivations that remained in place even once the madness had set in. All he had to do was pinpoint the right motivation.

Derek took a deep breath and plunged in headfirst.

"Mr de Ravel," he started, but then faltered at the first hurdle. "Or should I call you Doctor?" The inspector shook his head dismissively. Derek stumbled on. "Well, I feel I have to ask a very awkward question, and I'm not sure how to put it diplomatically. So as we're all of one mind when it comes to education, at least, I'm just going to come out with it. Is my understanding correct that you already know Sandra Lovelock in another guise?"

As the question tumbled out, the flicker of uncertainty that flashed in the man's eyes made Derek's heart begin to thump. There was definitely a hint of insecurity now lining the face staring back, and it was sending an odd mix of elation and shame coursing through his veins. But he held his gaze firm. He didn't want it to be this way, however desperate times called for desperate measures. He had to stand his ground.

There seemed to be no response.

"Well it strikes me," Derek then continued, but de Ravel suddenly found his voice.

"Hold on a second," the inspector interrupted, "are you trying to tell me that you don't know her in a different guise?" Derek noted the hint of inauthentic bravado in the voice and his confidence grew. He gave the man a brusque nod. "But you have said many times in the last twenty four hours, Mr Fitztumbleton," de Ravel continued "that Sandra Lovelock is a lady of many talents. You have said it with a glint in your eye and a spring in your walk. And we both know what a phrase like that means, don't we?"

Derek raised an eyebrow and cocked his head to the side.

"Yes, Mr de Ravel, I suspect we do," he said quietly, belying the panic he still felt. "It's just that a phrase like that clearly holds a different meaning for each of us, and I should imagine that Miss Bonniface could lend yet a third connotation to it if asked. Miss Bonniface?" Her head jerked up as he said her name. "Can you tell me what you would make of the phrase *Sandra Lovelock is a lady of many talents*?"

Diana Bonniface swallowed awkwardly.

"Err..." she mumbled, and then fired an appealing look for help at her colleague but it was to no avail. Her face fell. "Sorry," she murmured finally, "the Inspector Training manual doesn't cover that subject."

Derek sighed. He should have seen that one coming.

"Well, anyway," he mused, astonishing both himself and his audience, "needless to say, Mr de Ravel, it transpires that you have known Miss Lovelock in a capacity that I suspect you would prefer not to be made public, and we at the school have known Miss Lovelock in a capacity such that we would prefer, without prejudice, for the extracurricular activities of said teacher not to affect our ... our... inspection rating."

There, he thought, I've said it. It's out. Suddenly, he felt drained.

De Ravel grimaced and Derek could feel his heart banging in his chest as he waited, but finally the man shrugged and sighed.

"It's an interesting approach you have chosen to use, Mr Fitztumbleton, but as you are aware I generally admire people who can think outside the box. You'll be glad to know, therefore," Derek's heart pummelled away, "that in this instance, I believe that neither of us have any need to worry. If you get my drift."

Derek paused before replying; 'get my drift' could mean many things. His natural instinct was to nod agreeably to confirm that it was indeed gettable, but he immediately rationalised that natural instincts had gone out the window the moment the inspectors had arrived.

"So *neither* of us have any need to worry." he repeated, more to hear the phrase again than anything else, but the inspector seemed to take it as adequate confirmation. At this point, it seemed that the drift he had chosen to retrieve had indeed been the right one.

The whoosh of relief that flooded through his veins was exhilarating. Like the rush of all one's hopes culminating into a single huge explosion, it coursed around his bloodstream reaching the parts that even Heineken couldn't reach. It felt good. It felt surprisingly real. But it also felt, if he was being honest with himself, horribly tainted with shame. He was going to get what he'd been dreaming of ever since his career had begun, but it would come at the cost of his integrity. He'd had to blackmail a man whose weaknesses couldn't be controlled. It wasn't his finest moment.

Derek felt he should say something to lighten the atmosphere, but corruption wasn't a thing to follow up with a quip. So instead, he simply nodded.

"Now if you'll excuse me for a few minutes, I need to speak to the supply teacher. However I shall return soon."

Ignoring Bonniface's stunned expression, he backed out of the room. De Ravel's nonchalance seemed to have been restored, but what did that matter now, for they both had what they wanted.

Once out in the corridor, away from prying eyes, Derek leant against the wall and allowed a sigh of relief to escape. The ageing inflexibility of the partition pressed against his shoulders and he waited for his heart to settle down. My goodness he'd never been so bold. To coerce an inspector like that wouldn't have crossed his mind a week ago, but that was a week ago and a lot had happened since then; an awful lot. He decided to give himself another minute's peace before heading over to the secretary's office, and as he waited words filtered through the open door of the staff room.

"But we should not allow ourselves to be swayed so easily, Mr de Ravel. I confess I have been weak; I should never have influenced you as I have. I gave in to my own concerns last night and pledged inappropriately. Inspector Training should not have let me pass."

"What on earth are you talking about, Miss Bonniface? Who is being swayed? And, more importantly," the man added with an edge of disapproval, "who on earth has suggested that you have influenced me?!"

Derek imagined Bonniface's mouth opening and shutting and empathised.

"But when we spoke in the car going home last night..." she stuttered.

"When we spoke in the car going home last night," de Ravel cut in, "you were still reeling from the prospect of being seen in the papers next to a woman with a foot long plastic penis. And," it sounded as though Miss Bonniface wanted to say something in response, but the male inspector overrode her, "I think your actions were perfectly understandable given that we pledge to protect the good name of The Inspectorate at all times."

"But we can't go bending to Mr Fitztumbleton's request just to shut him up."

"Ah, but that is where your inexperience is showing through, Miss Bonniface," de Ravel replied, and Derek moved his head a little closer to the doorway. "What you suppose is happening isn't happening at all. Quite the contrary." Derek's ears pricked up. "Regardless of the extracurricular activities of its staff, this is an astonishing school in every way. Results, pupil progress, pastoral care. I'd go as far as to say that it is outstanding in fact, and every graph and bit of paperwork backs that assessment up. I haven't seen one better run in all my days as an inspector. You should count your blessings, Miss Bonniface. To have had the opportunity to come across such a superb school so early in your inspecting career will set you up for life. You now have a benchmark you should never, ever forget."

"So we aren't being blackmailed?"

De Ravel chuckled.

"Absolutely not! No doubt old Fitztumbleton thinks he is getting away with blackmail, and no doubt he will live with the guilt for the rest of his life, which from my perspective is adequate penance, but the truth still stands, Miss Bonniface; Lower Bushey Primary is a model institution, and it has earned the outstanding rating I'm going to give it entirely on its own merits."

Derek's heart swelled, and to think that he had doubted the school to the extent that he'd felt it necessary to resort to devious underhand methods. The thought tinged his inner rejoicing with remorse, but only slightly. In this instance, the end was indifferent to the means; a lesson had been learned, and, most significantly, his ticket out of this place was now guaranteed!

Mrs McFreece appeared out of her office, telephone message in hand.

"Your wife has just called, Mr Fitztumbleton. She'll be popping along later to speak with you about something. I told her that she wasn't to come before school had finished; you don't need any unnecessary distractions, eh? I think she got the hint."

Derek's stomach turned. Miranda, coming here? Unprompted? Was the timing of such an announcement a sign? Perhaps she now felt chastened to the point of not being able to cross their homely threshold without invitation. Perhaps she wanted to make amends. Perhaps dinner was on the cards after all. And for the first time since she'd left, he felt he had something with which to tempt her back.

Mrs McFreece continued oblivious of his thoughts.

"Well come on now, Mr Fitztumbleton," the woman urged. "Class Six are waiting. The new teacher has filled in all my forms and Billy Barber's Tourette's has moved up a gear because he's bored. She really needs to get cracking. Oh, and by the way," she added finally with a wry sparkle in her eye, "she's called Mrs Hound, and I think you'll find it's an appropriate name."

* * *

Derek did indeed grasp what The Fridge was implying as soon as he saw Mrs Hound, but his elation at hearing the inspectors' decision was enough to give him super human powers. He welcomed her with a face as straight as a Roman road, and not once did he have to hide a smirk. Within no time at all, she was ensconced within her classroom, teaching happily away. If she'd had a tail, it would have been wagging.

And oddly enough, bearing in mind the man's behaviour earlier on, the same could also have been said of John Bentwick.

Derek expected the farmer to wilt into his giant frame during the final official interview, but to his surprise it seemed to go as smoothly as muck spreading on a drizzly day. There was one moment of confusion when John asked de Ravel if he knew of any schools that might like a ram's testicles for research, and Derek had unconsciously put his hand in his pocket and squeezed Miranda's horseshoe scarf for comfort. But de Ravel had laughed the suggestion off in cavalier fashion, saying that Roger's scrotum were far too good for such treatment; they belonged in the Natural History Museum at least.

By the end of the meeting, as Derek already knew the outcome, the most significant thing that he got out of the exchange, was a sense of hope that the scarf was finally bringing him good luck. By the end of the same meeting, the most significant thing that John Bentwick appeared to gain, was a question about how one got a frozen carcass into the centre of London before it started to defrost.

But all the while, however, as the final meeting came to an end, the inspectors congratulated Derek and his staff on running such a truly magnificent institution, and as The Fridge gave him an impromptu kiss for achieving such success, Derek could only think of one specific thing; promotion. It was there now, on the horizon, he could smell it, and the waft of manure laden streets was swiftly substituting itself for car fumes in his mind's nose. No amount of unwanted snogging from a frosty secretary could dampen his spirit now; Miranda would be springing back home in no time.

He waved de Ravel and his dazed sidekick off from the school gate, thanking them for their time and masterfully controlling a wince as de Ravel barked an au revoir at Mrs Hound. There was no point in being churlish at this juncture; magnanimity was the word for the day.

John Bentwick sidled up to him.

"So do yer think 'e really meant it when 'e said that the Natural 'istory Museum might like to make a display of my ram?"

Derek reminded himself once again; magnanimity was the word for the day.

"Absolutely," he said without hesitation. "A beast as fine as yours should grace all zoological displays."

John appeared to appreciate the statement up to the word 'zoological' and was about to interject, but to Derek's relief they both then spotted Mabel walking across with Ashley and instantly John seemed to have something else on his mind.

"'ere," he said, and elbowed Derek lightly in the side, "'elp me out. Is 'er child a girl or a boy?"

Derek's stomach knotted but it was too late to make a strategic dash inside. Mabel reached them before he had a chance to answer.

"Are we allowed to know how it went?" she asked.

Derek cleared his throat.

"I'm sorry, Mrs Milner, but I am not permitted to tell anyone outside the governing body unfortunately."

"The bugger only went and got a standing ovation," John Bentwick interrupted and beamed a thrilled smile.

Derek cleared his throat again.

"Actually, the term is *outstanding*," he corrected and then bit his lip, but Mabel just grinned and gave him a wink.

"Mum's the word, Mr Fitztumbleton, don't worry. Miss Bonniface explained the set up to me last night. None of the parents will hear a thing from me, although I can't answer for anyone else." She glared at John as she said it, but there was a twinkle in her eyes. Derek saw it, believed her, and deep in his heart wished her and John good luck; of all the couples he'd seen together, they were going to need it.

A childish throat now cleared itself behind them.

"I thought *outstanding* meant something still left to do."

Three adult heads turned to see Ashley loitering a few feet away, smirking.

Derek flushed.

Then his stomach rumbled.

Until finally a burp of awkward wind forced itself up.

Mabel saw his discomfort and misconstrued it.

"Oh, don't worry, Mr Fitztumbleton, Ashley won't say a word either, will you, Ash?"

The child shrugged and shook its head. Out of the corner of his eye, Derek could see John frowning, the same question clearly in the forefront of his own mind only more visibly. He waited, hoping. Of all the times for John Bentwick's world-renowned faux pas to be of use, it was now.

The farmer bent down to speak to the child. Derek held his breath.

"Ashley," he said, his gruff voice softening kindly, "I need an 'and in making a decision." Ashley clearly didn't take too kindly to the patronising tone, so he coughed and spoke a little louder. "I'm thinking of suggesting to Mr Fitztumbleton that the school come and visit my farm some time. Do yer think that would be a good idea?"

Ashley managed a shrug and a hesitant nod.

"Well, I was thinking of offering rides on my tractor, " he continued, "just to keep the boys 'appy, and..."

"But the girls would like that too," *it* suddenly bloomed, and Derek felt a cautious whoosh of enlightenment. "I know I'd love to ride on a tractor. Don't just keep it for the boys."

John nodded sagely and then turned to Derek and winked.

"Well it's something else for yer to think about, Mr Fitztumbleton, before yer move on to pastures new, eh? Perhaps in the spring, when the lambs are frolicking around, as long as Roger did do 'is job properly, that is..." And Derek realised that it was probably time to step in.

"Well, quite, Mr Bentwick. Pastures new. Splendid idea. Thank you."

John nodded. "Right," he sighed, clearly satisfied. "Well best I 'ead off to do my chores. I'll pick yer up later, Mabel. Perhaps, before we go for a drink, yer'd like to see 'ow I've got 'im laid out in the freezer."

* * *

Derek heard the flap of pigeon wings a split second before Mabel and hastily managed a duck. The look of anguish on her face as he'd straightened up swiftly made sense; he felt a tinge of guilt. He'd wished the poor woman luck just a few moments before, but he'd not planned for it to be exacted in quite this way. The splat on her forehead was already beginning to drip towards her left eye.

He fumbled in his pockets for a hankie and pulled out Miranda's scarf. Without a second thought, he passed it across.

"Here, get it quickly before it dries," he instructed, and then pointed out where she'd missed some whilst she gently wiped the sludge away. Mabel looked down at the silky material, all navy blue and gold, horseshoes gleaming out their heady fortunistic predictions and wrinkled her nose.

"She's not right for you, you know, the sort of woman who goes for this stuff. This sort of woman could never make a deep and thoughtful man like you happy, Mr Fitztumbleton. What she's after is all too on the surface."

Derek looked at her. She meant it kindly but what did she know? It probably hadn't even occurred to her yet that he now was able to have plans; the sort of plans that a woman like Miranda would revere. The sort of plans that might just make his wife come back home.

"Oh, Derek," he could imagine Miranda saying. "Oh, Derek, there you are. I've been looking for you." That's what she would say and he'd be able to turn to look her in the eye with self-respect at last.

The lovely day dream continued.

"Derek?" he heard in his mind's ear.

"Derek?" There it was again, only this time it sounded extraordinarily real.

"Derek!" it repeated, and suddenly he felt a tug on his arm. "Derek, you oaf, what is that woman doing with my scarf?"

Derek's mind's eye realised that it was time to take a back seat and return him to reality. The two optical facilitators in his face took in what was presented and reluctantly passed the scene to his brain.

"Miranda," he gasped, and then for some reason looked apologetically across at Mabel. "What are you doing here?"

Miranda's eyebrows knitted with annoyance.

"I phoned your secretary earlier. She promised she'd tell you I was coming," she explained curtly. "I told her that I urgently need my scarf. I've looked all over the house for it." Derek felt himself bristle at the thought of

Miranda rifling through her own things in their house. "And then I remembered you saying that I'd left it in your car. I need it for a do in Nottingham tonight. Marcus and I are going to the Sheriff's Masquerade Ball and I want it for the pre-dinner drinks."

"Oooh, how exciting. Is it fancy dress?" Ashley asked innocently, and all heads turned. Her voice was as sugary as mead. Miranda frowned. "I reckon you'd make a lovely Maid Marion," the child added sweetly. "Is your friend going as Hobin Rood?" As the mistake tumbled out of her mouth, her eyes suddenly widened with mirth and she chuckled with embarrassment. "Oh, I am sorry, Mrs Fitztumbleton," she apologised, "Mrs Hound was teaching us about spoonerisms today. I'd meant to mix up Friar Tuck..."

Miranda's frown deepened, and whilst Mabel was quizzically mouthing the word 'spoonerism', Derek, to his surprise, found that he had to bite his lip. He gave Ashley a coy wink.

"Well, really!" Miranda exclaimed, determinedly ignoring the child's giggles and leaning across to snatch her scarf out of Mabel's hand. "No wonder your career is failing so badly," she growled. "If that's the sort of thing you are teaching them these days, there really is no hope." As she spat the words, she stared angrily across and tied the scarf expertly in a knot.

At that moment, with his spouse glaring in contempt, Derek felt many things. He felt mortified by his wife's rudeness. He felt awkward but amused by Ashley's clearly inherited sardonic sense of humour. And he felt desperate to tell the world the fantastic news about the inspection they'd just had. But there was one thing that he didn't feel, and it was the most striking thing of all; he didn't feel any inclination to warn Miranda that she now had bird poo smeared across her neck. It was a rather nice not-feeling to have.

Whilst he contemplated his silence, the pinstripe prince sidled up in his Jag. Giving Derek a look of victorious disdain, Miranda offered Marcus a little grin, reached inside her handbag and pulled out an envelope. Throwing him one final glance, she then thrust the package into his hand, jumped into the passenger seat, and the car sped off before he had a chance to say a word.

* * *

Derek stared at it. Manila, of course, not white. Official looking. It didn't bode well. Mabel shifted on her feet and cleared her throat.

"Divorce proceedings, I expect," she said quietly. "I'm sorry, Derek."

Derek looked at it again. Now was not the time to open it. He wasn't sure when the right time would be, but this 'now'; the 'now' when he'd thought he'd known how his future could pan out, only to be told that it simply could not be, this 'now' was not the time. So in this 'now' he just shook his head instead.

"But at least you have a way to move forward career wise," Mabel added. "I should image you'll be able to get any job you want. Cockerby Primary is crying out for a good headmaster, apparently. Although I expect you'll be looking for bigger and greater things in the city. Well anyway," she sighed finally, "Ashley's forgotten her trainers. I'm just going to pop inside and get them. Ash?" The young girl looked up as she called her name. "Can you keep Mr Fitztumbleton company whilst I nip back inside? Who knows, perhaps we can sweet talk him into giving us a lift home, huh?"

Mabel gave him a final, soft, thoughtful smile and then headed back to the main school building. Derek followed her with his eyes.

"You know," he said wistfully, still watching her disappearing form, "she's quite an amazing woman, your mother, and everything she does, she does for you, Ashley. She's bright, she's determined, and she loves you, which makes you a very lucky girl."

The child's shoes shuffled on the pavement. Derek turned. She too had a pensive look on her face.

"People don't usually see my mum in that way, Mr Fitztumbleton," she replied. "All they usually remember are her boobs." Derek thought back to his first memory of Mabel Milner only five days before and reckoned that buttocks were probably more accurate for him, but he wasn't going to argue.

"I think Mr Bentwick sees her as I do, though," he said instead.

That made Ashley laugh. "Oh, him, he's funny. I think my mum really likes him 'cos he's not like any of the men she knows." Again, Derek didn't feel in a position to argue. "I'm guessing he's the opposite of my dad too, which is probably no bad thing."

Derek caught her tone and noted the lack of melancholy. It made him think.

For an eleven year old, Ashley Milner was remarkably astute. She was also particularly pragmatic, and at moments surprisingly outspoken as well, which made her very like, very like... And then it suddenly struck him. Yes, Ashley Milner was astonishingly like her mother. She had a shrewdness of thinking that was unsullied by ignorant prejudice. She had a wisdom ahead of her years and an understanding of people that was second to none. She could spot the nub of a situation before anyone else had realised a situation was taking place, and why, he wondered, would that even come as a surprise? Why on earth wouldn't Ashley have those qualities? For she had learned them from an expert. Despite what the rest of the world thought, Mabel Milner wasn't just a mother, she was a role model.

Her young voice interrupted his thoughts.

"I know what you're thinking," she said, and he doubted that even she could really know what was going through his mind, but he let her carry on speaking uncorrected. "And you're right," she continued. "But the sad thing is that I've lived with my mum all my life and I've only just seen it, whereas you on the other hand, Mr Fitztumbleton, you have only known her a week and you've spotted it already. And I feel I should thank you. Thank you for helping *me* to see it. Because you're right, she really is amazing."

Derek chuckled. He should have known that he'd underestimate this child and that she'd get it right. It's exactly what her mother would have done.

"Yes, she is amazing," he agreed. "And I only wish I could be as good an example to others as she is."

"Oh but you are!" Ashley cut in, and her eyes widened with fervour. "This place would fall apart if you weren't here. We need you to hold it all together, Mr Fitztumbleton. We need your rules and your guidelines. We need you to open our eyes properly so that we don't just walk around with them closed. I mean come on," she scoffed finally, "if it hadn't been for you just now, I'd never have seen how brilliant my mum is." And with that last announcement, she turned her head wistfully back towards the school.

Derek pondered her words. Could she be right? Had he brought something to this tiny rural village without realising it? Could it really be true or was this just another one of Ashley's astute tricks? He wasn't sure. With all his highfalutin misguided beliefs, he had arrived in Lower Bushey convinced that he was the normal one, set to offer his paternal generosity to a flock that needed guidance, and yet it was they who had welcomed him with open arms; odd one out and outsider that *he* was. No one except Miranda had ever doubted that he would turn this place around. The people of Lower Bushey just didn't suffer from the small minded outlook that many townies wore as a badge of honour. They were simply not caught up with the minutiae of pointless detail. And it was only now he realised that he'd felt the way he had when he'd arrived, because it was *he* who had not accepted them. It had just taken him all this time to realise it.

Was it possible to transfer such broadminded thinking elsewhere? Take it with him? Spread the word, so to speak?

"But in a bigger school, I could..." he started, but to his surprise Ashley shook her head before he'd finished the sentence.

"This isn't a numbers game, Mr Fitztumbleton," she stated with striking maturity. "Helping a hundred city kids isn't any more worthwhile than helping one out here. We all deserve it; every single one. Us sad little village kids, with our unfashionable clothes and odd hobbies, we deserve the best just as much as those city kids do. And as you are the best, Mr Fitztumbleton," she added, dropping her voice just slightly, "and as we do deserve the best - please, please, please don't go..."

The heartfelt plea brought a lump to Derek's throat. He swallowed hard.

"Tell me," he mumbled, needing to move the subject on, convinced that his voice would crack if he wasn't careful, "would you really like to have a go on a tractor?"

Despite her seriousness, Ashley laughed.

"Nah," she said, and shook her head. "I just said it to help him 'cos I could see he wasn't sure if I was a girl or a boy. I get it all the time," she added indifferently. "I know my mum would like me to be more girly, but I am what I am, just as much as she is what she is. She'll learn that one day, but in the meantime it doesn't mean that I can't try to make things easier for her, and she need not ever know I'm doing it."

Suddenly, Derek realised what she'd been trying to get at when she'd asked what made a person great. It certainly wasn't what one *was* or what one *had* that made one great, and it wasn't what others thought of one either. No. And although the shape of one's greatness clearly had a lot to do with what one *did,* that was only the tip; the visible bit. The bedrock upon which greatness actually rested was *why* one did something at all. Helping a hundred children was fantastic, but no more admirable than helping one; for that one child still needed that help; it simply came with less glory. Greatness could see past that.

Part of him wanted to convey this unexpected revelation to this eleven year old child, but he guessed there was little point. She knew it already. It was probably the most obvious thing in the world to her, perhaps would have been the most obvious thing in the world to him too at that age, but he'd lost touch. The numbers game had begun to mean too much; bigger was better, more meant more to too many, and he'd been seduced by the need for other peoples' esteem because he'd not managed to find it within himself.

Hearing Mabel's heels tripping back to meet them, Derek looked around at all that was his domain; the cracked playground, the crumbling school building, the resident pigeon chuckling to himself perched on top of the roof, and for the first, time he realised that this was where he belonged. He clenched his fists with excitement. The envelope crumpled in his hand.

I'm not leaving these buggers to fend for themselves, he decided suddenly.

Fuck 'em! Fuck 'em all!

Printed in Great Britain
by Amazon